Pupil's Book
Second Edition

Nigel Heslop
David Brodie
James Williams

Hodder Murray

A MEMBER OF THE HODDER HEADLINE GROUP

The Publishers would like to thank the following for permission to reproduce copyright material:

p.2 *a)* Centre Jean Perrin/Science Photo Library, *b)* Dr Yorgos Nikas/Science Photo Library, *c)* Eye of Science/Science Photo Library, *d)* Dr Jeremy Burgess/Science Photo Library, *r* L Willatt, East Anglian Regional Genetics Service/Science Photo Library; **p.3** © Hulton-Deutsch Collection/Corbis; **p.4** *l* Dave G Houser/Corbis, *r* Mrs E. B. Carpenter; **p.6** © Guntr Marx Photography/Corbis; **p.9** Holt Studios; **p.10** *l* The Zoological Society of London, *r* Reinhold Rau; **p.11** *l* Reinhold Rau, *r* Peter Scoones; **p.12** Science Photo Library; **p.13** Monica Grady; **p.14** © Bettmann/Corbis; **p.16** *a)* © Robert Holmes/Corbis, *b)* Elizabeth Whiting, *c)* Ruth Hughes, *d)* Hodder Murray, *e)* © Francis G. Mayer/Corbis, *f)* Hulton Archive/Getty Images; **p.20** *all* Andrew Lambert; **p.22** Andrew Lambert; **p.23** *all* Andrew Lambert; **p.27** *all* Andrew Lambert; **p.28** *tl* George Hall/Corbis, *bl* Mehau Kulyk/Science Photo Library; **p.29** *tl, cl, bl* Andrew Lambert, *tr, tl* New Media; **p.30** *tl* © Jim Richardson/Corbis, *tr, br* Andrew Lambert; **p.31** *t* British Alcan, *c, b* Andrew Lambert; **p.34** Saturn Stills/Science Photo Library; **p.35** *t* Emma Lee/Life File, *b* Andrew Lambert; **p.38** © Peter Bowater/Alamy; **p.42** *all* Centre for Alternative Technology; **p.43** Centre for Alternative Technology; **p.45** Ingram; **p.49** Tek Image/Science Photo Library; **p.50** *l*, Ruth Hughes, *tr* Life File, *cr* Matt Meadows, Peter Arnold Inc./Science Photo Library, *br* H Schleichkorn, Custom Medical Stock/Science Photo Library; **p.51** Dr. E. Walker/Science Photo Library; **p.52** *both* Wellcome Trust; **p.53** Hodder Murray; **p.54** *l* Ruth Hughes, *r* Life File; **p.56** *tl* Voisin/Phanie/Rex Features, *bl* Annabella Bluesky/Science Photo Library, *tr* Sinopix/Rex Features, *br* Rex Features; **p.57** © Bettmann/Corbis; **p.58** Mark Edwards /Still Pictures; **p.59** Andrew Lambert; **p.60** *t* J. P. Vantighem /Still Pictures, *b* Emma Lee/Life File; **p.62** *t* Nigel Sitwell/Life File, *b* Hodder Murray; **p.64** *t* NASA/Science Photo Library, *b* Emma Lee/Life File; **p.67** Kathy Sykes; **p.68** A C Searle/Rex Features; **p.70** Gunter Marx/Corbis; **p.72** The Ronald Grant Archive/Ron Batzdorff; **p.76** David Brodie; **p.77** *tl* Science Photo Library, *bl* © Bettmann/Corbis, *tl* Space Telescope Science Institute, NASA/Science Photo Library; **p.78** *l* European Space Agency/Science Photo Library, *r* University of Dundee/Science Photo Library; **p.79** *t* CNES, 1997 Distribution Spot Image/Science Photo Library, *b* NASA; **p.80** *l* NOVOSTI/Science Photo Library, *r* © G. P. Bowater/Alamy; **p.81** Scott Sinklier/Agstock/Science Photo Library; **p.84** *l, tr* Science Photo Library, *br* Sheila Terry/Science Photo Library; **p.85** *t* © Hulton-Deutsch Collection/Corbis, *b* Lawrence Berkeley National Laboratory/Science Photo Library; **p.86** Holt Studios; **p.87** Holt Studios; **p.88** Ruth Hughes; **p.89** Holt Studios; **p.90** *all* Holt Studios; **p.92** *a, d* Bruce Coleman Collection, *b* © John Cancalosi/Bruce Coleman Collection, *c* © Johnny Johnson/Bruce Coleman Collection; **p.94** *t* NASA/Science Photo Library, *b* Emma Lee/Life File; **p.98** *both* Andrew Lambert; **p.99** © Richard Hamilton Smith/Corbis; **p.100** *tl, bl,* Andrew Lambert, *tr* Hodder Murray, *br* Life File; **p.101** *t* British Alcan, *b* Nigel Heslop; **p.103** Andrew Lambert; **p.106** *tr* Life File, *br* Weston Point Studios Ltd, *tr, cr* Ruth Hughes, *br* Jeremy Hoare/Life File; **p.111** © Wendy Drake/Naturepl.com; **p.112** TCF/Lucasfilm (Gary Kurtz)/Moviestore Collection; **p.114** Action Plus; **p.115** *l* Getty Sport, *tr, br* Phil Noble/EMPICS/PA; **p.118** *t* Tony Bomford/Oxford Scientific Films, *b* Johnny Johnson/Bruce Coleman Ltd; **p.120** Takeshi Takahara/Science Photo Library; **p.121** Fraser Ralston/Life File; **p.124** Johnny Johnson/Bruce Coleman Ltd; **p.126** *l* NASA/Science Photo Library, *r* Carl & Ann Purcell/Corbis; **p.128** t Charles O'Rear/Corbis, *b* Vaughan Piccolo; **p.129** Ruth Hughes; **p.132** *t* Action Plus, *bl* Wellcome Trust, *br* AP Photo/Jens Hartmann; **p.137** *l* Carlos Munoz-Yague, Eurelios/Science Photo Library, *r* David Parker/Science Photo Library; **p.138** *l* Science Photo Library, *tr* Science Source/Science Photo Library, *br* Science Source/Science Photo Library; **p.139** *l* Andrew Lambert, *tc* Emma Lee/Life File, *bc, r* Andrew Lambert; **p.140** *both* Andrew Lambert ; **p.145** Jen and Des Bartlett/Oxford Scientific Films; **p.149** *all* Lynda King; **p.150** *both* Andrew Lambert; **p.151** *all* Ruth Hughes; **p.152** Emma Lee/Life File; **p.153** Dave Thompson/Life File; **p.155** *Monera* John Pacy/Science Photo Library, *Protista* Michael Abbey/Science Photo Library, *rest* Hodder Murray; **p.157** © Bettmann/Corbis; **p.158** Custom Medical Stock/Science Photo Library; **p.159** *t* Mike Birkhead/Oxford Scientific Films, *b* Science Photo Library; **p.161** Martin Dohrn/IVF Unit, Cromwell Hospital/Science Photo Library; **p.162** Science Photo Library; **p.163** *t* Martin Dohrn/Science Photo Library, *b* Ruth Hughes; **p.164** Ruth Hughes; **p.166** Anthony Cooper/Science Photo Library.

t = top, *b* = bottom, *l* = left, *c* = centre

The Publishers would also like to thank the British Library for permission to use the pictures of the heliocentric and geocentric universe (page 76) from *A perfit description of the Caelestiall Orbes 718g52* and *Cosmographia 1007.g.24*, respectively.

Although every effort has been made to ensure that website addresses are correct at time of going to press, Hodder Murray cannot be held responsible for the content of any website mentioned in this book. It is sometimes possible to find a relocated web page by typing in the address of the home page for a website in the URL window of your browser.

Orders: please contact Bookpoint Ltd, 130 Milton Park, Abingdon, Oxon OX14 4SB. Telephone: (44) 01235 827720. Fax: (44) 01235 400454. Lines are open 9.00–6.00, Monday to Saturday, with a 24-hour message answering service. Visit our website at www.hoddereducation.co.uk.

© Nigel Heslop, David Brodie, James Williams 2000, 2005
First published in 2000. This edition published 2005 by
Hodder Murray, an imprint of Hodder Education,
a member of the Hodder Headline Group
338 Euston Road
London NW1 3BH

Impression number   10 9 8 7 6 5 4 3 2 1
Year   2010 2009 2008 2007 2006 2005

Cover photo Science Photo Library
Typeset by Fakenham Photosetting Limited, Fakenham, Norfolk
Printed and bound in Italy

A catalogue record for this title is available from the British Library

ISBN-10: 0 340 88680 3
ISBN-13: 978 0 340 88680 9

Contents

Dedications

To my family, especially Will, for their inspiration and their perspiration.

Nigel Helsop

To my wife Joan, for her patience, understanding and practical advice, and to Laura and Sarah Grant for their expert advice in choosing the photographs.

James Williams

To Tom, Eleanor and Claire, not so much for being supportive as for being.

David Brodie

Picture this . . .

This section is to help you work out 'not understanding'.

Start off by reading this:

Everybody was there at junior school sports day. Luis, Maria, Vince and Serena had been friends since they all arrived in Britain with their parents, looking for a safe community to live in.

They lined up for the 60 metres sack race with two boys from another class. Maria had 'grown up' earlier than the others. She was much bigger and taller than her friends – her long legs seemed twice as long as theirs. She was bigger and stronger when they played games and they knew she would win for sure.

Miss Jack was the starter official. She was new to the school this year. They thought she looked cool with her bleached, braided hair and white Nike tracksuit. They concentrated on listening to her instruction.

The whistle blew and they were off. Some scuttled along and some hopped. The scuttlers put their feet in the corners of the sacks and ran. The hoppers pulled the sack up tight to their waist and hopped. Maria was a hopper, and a good one. By half-way she was well in front of the others, but then there was a crack and Maria fell to the ground with a scream.

The others were past her in no time and heard her whimper. At that moment the three friends turned, like synchronised swimmers, forgot the race and went back to comfort their friend.

Did you see the pictures in your head?

- School sports day
- Maria bigger and stronger than the others
- Miss Jack, the cool young teacher

And did the race play like a video in your head?

When you SEE THE PICTURES IN YOUR HEAD it means you understand what you are reading.

When you read or have something explained in science, try to make the pictures of what is happening appear in your head.

At first, perhaps it's just still pictures, of each stage in a description. You might see still pictures of Maria, the race, and Miss Jack. Then, if you concentrate hard, you can 'animate' the picture to make them play like a video. This is what UNDERSTANDING is like.

Task

Draw six boxes like this on your page. Look at each box in turn and imagine still pictures of the stages of making a cup of coffee for mum.

For example:

Coffee jar, milk and sugar	Kettle boiling	Spoon of coffee and sugar into cup
Add boiling water from kettle	Add milk	Stir and give to mum

Now imagine these still pictures and animate them to make them play together like a video. Can you see the whole process?

Working with words

Words usually have one meaning, but a word can have more than one meaning. This makes life a little bit complicated. So how are words constructed and can we work out what words mean in science?

Some words are constructed like this.

A root is the main part of the word. We can add to the root to change the word. The bits that we add are either prefixes (added in front of the word) or suffixes (added to the end of the word).

If we take the word 'carnivore' apart we can look at the root and see what's been added.

The root of this word is 'carni': it means flesh or meat.

The suffix '-vore' means feeding.

When we add the two together we get the word 'carnivore' which means meat eater or meat feeder. The word Bronchitis is made up in the same way. The root of the word is 'bronch' meaning windpipe and the suffix 'itis' simply means inflamed or diseased. So 'bronchitis' means that your windpipe is inflamed – something that gives you a cough!

Task

First here are some examples. See how many meanings of the words below you can work out from the table of roots, prefixes and suffixes shown.

- kilometre
- voltmeter
- thermograph

- input
- photosynthesis

Root	Meaning
photo	to do with light
thermo	to do with heat or temperature
electro	to do with electricity
ultra	extreme
volt	electrical unit

Prefix	Meaning
milli	thousandth
kilo	thousand
mega	million
in	in
out	out

Suffix	Meaning
metre	unit of distance
meter	measuring instrument
graph	picture
synthesis	making
sound	sound
magnetic	magnetic
sensitive	able to respond
joule	unit of energy
put	put

CHAPTER 1

Inheritance and selection

We usually identify our family and friends by the way they look. Humans can recognise faces quite accurately, but if we are trying to identify strangers or identify criminals and terrorists we may have to use other methods. Photographs date quickly, and if you change your hair colour or style it is harder to compare the person to their passport photo. Airports are now using biometric data to help identify individuals. From 2007, in order to obtain a passport or driving licence you may have to provide biometric data to be coded onto a computer chip.

The following things could be coded onto a chip for your passport, driving licence or possibly an ID card:

- **Fingerprint scan** – this records the ridges, furrows and patterns that appear on your fingertips. Fingerprints are unique to each person. The scan is done by a laser light passing across your fingertip while it is pressed onto a glass plate.
- **Iris scan** – this records the patterns in the coloured part of the eye, the iris. No two iris patterns are the same, and even the iris patterns in twins are different. Scans can be done from a distance of up to 40 cm. Your

Facial scan
Software reads image from camera

Iris scan
Camera produces an image of the iris, which is coded and analysed by the computer

Fingerprint scan
Scanner reads individual prints. The resultant mapping is converted into code, which is checked against database

iris pattern is fixed from about the age of 1 year.
- **Retinal scan** – this scans the pattern of blood vessels at the back of the eye. Again these patterns are unique to individuals. Scans require you to look directly into a scanner. Your retinal pattern is fixed from about the age of 1 year onwards.
- **Facial scan** – the surface contours of the face are scanned. A high definition camera takes your picture and computer software turns this into a digital map.
- **Voice scan** – the pitch, tone and pattern of your speech is scanned and recorded for comparison. A microphone records your speech.

Questions

1 Which of the above scans do you think are likely to be the easiest to obtain?

2 Which biometric data are most likely to change as you grow from childhood to adulthood?

3 Some people are against ID cards. Think about some of the issues surrounding the introduction of ID cards.

a) Write down at least three good reasons why we should have ID cards.

b) Write down at least three good reasons why people may object to having ID cards.

Why are we all similar, but not identical?

When most cells divide, the nucleus makes a copy of itself and each cell produced is identical to the cell it came from. All of the information needed to produce an identical copy of us is contained in the nucleus of each cell.

For a new life to begin, a sperm cell from the father and an egg cell from the mother must join together. This process is known as **fertilisation**. A similar thing happens in most plants. A pollen grain (the male cell) joins with an ovule (the female cell) and seeds are produced that can grow into new plants. This type of reproduction is known as **sexual reproduction**. In animals and plants it leads to new plants and animals that are similar, but not identical, to the parent plant or animal.

What living things look like and how they grow is controlled by **DNA** in the nucleus of the cell. In particular, it is controlled by small sections of DNA called **genes**. Every nucleus contains many thousands of genes – the genetic information, needed to produce an individual. Genes will control the colour of your eyes and hair, the shape of your nose, the production of protein in your muscles and many other things.

The genes are found on strands of DNA called **chromosomes**. The chromosomes occur in pairs. Each of our cells contains **23 pairs** of chromosomes, like the ones shown in Figure 2. Egg cells and sperm cells are specialised cells and they only have **23 single chromosomes**.

Stop and think!

Can you remember where the egg cells and sperm cells are produced? How are they specialised for the job that they do?

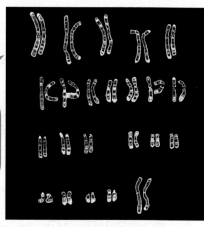

Figure 2 Human beings have 46 chromosomes in 23 pairs.

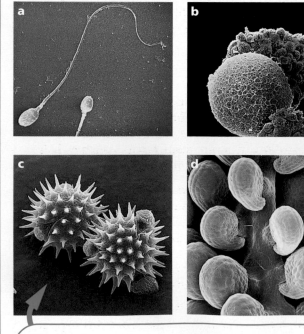

Figure 1 Sex cells: a) sperm cells, b) an egg cell, c) pollen grains, d) ovules. The colours are added.

Figure 3 shows how sperm cells would be produced in an animal with only four chromosomes (two pairs). In step 1 the cell divides just like a normal cell, making two cells each with four chromosomes. In step 2 the cell divides again, but this time one chromosome from each pair ends up in the new cell, making four cells each with two chromosomes.

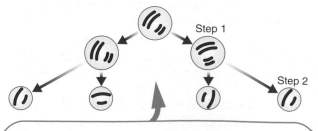

Step 1

Step 2

Figure 3 Producing sex cells from an animal with only four chromosomes.

When fertilisation takes place, chromosomes pair up again. A fertilised egg in this animal would have four chromosomes again, two from the father and two from the mother. In other words, there is a mixture of genes and chromosomes from the mother and father, so the offspring would have a mixture of features from the mother and father. This explains why offspring produced in this way are similar, but not identical, to the parents.

Twins

When two babies are born on the same day to the same mother, we call them **twins**. There may even be some pairs of twins in your school. There are two types of twins – **identical** and **fraternal**.

Identical twins can be exactly the same, or there may be small differences. Just after the egg is fertilised inside the mother, it begins to divide and grow. Before it gets too big, the egg splits completely into two. Because the DNA in each is identical, two identical babies develop. If the egg doesn't completely split, then conjoined twins can develop. These are often referred to as **Siamese twins** after the most famous pair Eng and Chang, born in Siam (now Thailand).

Figure 4 Eng and Chang, conjoined or Siamese twins, were born in Siam in 1811.

Fraternal twins happen when two different eggs in the mother are fertilised by two separate sperm. Because the DNA is not identical, the twins may be no more similar than normal **siblings**. They can even be of different sexes. The word fraternal actually means 'brother' but we use it to explain twins that are not identical, even if they are a brother and sister.

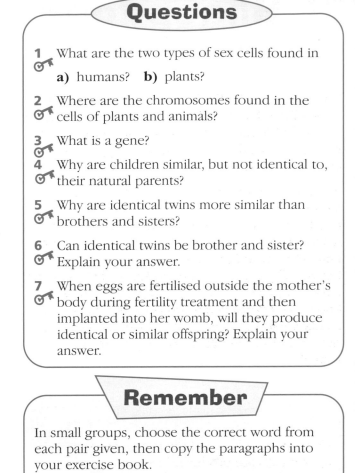

Questions

1 What are the two types of sex cells found in
   a) humans? **b)** plants?

2 Where are the chromosomes found in the cells of plants and animals?

3 What is a gene?

4 Why are children similar, but not identical to, their natural parents?

5 Why are identical twins more similar than brothers and sisters?

6 Can identical twins be brother and sister? Explain your answer.

7 When eggs are fertilised outside the mother's body during fertility treatment and then implanted into her womb, will they produce identical or similar offspring? Explain your answer.

Remember

In small groups, choose the correct word from each pair given, then copy the paragraphs into your exercise book.

Children are often SIMILAR/IDENTICAL to their natural parents. Many of your features are inherited from your parents. They are inherited through the CYTOPLASM/DNA found in the CELL MEMBRANE/NUCLEUS of nearly every adult cell. Specialised sex cells contain copies of the CYTOPLASM/DNA that are passed on to the offspring.

The DNA in the nucleus makes up strands called GENES/CHROMOSOMES. Small sections of these are called CHROMOSOMES/GENES. These control many of our characteristics such as hair colour, eye colour and the shape of our noses.

The male sex cell in humans is a SPERM/CHEEK CELL. In females, it is an egg or ovum. In plants, the male sex cell is NECTAR/POLLEN and the female sex cell is an ovule. Sex cells are specialised in a number of ways. One important way is that the amount of DNA is HALF/DOUBLE that found in an ordinary cell.

Identical twins happen when one fertilised egg completely splits in two. Fraternal twins happen when two different eggs are fertilised by two different sperm.

Sheepdogs

Sheepdogs are a good example of how we have bred traits, physical features or types of behaviour, into animals to create a breed that is useful to us.

Sheep and sheepdogs have been around in Britain since the Romans brought them when they invaded over 2000 years ago. In 1570, a Dr Caius wrote about the 'shepherd's dogge'.

Figure 1 A Border collie like this one is the breed of dog specially created for working with sheep. Crouching is one of the traits of a good sheepdog.

Hundreds of years ago, there were many breeds of working dog. Most of these breeds have now become **extinct**. Many disappeared when sheep and cattle were no longer being driven to market but were taken by rail and later lorries. Dogs were no longer needed to drive the animals over long distances.

Old paintings show dogs similar to the Border collie that we know today. The trick was to find dogs that had the traits that shepherds needed. A Northumbrian farmer, Adam Telfer, mated two collies, called Roy and Meg. Roy was a gentle dog, but not very good at herding, and Meg was a good herding dog. She gave birth to a puppy dog called 'Old Hemp' on 15th September 1893.

ADAM TELFER'S HEMP (9)

Figure 2 Old Hemp, the first true Border collie.

The Border collie as we know it today is descended from Old Hemp, who fathered over 200 puppies until his death in 1901.

Every dog has its day

Dogs have been both pets and working animals for centuries. We use dogs in a variety of ways – to aid the blind and the deaf, to guard premises and people and as companions. The ways in which we use the different traits dogs display can be quite inventive. Small dogs were used by hunters and poachers to flush animals out of their burrows. Large dogs are used to instill fear in people. Easily trained dogs that have a good temperament are used perhaps as seeing dogs for the blind and hearing dogs for the deaf. Others that used to be used for hunting and sniffing out prey may have traits that make them useful as sniffer dogs searching out explosives or drugs at airports. In your exercise book why not make a list of as many working dogs as you can and the traits that they would need to have in order to be good at their job. Use the following working dogs to start off your list. You could discuss in small groups the

Trait	Why it's important
A. Eye	Border collies control sheep with 'eye'. The dog concentrates on the sheep by staring at it. The sheep are 'held' by the dog's eye and a dog in which this characteristic is well developed is called 'strong-eyed'.
B. Crouch or clapping	Border collies have a tendency to 'clap' or go down and face the sheep with their stomachs close to the ground. This, along with 'eye', makes the dog look like a predator. Dogs were bred for clapping and strong eye for many years. Now some are being bred or trained to stay more on their feet so that they are ready to move quickly if necessary.
C. Balance	Border collies need to work rapidly and often have to change direction quickly to stop sheep from straying. To do this they need a keen sense of balance. For newer breeds of Border collie, where crouching is done more on their feet, balance is even more important.
D. Power	Border collies often need to cover a lot of ground in order to gather the sheep in fields scattered over the mountains. Powerful leg muscles are needed.
E. Speed and agility	Sheep can scatter very fast if they are startled or frightened. The Border collie needs to react quickly and be able to turn and twist.
F. Interest in moving targets	Border collies need to be alert and be able to pick up stray sheep that have split away from the main herd. If the dog didn't take any interest in moving targets, they could easily miss a stray sheep.

Table 1 Behaviour traits which make up the Border collie.

various traits and also whether or not we should train dogs to do some jobs.

- Guide dogs for the blind
- Hearing dogs for the deaf
- Sniffer dogs for drugs and explosives
- Dogs that perform tricks for TV, film or stage work
- Police dogs
- Guard dogs

Questions

1   The Border collie is a working dog, used to being very active in the countryside. What do you think you would have to do about the following if you kept a Border collie as a pet?

   a) Exercise

   b) Meals

   c) Training

2   What do we mean by the term 'trait'?

3   What traits do you think humans have bred into the following animals:

   a) a racehorse?

   b) a dairy cow?

4   Border collies, sometimes known as Welsh Sheep Dogs, were specially bred for herding farm animals. Is this an example of natural selection or artificial selection? Explain your choice.

Remember

Copy the following paragraph into your exercise book and write down the meaning of the words printed in bold type.

Animals can be specially bred to do a job. Sheepdogs are a good example of this. They have **traits** that make them suited to herding sheep. Some of the traits are **eye**, **crouch**, speed and **agility**, power and balance. We have used dogs to do different jobs for hundreds of years. As each **generation** of dog is bred for a purpose, we improve the breed. Sheepdogs are a breed called Border collies. The first Border collie was a dog called Old Hemp. All modern day Border collies are related to him. Breeding animals in this way is referred to as **artificial selection**. Dogs are used for many things, such as guide dogs for the blind and hearing dogs for the deaf. They also help the police and customs officers detect explosives and drugs or to track suspects and help **apprehend** them.

Farmer's beef

For many years, farmers have been selectively breeding animals for particular traits. One of the most famous examples of this is the Hereford breed of cattle.

If you visited a farm in the Middle Ages, the animals you would see would look similar to the ones we have today. You would recognise a cow, a sheep, a chicken and a pig but you'd also notice a lot of differences. Over hundreds of years, farmers have selected for breeding those animals that contain the traits that are most desirable to the farmer and their customers – i.e. us the consumer.

Where's the beef?

Almost 250 years ago, the Tomkins family of Herefordshire wanted to create a breed of cattle that could quickly and efficiently turn the grass of the local hills into beef. After years of selective breeding, the Tomkins finally produced a herd in 1756, and the line of the present-day Herefords was begun.

Figure 1 A modern-day Hereford cow.

In the 1700s and early 1800s, Herefords in England were much larger than they are today. Many weighed 1350 kg or more. Gradually, they were selectively bred smaller and smaller in order to get more quality and efficiency. Today's Miniature Herefords weigh between 450 and 550 kg.

Questions

1 Copy Table 1 into your exercise book and think of the traits or characteristics that the following common farm plants and animals need in order to be useful to us as food.

Plant/animal	Most desirable characteristics or features
Wheat	
Maize (corn)	
Potato	
Strawberry	
Dairy cow	
Pig	
Chicken (egg laying)	
Chicken (meat)	
Sheep (wool producer)	
Lamb (meat)	
Beef cattle	

Table 1

The Hereford Cattle breed is very common in America. Read the following account of how breeders have changed the breed and answer the questions at the end of the page.

Hereford Cattle changes

Following World War II, the compact, fatter type of cattle continued to be favoured in the show-ring, but there was a change taking place in the meat-packing industry and in the basic American diet. The commercial market for fat (beef tallow, which was used to make a type of wax and as an ingredient in other foods) had declined, and people were unwilling to buy the excess fat on joints of meat. The result was that beef packers paid less for over-fat cattle and the industry preferred a different type of animal. Demand was growing for a trimmer, leaner, more heavily-muscled kind of cattle. The once-preferred wide-backed, over-fat cattle no longer fetched a high price in the market place.

This change in the market meant two things had to happen to the cattle:

- they had to have a faster daily weight gain at less cost
- they had to increase conversion of feed to muscle instead of fat.

This presented breeders with a big challenge to modernise the breed and turn it into a new kind of Hereford. Breeders began using new-found tools such as artificial insemination and embryo transfer from one cow to another. This resulted in a faster change in the breed. Millions of animal records were kept on computer files to help breeders make improvements for generations to come.

In the late 1960s, breeders found that too many cattle did not have the growth rate and adult size found in some of the European breeds. They imported cattle from Europe to improve the Hereford breed.

The result is a breed of cattle called the Miniature Hereford that meets the needs of the meat packers and, therefore, the consumers. The breed efficiently converts feed to beef, grows at a relatively fast rate and has meat with the taste, look and properties that people want to buy in the supermarket.

Cows in the city

In Britain we are used to seeing herds of cows grazing in the fields. Dairy farmers have specialised milking sheds and produce millions of litres of milk that is collected by tankers, processed, bottled and ends up in our supermarkets or delivered to our doorstep. The farmers buy special food supplements and feeds for the cattle to make sure that they have a balanced diet and produce the best quality milk and greatest quantity of milk. In Britain we have room for the herds of cattle to graze in the summer months, and farmers cut grass and store it to use as feed during the winter months. But what if you lived in a large city in an area of the world where green fields and open spaces are not that easy to come by?

In Mexico City, many households keep their own dairy cows to provide a source of fresh milk. Over 60% of the households in an area to the east of the city have cattle in the backyard. They have between three and 19 cows. The problem is that many of these households do not have lush green fields on which the cattle can graze. Feeding the small herds of cattle is difficult so much of the feed comes

from vegetables that were rejected by the local markets for sale to humans or from by-products of foods processed for human consumption.

Most of the milk produced is sold locally. The milk is usually watered down, four parts water to one part milk. Any other milk not sold is processed to make cheese, cream, jelly and custard or given to calves to help them gain weight quickly. Herding cows in Mexico City is a good example of adapting farming to fit in with the conditions of the city.

In small groups decide which word to use from the pairs given below to complete the paragraph. Once you have checked it with your teacher, copy the paragraph into your exercise book.

For many years farmers have been using NATURAL SELECTION/ARTIFICIAL SELECTION to breed cattle that produce good quality MEAT/FUR. Another name for NATURAL SELECTION/ARTIFICIAL SELECTION is SELECTIVE BREEDING/CLONING. As well as cattle, many other plants and animals have been bred to produce better quality food or greater quantities of food or other useful products. Sometimes the CONSUMER/PRODUCER demands changes in the way that their food is produced. Today, people know that having too much fat in their diet can be unhealthy. As a result cattle that have LESS/MORE fat are produced.

In some countries cattle are kept in less than ideal conditions, such as in a poor area of Mexico City. Here, cattle are given a poor diet. This can lead to LESS/MORE milk being produced and the milk is often not of a HIGH/LOW quality. To compensate for LESS/MORE milk being produced, the farmers water the milk down.

Questions

2   What is beef tallow?

3   What reasons can you think of for people wanting leaner, less fatty joints of meat?

4   How do the cows 'efficiently turn the grass of the local hills into beef'?

5   What do you think is meant by the phrase 'embryo transfer from one cow to another'?

6   Why do the dairy producers water down the milk?

How do you grow a seedless grape?

Next time you eat a seedless grape, think about how it grew. Seedless grapes, oranges and other fruits are nice to eat and do not taste any different to fruits with seeds. You know that plants grow from seeds, so just how do you grow a seedless grape?

To understand how it is possible to grow a seedless grape, we first need to understand what happens when plants produce seeds.

Flowers normally produce either male sex cells, **pollen**, or female sex cells, **ovules**. After pollination has taken place, the pollen that sticks to the stigma begins to grow a **pollen tube**. This grows down the inside of the style, towards the ovules which are found in the ovary of the plant. Once an ovule has been reached, the male nucleus travels down the pollen tube and fuses with it. Seeds develop from the fertilised ovule and can then germinate into new plants.

Stop and think!

Can you remember how pollen is spread from one plant to another? Plants can reproduce either asexually or sexually. What is the difference between the two?

Can you remember how different types of plants scatter their seeds?

So plants normally only produce seeds once fertilisation of the ovule has taken place. The seeds can be contained in fruits, such as grapes, oranges and lemons. The fruits can then be eaten by animals and the seeds within the fruits are scattered in their droppings. Seeds are a nuisance to us, however, as we normally have to spit them out. So, just how do you grow a seedless grape or orange?

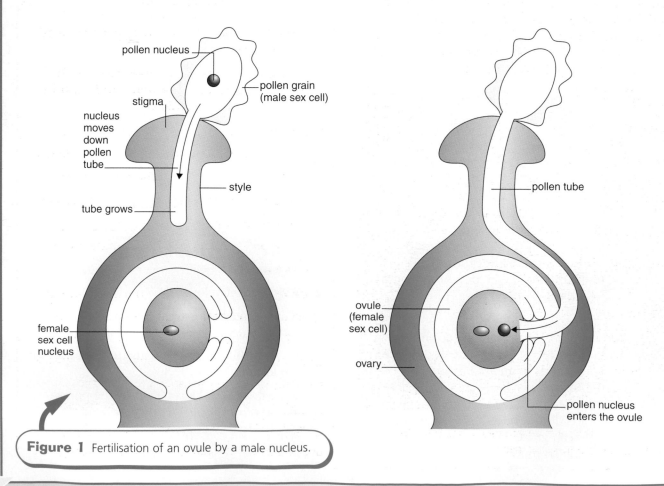

Figure 1 Fertilisation of an ovule by a male nucleus.

The answer is really quite simple. Plants have special chemicals called **hormones** that control how they grow as well as other things such as producing fruit, dropping leaves and fruit at the right time of year or simply growing roots. By spraying the grapevines with the hormone that controls fruiting, the plant can be forced to produce fruits, even though no fertilisation has taken place.

Not all plants produce fruits with seeds. Bananas, for example, are naturally seedless. The male flowers are sterile – which means that they cannot produce the male sex cell or pollen. It is the female flowers that produce the fruit. You may have thought that bananas grow on trees, but strictly speaking, this is not true. The banana plant has no wood fibres and so cannot be considered a tree. It is in fact the world's largest herb, related to the lily. The plant grows from an underground stem called a **rhizome**. New shoots grow up and clumps of bananas called 'hands' grow where the female flowers were. Banana plants only live for one year and produce one crop of bananas then they die off. A new banana plant pops up from the underground shoot to make a new plant.

Plantain is a very similar fruit to a banana but is used for cooking rather than eating raw. Plantain contains much more starch than a banana and the fruit is usually bigger. It is cooked when it is green so the starch can be broken down.

Figure 2 The banana plant might look like a tree but it is in fact a flowering plant.

1 Draw a simple strip cartoon to show how a pollen tube travels down the stigma and style to reach the ovules. (You might want to turn this into a flick book. Ask your teacher if you are unsure of what a flick book is and how to make one.)

2 What do the ovules normally develop into after they are fertilised?

3 What type of chemical do you think rooting powder contains to help cuttings from plants grow?

4 Plantain looks very much like a banana and is closely related. What is the main difference between them and what is plantain mainly used for?

5 What does the starch in plantain break down into when it is cooked?

6 What evidence do we have that bananas are not trees but are more like flowering plants?

Remember

Copy and complete the following paragraph into your exercise book.

**hormones stigma bananas style
ovules rhizomes pollen pollen tube
seedless**

Seeds develop once the female sex cells, the ____1____, have been fertilised by the male sex cells, the ____2____. Once the right type of pollen lands on the sticky ____3____ of a plant, the pollen develops a ____4____ that travels down the ____5____ to the ovary containing the ovules.

In order to grow ____6____ fruits, you have to spray the plants with special chemicals called ____7____. These chemicals make the plant grow fruit without being pollinated. Some plants naturally grow fruit without seeds, such as ____8____. New banana plants grow because special underground stems called ____9____ break through the surface and a new plant grows.

Bringing the quagga back to life

Once a species is extinct, we have lost it forever. In the film *Jurassic Park*, science was supposed to be able to recreate dinosaurs from their DNA found inside insects trapped in amber. The truth is that the methods used in the film are just not possible. But one man believes he can bring back an extinct animal using selective breeding.

Figure 2 Reinhold Rau (far right) with the quagga foal he remounted.

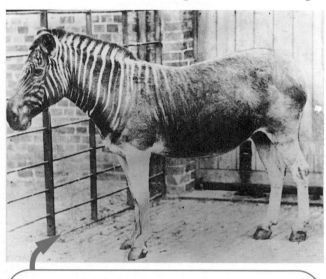

Figure 1 The only live quagga ever photographed lived in London Zoo in 1870.

Horses and zebras are very close cousins. The quagga is a variety of zebra. Figure 1 shows one of the last known quaggas.

Quaggas fed mainly on grasses growing on the Karoo plains of South Africa. Early settlers in the 1800s saw them as a competitor for the food they needed for their sheep, goats and horses to survive. Quaggas were hunted by the settlers and the hides exported or turned into leather for bags. Nobody gave any thought to saving the animal from extinction. By the 1860s there were few, if any, quaggas left in the wild. Some quaggas were still to be found in zoos. Unfortunately zoos then did not do much work on saving species. The last quagga, a mare kept at the Artis Magistra zoo in Amsterdam, died on the 12th August 1883.

Reinhold Rau, Head Taxidermist at the South African Museum, discovered a quagga foal in the museum in 1969. It was a little moth-eaten and badly mounted. He remounted it, and the results are shown in Figure 2.

What is a species?

For two plants or animals to be the same species, they must be able to breed with each other to produce fertile young. For example, all domestic cats belong to the same species (*Felis domesticus*). No matter what the variety of cat, Siamese, Persian etc., they can all mate with one another and produce kittens that can also mate with other cats and have kittens.

The quagga was originally thought to be different from the three other zebra species, but Rau was not convinced. He set out to prove that the quagga was a sub-species or variety of the plains zebra. He had noticed that some plains zebra had incomplete striping and were coloured a similar brown colour to the quagga. Unfortunately, because quaggas became extinct in 1883, we don't really know whether or not they could have produced fertile foals when mated with plains zebras. Reinhold Rau, however, had a piece of evidence that he couldn't use in 1969 but today proves that the quaggas were a variety of plains zebra. When he remounted the quagga foal in the museum, he found small pieces of quagga flesh stuck to the inside of the hide. When the quagga DNA was tested in the early 1980s, it was found to be almost identical to that of the plains zebra. That meant that quagga genes were still around in the DNA of the plains zebra.

Rau began recreating the quagga in 1987. By carefully selecting plains zebras with characteristics similar to quaggas, such as reduced striping or legs with no stripes, he has managed to breed zebra that are beginning to look like quaggas.

Figure 3 This specially-bred zebra foal has few stripes on its hind quarters.

Can we clone a quagga?

The quagga that Rau is trying to breed is not a clone. Clones are created using the DNA of a plant or animal to make an individual that is identical to its parent, like Dolly the sheep. To clone a quagga we would need to have a complete copy of its DNA. The problem with DNA is that it breaks down in time – the older the DNA is, the less complete it is.

Stop and think!

Can you remember how scientists cloned Dolly the sheep?

The coelacanth

One animal that we thought was extinct actually came back to surprise us less than 100 years ago. Just before Christmas in 1938 a large fish was caught off the coast of South Africa. Scientists had never seen such a strange looking fish, until one scientist, JLB Smith, remembered seeing similar fossilised fishes. He eventually identified it as a coelacanth – a fish thought to have been extinct for 70 million years. It lives deep in the oceans and only comes out from underwater caves at night. There are very few coelacanths in the ocean compared with other fish species, so catching one has proved very difficult.

Figure 4 A coelacanth – a genuine 'living fossil'.

Questions

1 What do biologists mean when they call an animal a 'variety'?

2 What was the main purpose of zoos in the 1860s and what do you think is different about what zoos do today?

3 How would we know that two plants or animals came from the same species?

4 Where would scientists find the DNA in the quagga flesh?

5 What are the problems in trying to clone new animals from the old DNA of extinct animals?

Remember

Put the following sentences into an order that makes a sensible paragraph.

However, when two animals of the same species look very different to each other, we say that they are two varieties of the same species.

When a species is extinct, it means that there are no more animals of that species left on Earth that can reproduce.

Animals that are of the same species do not have to look exactly like each other.

A quagga and a plains zebra are two varieties of the same species.

It may be possible to recreate a lost variety of a species using selective breeding.

Two dogs can look very different, such as a Great Dane and a terrier, but they are still the same species.

For two plants or animals to be of the same species, they must be able to breed and produce offspring that can also breed.

The forgotten evolutionist

Alfred Russel Wallace

You might remember the name of Charles Darwin. Most people know of him because of what is called Darwin's theory of evolution. Alfred Russel Wallace also came up with the theory of evolution by **natural selection**. In fact the theory could be known as the Wallace–Darwin theory. This is the story of Wallace and how the theory of evolution was published on 1st July 1858 to explain how plants and animals survived and changed over time, some to evolve into new species.

Alfred Russel Wallace was born on 8th January 1823 in the village of Llanbadoc, near Usk in Monmouthshire. He was the seventh of eight children. When Wallace was five, his family moved to Hertford, and he went to the local grammar school. He didn't like school but was interested in a wide range of subjects. After leaving school he worked with an elder brother, William, and trained as a surveyor. He eventually ended up in the market town of Neath in South Wales following the death of his brother. Using his surveying skills and his self-taught skills in architecture, he raised money by building a library and teaching in a local school to fund a trip to South America to find the origin of species. He had read the books of many travellers, including Darwin's *The Voyage of the*

Beagle, and decided that South America looked like the most interesting place to explore. He went in 1848 as a professional collector and sent back collections of birds, insects and other animals for sale to museums. In 1850, his younger brother Herbert joined him, but died of yellow fever in 1852. This upset Wallace and he decided to come back to England with all of his collections. He set sail from South America, but 25 days later the ship caught fire and sank, and with it went all of Wallace's belongings and all of his **specimens**. After being set adrift for 10 days, the crew and passengers were rescued and returned to England.

In 1854 Wallace set off again, this time to the other side of the world – the Malay Archipelago in the Pacific Ocean. It was here that he was to come up with his theory of evolution by natural selection. He spent some time collecting birds, mammals, insects and plants, sending them back to England to be sold to fund his trip. In 1855 he wrote an essay on evolution which was published in a scientific journal. Charles Darwin read this essay and was so impressed by it that he wrote to Wallace to congratulate him. The problem with the essay was that it didn't prove *how* evolution took place, it only really showed evidence that it had taken place. In 1858, Wallace had an attack of what was probably malaria, a tropical disease spread by mosquitoes. While he lay sick in his bed, he remembered an essay he had read about 10 years earlier written by Thomas Malthus. Malthus had written that the human population was kept down by war, disease and **famine**. Wallace realised that some of these would also affect animals. The weak ones would die but the strong ones would survive. When he had recovered enough from his attack of malaria, he wrote another essay, outlining his theory of evolution by natural selection.

Wallace was not a well-known scientist. In fact **he was not of the same social class as Charles Darwin**, whose rich family included doctors. Wallace, the son of a **bankrupt**, needed someone to help him publish his ideas. He remembered that Charles Darwin, a famous and **respected** scientist, had liked his earlier essay and so he sent it to him in February 1858, asking him to send it for publication if he thought it was good enough. When Charles Darwin received Wallace's letter and essay in June 1858 and read it he was very upset. He could see that Wallace had exactly the same explanation for how evolution took place as he did. In fact Darwin had also been **inspired** by Malthus's essay on population. Darwin called on two friends, the

Scientists

geologist Charles Lyell and the botanist Joseph Dalton Hooker to decide what should be done about Wallace's essay. They decided that rather than publish the essay on its own, which would have meant Wallace getting all the credit for the theory, they should publish some letters from Darwin that outlined his theory, and a short essay by Darwin written some years earlier but never published. On 1st July 1858 **the theory was announced to the world** at the Linnean Society of London. Lyell and Hooker presented the theory, as Wallace was still abroad and Darwin was too ill and upset to attend. Darwin had suffered from all sorts of illnesses for many years. Some people claim he was a **hypochondriac**. Added to this, his young baby was ill and died 2 days before the theory was presented.

Lyell and Hooker persuaded Darwin to write his now famous book *On the Origin of Species by means of Natural Selection* the following year. Wallace was unaware of what had happened until he received a letter in September 1858. Wallace never questioned Darwin's claim to be the man who thought of the theory of evolution. Many people say that the theory is about '**survival of the fittest**'. Darwin didn't actually think this phrase up. He was **persuaded** to use it by Wallace who borrowed it from another writer called Herbert Spencer.

Alfred Russel Wallace died on 7th November 1913 at Broadstone, Dorset, where his grave is marked by a large fossilised tree trunk. Charles Darwin, on the other hand, is buried along with many other famous scientists, poets and authors in Westminster Abbey.

Questions

1 Make a list of the words and phrases in bold and write down what they mean.

2 Why do you think Wallace needed to work as a professional collector selling collections of animals to zoos, unlike Charles Darwin who simply went on the *Beagle* as a companion to the captain and later as the ship's biologist?

3 If Wallace's letter was sent in February 1858, why might Darwin not have received it until June 1858?

4 Why do you think Wallace was unaware of what was happening to his theory during July 1858?

5 Who do you think should be given the credit for the theory of evolution by natural selection – Darwin, Wallace or both? Write down the reasons for your choice.

Scientists

Monica Grady – 'Dr Meteorite'

Monica Grady studies meteorites. She is fascinated by the rocks that fall from space onto the surface of the Earth. In particular she is interested in Martian meteorites, rocks that formed originally on Mars and were blasted into space by other meteorites hitting the surface of Mars. She has worked on the Martian meteorite ALH84001 – which may or may not show evidence of life on Mars. Monica studied chemistry and geology at the University of Durham, graduating in 1979. She then studied meteorites for her PhD, so she really is Dr Meteorite. She has travelled the world looking for meteorites, including to Antarctica, where ALH84001 was found, and the Nullarbor region in Australia. She has an asteroid named after her – asteroid number 4731 – now known as Monica Grady, and in 2003 she gave the Royal Institution Christmas lectures, *A Voyage in Space and Time*. Her book, *Search for Life,* is about looking for alien life in our universe. She believes that we are not alone in the Universe, but she hasn't seen any aliens or spaceships – yet.

Gene therapy

Genes control how your body looks and works. If your genes do not work properly, or if you have genes that have changed or **mutated** you may suffer from an illness that could be fatal. Gene therapy replaces the faulty genes with working genes. Gene therapy is a new development. It is hoped that eventually it will be able to cure a wide range of illnesses. SCID is one such illness.

SCID

A rare condition, called severe combined immunodeficiency (SCID), means that people born with a defective gene are unable to develop

David Vetter playing in his plastic bubble.

an immune system. In 1971 David Vetter was born with SCID. He lived for 12 years in a plastic, germ-free bubble and died in 1984. Recently SCID has been treated by gene therapy.

Some forms of cancer may also be treated using gene therapy.

How gene therapy works

For gene therapy to work scientists must get new genes into existing cells. They can do this in a number of ways.

- **Viruses:** Some viruses can inject their DNA into the cell where it can combine with the cell's own DNA. They are similar to the flu virus, but do not make you ill. The genes are inserted into the virus. Viruses are easy to introduce into the body and small enough to attach themselves to cells and deliver the genes to the cell.
- **Direct injection:** Small, circular pieces of DNA are injected directly into the cell. This can be less effective than using viruses. For cancer, the DNA has to be injected directly into a tumour.
- **Tumour cells:** A third method is to take tumour cells out of the body before adding new genes. This may be useful in making the cells more "visible" to the immune system. The cells are then injected back into the patient in the hope that immune cells will destroy them and any other cancer cells that look like them.

Activity

1 What sorts of things do genes control in humans?

2 What is a mutation?

3 Why might viruses be the best way to deliver genes to cells?

4 Briefly explain why it would be easier to treat skin cancer than a tumour inside the body using direct injection gene therapy.

5 Gene therapy could also be used to alter other genes such as eye colour, hair colour or skin colour to produce 'designer babies'. Do you think this is a good use of science? Write a brief argument either for or against using gene therapy to alter a baby's looks.

Reactions of metals and the reactivity series

Opener Activity
Reactions

Chemistry is like cooking. You mix stuff together, often add energy to start the changes, and end up with substances that are more useful at the end.

The building blocks of these substances are the elements listed in the Periodic Table (see page 167). The atoms of these elements are just rearranged in chemical reactions. They don't get changed. You have the same atoms at the end, just in different combinations.

Questions

1 Deepak works as a structural engineer. He uses a huge machine that tests steel bars until they break. Many steel bridges are getting rusty, so Deepak is testing the strength of samples of old steel. He makes his test fair by cutting 1 cm × 1 cm × 10 cm samples. The table shows his results.

a) Draw a chart to display the results.

b) How reliable are the test results

  i) after 10 years

  ii) after 150 years?

c) Write a short report, based on the results, about replacing the bridges.

d) Until the 150 year old bridge gets replaced, what is the maximum safe load that it can take?

	Breaking strength in tonnes		
	1st test	2nd test	3rd test
New	12	12	11
10 years old	12	11	11
20 years old	10	11	11
30 years old	11	12	11
50 years old	8	9	10
100 years old	7	7	8
150 years old	1	4	5

We need metals

Of the 90 elements that occur naturally, about 70 are metals. Of these 70, only a few are in common use.

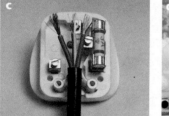

Figure 1 Uses of the six most common metals:
a) Iron is used to make steel. b) Manganese is used in stainless steel. c) Copper is used for electrical wiring. d) Aluminium is used for airframes. e) Silver is used to make expensive ornaments. f) Gold stays shiny, so is used for jewellery.

Metals are very important to us. Iron, in the form of steel, holds up most of our buildings, bridges and roadways. Steel is also used for trains, videos, dishwashers, forks and bedsprings. Iron in the form of steel is **strong**, **hard** and **tough**.

Other metals, like copper, can be **drawn out** into wires. **Shiny** metals, such as silver and gold, can be **bent** into decorative shapes for jewellery.

Alloys are mixtures of metals. It's as if one metal dissolved in another when molten. When the mixture is cooled down, the new mixed metal has better properties. Alloys, such as brass, make a **nice noise** when hit.

Magnetic materials are needed for motors and loudspeakers, and **conducting** metals are used for lighting, heating and making entertainment.

Questions

1 What are the properties of metals mentioned in the text? (*Hint*: there are nine properties. Look at the words given in **bold**.)

2 Explain what alloys are.

3 Explain how alloys might be made.

Non-metals

There are only about 20 non-metal elements. Of these, the six noble gases are involved in hardly any chemical reactions. But living organisms are mainly made from the non-metal elements carbon, oxygen, hydrogen and nitrogen. In addition, chlorine, sulphur and phosphorus have essential roles in the way our bodies work. Silicon is the main element in most rocks on the surface of the Earth. So, although there are few non-metals, they are the most important elements in our lives.

Questions

4 Make a list of the non-metal elements in the text above.

5 Use the list you made in Question 4 to fill in the first column of this table. Then fill in the other columns.

Non-metal element	What state of matter is it?	Description of what it looks like

Comparing metals and non-metals

	Metals	Non-metals
Surface texture	All metals are shiny	Most solid non-metals have a dull surface
Melting point	Most metals melt at high temperatures	Most non-metals melt at low temperatures
Hardness	Most metals are hard	Solid non-metals tend to be soft and easy to cut
Tensile strength	Many metals are strong	Most solid non-metals have a weak structure
Brittleness	Metals do not break, they bend (flexibility) Metals can be drawn into wires (ductility) and hammered into flat sheets (malleability)	Solid non-metals break very easily
Sound	Metals ring like a bell when hit	Solid non-metals make a dull thud when hit
Magnetism	Iron (steel), nickel and cobalt are the *only* magnetic materials	No non-metals are magnetic
Electrical conductivity	*All* metals conduct electricity	Non-metals do not conduct electricity except carbon in the form of graphite
Heat conductivity	Metals allow energy to flow through them, causing heating	Non-metals are poor at conducting energy to cause heating

Table 1 Comparing the properties of metals and non-metals.

Remember

Iron is 100% iron atoms. Steel is 99.6% iron atoms and 0.4% carbon atoms. Steel is much harder than iron.

Metal	Chemical symbol	World production (thousand tonnes per year)
Aluminium	Al	20 000
Antimony	Sb	130
Arsenic	As	40
Chromium	Cr	11 000
Cobalt	Co	20
Copper	Cu	12 000
Gold	Au	2
Iron	Fe	500 000
Lead	Pb	6000
Magnesium	Mg	300
Manganese	Mn	22 000
Molybdenum	Mo	120
Nickel	Ni	900
Silver	Ag	10
Tin	Sn	200
Tungsten	W	20
Uranium	U	35
Zinc	Zn	7000

Questions

6 What is the difference in composition between iron and steel?

7 What is the total world production of metals?

8 What are the four metals with the highest production figures?

9 What are these metals used for?

10 Using your answer from Question 7, what percentage of total metal production is iron production?

11 What metal is used to make most electrical wires?

12 a) Which two metals have the lowest production figures?

b) Suggest a reason for this.

Remember

Draw a series of cartoons to illustrate these two sentences:

'The properties of metals are shininess, toughness, flexibility, tensile strength, ringing like a bell, electrical conductivity and heat conductivity. Some metals (iron, cobalt and nickel) are magnetic.'

Table 2 World production of some common metals.

Acid patterns

All acids react in similar ways. This is because only the hydrogen ion in the acid does the reacting. All alkali reactions are the same for a similar reason.

When acids dissolve in water, they all split up to make **hydrogen ions**. These hydrogen ions are the 'acid reacting' particles. The other part of an acid is a '**spectator ion**'.

When acids and alkalis react in a **neutralisation** reaction, the spectator ions take no part. They stay dissolved in the solution.

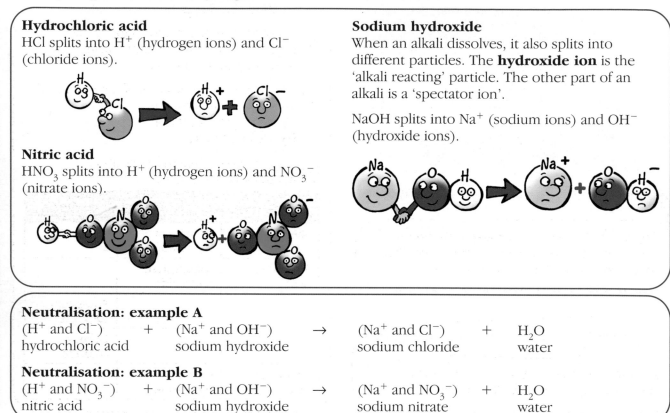

Hydrochloric acid
HCl splits into H^+ (hydrogen ions) and Cl^- (chloride ions).

Nitric acid
HNO_3 splits into H^+ (hydrogen ions) and NO_3^- (nitrate ions).

Sodium hydroxide
When an alkali dissolves, it also splits into different particles. The **hydroxide ion** is the 'alkali reacting' particle. The other part of an alkali is a 'spectator ion'.

NaOH splits into Na^+ (sodium ions) and OH^- (hydroxide ions).

Neutralisation: example A

$(H^+$ and $Cl^-)$	+	$(Na^+$ and $OH^-)$	→	$(Na^+$ and $Cl^-)$	+	H_2O
hydrochloric acid		sodium hydroxide		sodium chloride		water

Neutralisation: example B

$(H^+$ and $NO_3^-)$	+	$(Na^+$ and $OH^-)$	→	$(Na^+$ and $NO_3^-)$	+	H_2O
nitric acid		sodium hydroxide		sodium nitrate		water

If you remove the spectator ions, both neutralisation equations are exactly the same:

$$H^+ + OH^- \rightarrow H_2O$$

Only one change happens in any acid–alkali reaction – hydrogen ions join with hydroxide ions to make water molecules. The spectator ions are left over. They form the **salt** in the reaction.

Sulphuric acid is slightly different when it dissolves. It splits up to make two hydrogen ions from each sulphuric acid particle.

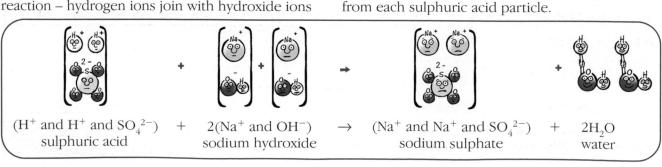

$(H^+$ and H^+ and $SO_4^{2-})$	+	$2(Na^+$ and $OH^-)$	→	$(Na^+$ and Na^+ and $SO_4^{2-})$	+	$2H_2O$
sulphuric acid		sodium hydroxide		sodium sulphate		water

Making salts

When acids get neutralised and water molecules get left, the 'spectator ions' are left as a solution.

These make a salt. There are lots of different salts – some of them have common names as well as chemical names.

Reactions of metals and the reactivity series

Common name	Chemical name
Table salt	Sodium chloride
Epsom salts	Magnesium sulphate
Saltpetre	Potassium nitrate
Lo salt	Contains potassium chloride
Sea salt	Contains sodium iodide

Table 1 Names of some common salts.

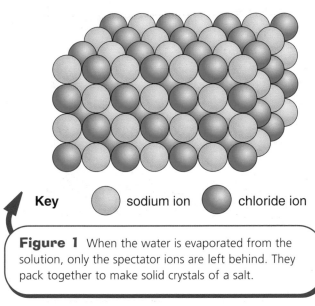

Key ○ sodium ion ● chloride ion

Figure 1 When the water is evaporated from the solution, only the spectator ions are left behind. They pack together to make solid crystals of a salt.

Remember

You can work out the name of the salt from the names of the acid and alkali that made it.

Questions

1 What particle is present in all acid reactions?

2 What particle is present in all alkali reactions?

3 What is a spectator ion?

4 Draw particle pictures for nitric acid (HNO$_3$) being neutralised by calcium hydroxide solution (Ca(OH)$_2$).

5 Draw particle pictures for sulphuric acid (H$_2$SO$_4$) being neutralised by calcium hydroxide solution (Ca(OH)$_2$).

6 How many new molecules of water are made in the reaction between:
   a) H$_2$SO$_4$ and Ca(OH)$_2$
   b) HCl and KOH?

7 Copy and complete this table about neutralisation and salts.

Name of acid	Name of alkali	Name of salt
Nitric acid	Potassium hydroxide	
Sulphuric acid	Magnesium hydroxide	
		Potassium sulphate
		Lithium chloride
Phosphoric acid	Calcium hydroxide	

First part of name from alkali		Second part of name from acid
sodium hydroxide makes a 'sodium' salt	with	hydrochloric acid makes a 'chloride' salt
potassium hydroxide makes a 'potassium' salt	with	sulphuric acid makes a 'sulphate' salt
calcium hydroxide makes a 'calcium' salt	with	nitric acid makes a 'nitrate' salt
magnesium hydroxide makes a 'magnesium' salt	with	ethanoic acid makes an 'ethanoate' salt

Table 2 Naming salts.

Remember

Complete the paragraph using the words below.

looks on part idea acid alkali spectator different hydrogen hydroxide

When acids react, only the ___1___ ion particles in the ___2___ solution take part in the change. The other part of the acid particle just ___3___ and takes no ___4___ in the change. It is often called a ___5___ ion. This is why ___6___ acids have the same type of reaction. The same general ___7___ applies to ___8___ reactions. Only the ___9___ ion takes part in the change.

Acid treatment

There are several types of substances that will neutralise acids. They are called bases.

Acid + alkali (soluble base) → salt + water
Acid + metal oxide (base) → salt + water
Acid + carbonate (base) → salt + water + carbon dioxide

Metals also react with acids but they are not bases.

Acid + reactive metal → salt + hydrogen

You have learnt about alkalis that neutralise acids. Any chemical that will neutralise an acid *to make a salt plus water* is called a **base**. An alkali is a **soluble base**.

Don't confuse the chemical word 'base' with all the other meanings of the word base e.g. in sports, part of apparatus, in mountain climbing, in 'back to base' etc. Alkalis are a particular sort of chemical base. They are metal oxides that dissolve in water to form a 'hydroxide' solution.

Many reactive metals will also react with some acids, but metals are not called bases. They do not react to produce water molecules. Reactive metals combine with acids by displacing hydrogen from the acid compound. So the reaction is a **displacement reaction** not a neutralisation reaction. Be careful though, this reaction does not work for the less reactive metals, such as copper or gold, or for certain acids such as nitric acid.

Figure 1 Rust remover. Phosphoric acid is used to dissolve rust off iron and steel. It's exactly the right strength to work. The iron oxide is dissolved quickly by the acid but the acid is weak and only dissolves the iron metal slowly. When all the rust has gone, the acid is washed off with lots of water, leaving clean metal.

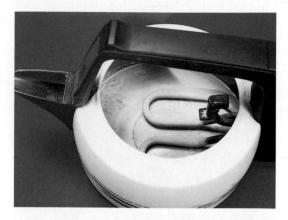

Figure 2 Kettle scale (top). Acids are also used to dissolve the limescale that gets on kettle elements (bottom). Limescale is calcium carbonate (like chalk). The acid dissolves it with a fizz to show it is working. Tartaric acid is used as it dissolves the limescale but doesn't attack the metal and won't make the tea taste nasty.

1 Acid plus metal oxide

Alkalis are metal oxides that dissolve in water. Some metal oxides don't dissolve, but they all react with acids in a similar way. All metal oxides are called bases because they neutralise acids.

$$(H^+ \text{ and } H^+ \text{ and } SO_4^{2-}) + MgO \rightarrow$$
$$\text{sulphuric acid} \quad\quad \text{magnesium oxide}$$

$$(Mg^{2+} \text{ and } SO_4^{2-}) + H_2O$$
$$\text{magnesium sulphate} \quad\quad \text{water}$$

The oxygen in the oxide neutralises the hydrogen ions in the acid. A water molecule gets made and the 'spectator ions' are left. They make magnesium sulphate.

Reactions of metals and the reactivity series

2 Acid plus carbonate

Magnesium carbonate has the formula $MgCO_3$. It is a base – it dissolves in acids and neutralises them. It's as if MgO (magnesium oxide) had absorbed a molecule of CO_2 (carbon dioxide). When any carbonate reacts with any acid, a molecule of carbon dioxide gets set free.

So the reaction between an acid and a carbonate is similar in pattern to the reaction between an acid and a metal oxide.

$$(\text{H}^+ \text{ and } \text{H}^+ \text{ and } \text{SO}_4{}^{2-}) \quad + \quad MgCO_3 \quad \rightarrow$$
$$\text{sulphuric acid} \qquad\qquad\qquad \text{magnesium}$$
$$\text{carbonate}$$

$$(\text{Mg}^{2+} \text{ and } \text{SO}_4{}^{2-}) \quad + \quad H_2O \quad + \quad CO_2$$
$$\text{magnesium} \qquad\qquad \text{water} \qquad \text{carbon}$$
$$\text{sulphate} \qquad\qquad\qquad\qquad \text{dioxide}$$

3 Acid plus metal – a less predictable reaction

Acids react quickly with reactive metals. A metal atom reacts like a metal oxide – but leave the oxygen out of the equation. So instead of H_2O (water), the product is H_2 (hydrogen).

$$(\text{H}^+ \text{ and } \text{H}^+ \text{ and } \text{SO}_4{}^{2-}) \quad + \quad \text{Mg} \quad \rightarrow$$
$$\text{sulphuric acid} \qquad\qquad\qquad \text{magnesium}$$

$$(\text{Mg}^{2+} \text{ and } \text{SO}_4{}^{2-}) \quad + \quad H_2$$
$$\text{magnesium} \qquad\qquad \text{hydrogen}$$
$$\text{sulphate} \qquad\qquad\qquad \text{gas}$$

This reaction is like a displacement reaction. The magnesium metal takes the place of the hydrogen in the sulphuric acid and steals the sulphate ion away from the hydrogen.

Magnesium reacts quickly with acids and makes lots of fizz. Zinc and iron react less quickly and lead reacts so slowly that you need strong acid to be able to see anything.

Metals such as copper, silver and gold are too unreactive to take the place of the hydrogen. They don't react with acids.

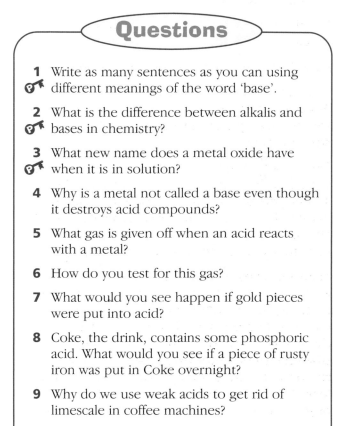

Questions

1 Write as many sentences as you can using different meanings of the word 'base'.

2 What is the difference between alkalis and bases in chemistry?

3 What new name does a metal oxide have when it is in solution?

4 Why is a metal not called a base even though it destroys acid compounds?

5 What gas is given off when an acid reacts with a metal?

6 How do you test for this gas?

7 What would you see happen if gold pieces were put into acid?

8 Coke, the drink, contains some phosphoric acid. What would you see if a piece of rusty iron was put in Coke overnight?

9 Why do we use weak acids to get rid of limescale in coffee machines?

10 What is the fizzy gas given off when acids are used to remove limescale?

Remember

Copy and complete this table using the information from the text, then learn the names and formulae of these particles.

Particle name	Particle formula	Particle name	Particle formula
Hydrogen ion		Hydrogen molecule	
Hydroxide ion		Water molecule	
Chloride ion		Sodium ion	
Nitrate ion		Carbon dioxide molecule	
Sulphate ion		Sulphuric acid	
Magnesium ion		Magnesium carbonate	

Metal and non-metal oxides

Every element's favourite partner is oxygen. Oxygen is very reactive and will oxidise metal and non-metal alike. Non-metal oxides are acidic.

Strong chemicals

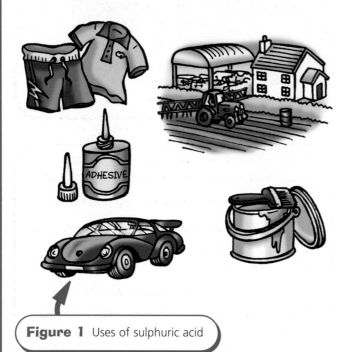

Figure 1 Uses of sulphuric acid

Sulphuric acid is probably the most important chemical to industry. It is used in the manufacture of nearly everything we use. Take yellow sulphur powder and burn it in air. The gas given off would choke you if you breathed it in, but it's the starting material for sulphuric acid.

Sodium hydroxide is not just a laboratory chemical. Its common name is caustic soda. It is used as paint stripper, oven cleaner and to unblock drains. It makes other materials squishy and soapy. In fact making soap has always been one of its biggest uses.

Figure 2 Uses of sodium hydroxide

TAKE CARE: BOTH SULPHURIC ACID AND SODIUM HYDROXIDE ARE DANGEROUS

Rainbow chemicals

Look at Figure 3 below. It's easy to recognise the metals. They are shiny solids that conduct heat and electricity well. They are found on the left-hand side of the Periodic Table. The shininess is true for sodium when it is freshly made or cut, but it corrodes in seconds when water or air gets to it. That's why it's stored in oil.

The non-metals are on the right. The non-metals are gases or dull-coloured solids that melt easily. Phosphorus is stored in water. If it's exposed to air, it oxidises so easily that it bursts into flame. Silicon is a puzzle. It is a shiny non-metal with a high melting point.

| Sodium | Calcium | Aluminium | Silicon | Phosphorus | Sulphur | Chlorine | Argon |

Figure 3 These are the elements of the third row of the Periodic Table. All of them except argon will easily react with oxygen. Argon is a very unreactive element and forms no compounds at all. Because it is unreactive it is used to fill light bulbs.

Figure 4 The oxides are rather dull looking, but put an indicator in the solution and a rainbow of colour results. Aluminium oxide and silicon oxide are not soluble, so the yellowy-green colour of jars three and four is the colour Universal Indicator goes with water.

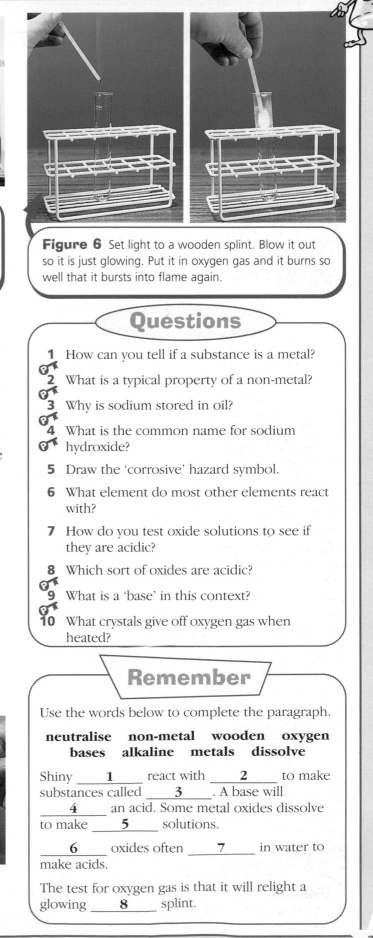

Figure 6 Set light to a wooden splint. Blow it out so it is just glowing. Put it in oxygen gas and it burns so well that it bursts into flame again.

The metal oxides all neutralise acids. Substances that neutralise acids are called **bases**. Aluminium oxide is insoluble, but neutralises acids so it is a base. Sodium oxide and calcium oxide are bases and they dissolve to form **alkaline** solutions.

Phosphorus oxide and sulphur dioxide dissolve to produce strongly acidic solutions. Chlorine oxide is also acid. Silicon dioxide will react like an acidic oxide but is insoluble. So non-metal oxides act like acids.

Testing a gas: oxygen

(a)

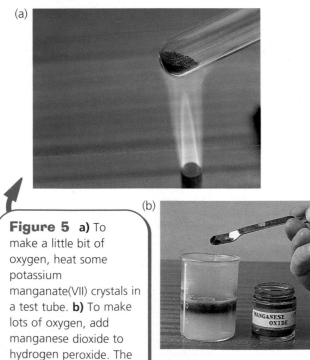

(b)

Figure 5 a) To make a little bit of oxygen, heat some potassium manganate(VII) crystals in a test tube. **b)** To make lots of oxygen, add manganese dioxide to hydrogen peroxide. The peroxide molecules break up to produce oxygen.

Questions

1 How can you tell if a substance is a metal?

2 What is a typical property of a non-metal?

3 Why is sodium stored in oil?

4 What is the common name for sodium hydroxide?

5 Draw the 'corrosive' hazard symbol.

6 What element do most other elements react with?

7 How do you test oxide solutions to see if they are acidic?

8 Which sort of oxides are acidic?

9 What is a 'base' in this context?

10 What crystals give off oxygen gas when heated?

Remember

Use the words below to complete the paragraph.

**neutralise   non-metal   wooden   oxygen
bases   alkaline   metals   dissolve**

Shiny ____1____ react with ____2____ to make substances called ____3____. A base will ____4____ an acid. Some metal oxides dissolve to make ____5____ solutions.

____6____ oxides often ____7____ in water to make acids.

The test for oxygen gas is that it will relight a glowing ____8____ splint.

Metals

Most elements are metals. All metals are useful materials. Metals are found in rocks, but except for gold, they are usually in the form of metal compounds. These compounds are chemically changed to give us the pure metals.

Over millions of years, all the metals in the earth except **gold** reacted with oxygen. They became metal oxides and were part of the rocks. The metal oxides are no use to us, but the metals are very useful. Gold was rare and precious.

Ten thousand years ago every home, big or small, cave or palace had a fire. Man built his fire on rocks to keep it under control. When he cleaned out the fire, he found shiny blobs of copper metal. He made a necklace out of them.

Seven thousand years ago the Afghan people were deliberately 'smelting' rocks with charcoal to get copper. The carbon in the charcoal changed the copper oxide to copper. The carbon is more reactive than the copper. It will **steal** the oxygen away from it. Copper oxide and carbon became carbon dioxide and copper.

Five thousand years ago people found out about bronze. Mixing rocks containing copper and tin made a metal that was much harder than either copper or tin.

Three thousand years ago people living near the Black Sea in Eastern Europe could make iron. Making iron needs high temperatures. Carbon is used to reduce iron oxide to iron. People used the iron to make tools and weapons. Iron was very much harder than bronze.

The Romans came to Britain 2000 years ago. They used the copper and tin mines here. They also made lead metal. Lead pipes have been found in Roman remains.

The more **reactive** metals can only be produced by ripping compounds apart with **electricity**. Aluminium was a precious metal in the time of Napoleon in the early 1800s.

Now we know about 70 or more metals. Most were discovered in the last 150 years.

Questions

1 What metal is found naturally as an element?

2 Where are other types of metals found?

3 What were people doing when they accidentally made metal?

4 Which metals were discovered first?

5 What element was used to remove the oxygen from metal compounds?

6 Why was iron more difficult to make?

7 Which common metal was once precious?

8 How are the more reactive metals like aluminium made?

Remember

Complete the spaces using words from the text.

_____1_____ are man-made materials. Only _____2_____ is found naturally as an element. Metals are found in the _____3_____ as compounds with _____4_____. The metals are released from the compounds by removing the oxygen. _____5_____ *carbon* will _____6_____ *steal* the oxygen from many metal compounds. More _____7_____ *reactive* metals are made using _____8_____ *electricity*

Making metals from rock

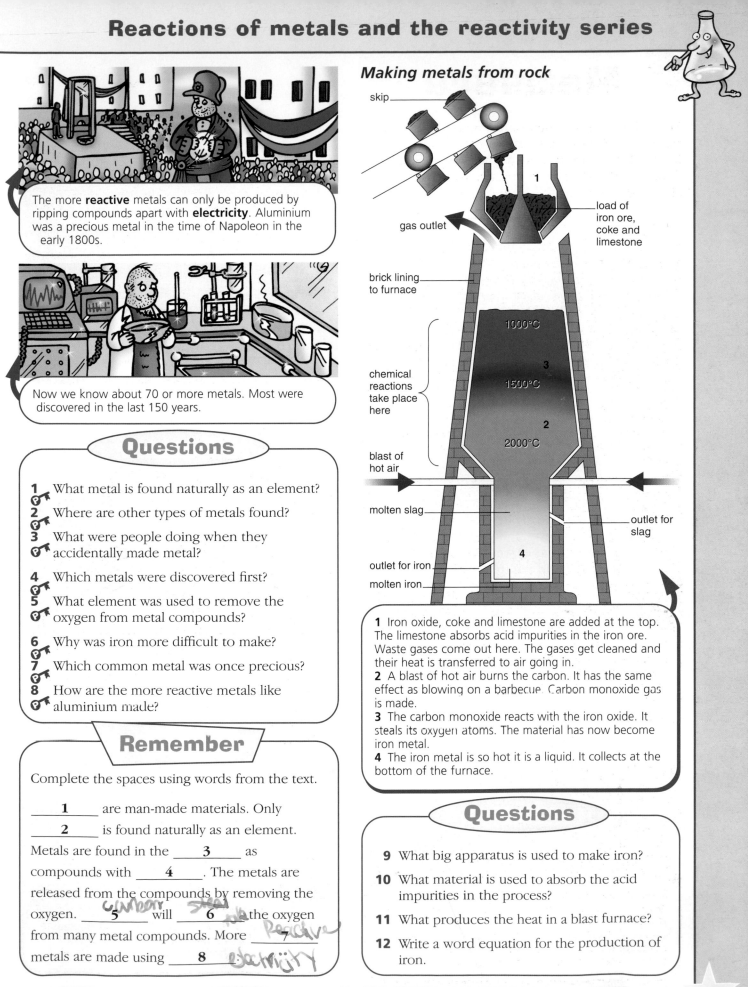

skip

gas outlet

load of iron ore, coke and limestone

brick lining to furnace

1000°C

3 1500°C

chemical reactions take place here

2 2000°C

blast of hot air

molten slag

outlet for slag

outlet for iron

molten iron

4

1 Iron oxide, coke and limestone are added at the top. The limestone absorbs acid impurities in the iron ore. Waste gases come out here. The gases get cleaned and their heat is transferred to air going in.
2 A blast of hot air burns the carbon. It has the same effect as blowing on a barbecue. Carbon monoxide gas is made.
3 The carbon monoxide reacts with the iron oxide. It steals its oxygen atoms. The material has now become iron metal.
4 The iron metal is so hot it is a liquid. It collects at the bottom of the furnace.

Questions

9 What big apparatus is used to make iron?

10 What material is used to absorb the acid impurities in the process?

11 What produces the heat in a blast furnace?

12 Write a word equation for the production of iron.

Treasure

Some metals react much more easily and more vigorously than others. There is a league table for the reactivity of metals called the reactivity series.

> *I brought a treasure chest back from my travels and I have hidden it deep in the cellars below the house. It was full of objects made from valuable metals.*
> *There was gold and silver.*
> *There was the finest ironware we had ever seen.*
> *There were beautiful copper drinking vessels.*
> *There were plates of a strange new metal.*
> *This metal was very light in colour and weight.*
> *But I am badly ill and will not survive the winter...*

Two sisters were visiting their grandparents at their old seaside house. They made an exciting discovery. This note was among the papers of an ancestor of theirs. So they went exploring in the deep cellars and found the treasure chest.

Sea water had been washing over the chest at high tide. The chest was covered in lead sheeting to protect the wood. This had been badly corroded by the sea, but was still intact. When they opened the chest they had some disappointments.

Figure 1 What the girls found in the chest.

The gold ornaments were in perfect condition. Their surface was as shiny and beautiful as the day they were made. The silver helmet and buckles were very fine. The silver lattices on the sides of the helmet were intact. The silver was dark and black, but only on the surface.

The copper goblets were heavily pitted by the sea water. It had corroded the metal in many places. But they were still useable, and they cleaned up well.

The thin iron daggers with fine handles were useless. They were a mess of crumbly rust. Worst of all were the metal plates. They had been reduced to a white powder. The sea water had completely corroded them away.

Figure 2 The girls' aunt explained what had happened: 'Metals have different reactivities. The salt in sea water makes it quite corrosive to metals. Gold is the least reactive of the metals. It stays shiny for centuries. Silver reacts very slowly. Usually it only tarnishes on the surface. Copper and lead corrode slowly. But this is speeded up by sea water. Lead corrodes faster than copper. Iron is actually quite a reactive metal. Corrosion damages car exhausts very quickly. Aluminium was the light metal used for the plates. Normally it has a protective layer of oxide on the surface. But the sea water dissolves this away. The aluminium will have reacted quickly with the sea water.'

Reactions of metals and the reactivity series

Questions

1 Make a list of all the metals mentioned in the passage.

2 Which metal has reacted least with the sea water?

3 Which metal must have reacted fastest?

4 Fill in a list of all the metals in order of reactivity. Start with the fastest or most reactive at the top.

5 Which two metal objects became useless when in sea water?

6 What is the word used for the damage caused to metal objects by sea water?

Magnesium is a metal that reacts more strongly than copper and iron. There is a league table of reactivity for metals. It is called the **reactivity series**.

Magnesium
Aluminium
Zinc
Iron
Lead
Copper
Silver
Gold

Metals that are higher in the reactivity series will displace metals that are lower than them from their compounds. Displacement reactions are often used to find out where an element is in the reactivity series.

A league table

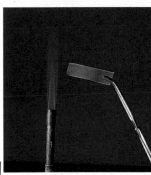

Figure 3 Metals react differently with the oxygen in the air when heated. Copper (a) goes black but magnesium (b) bursts into flame.

(a)   (b)

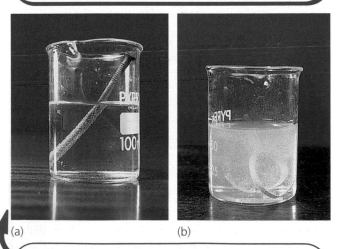

(a)   (b)

Figure 4 Metals react at different rates with acids. Iron (a) fizzes very slowly, but magnesium (b) dissolves very quickly. They both displace hydrogen from the acid.

Figure 5 Zinc has displaced copper from copper sulphate solution.

Remember

Complete the spaces below using the words from the text.

Some chemical changes like the ____1____ of metals are not useful.

Most ____2____ will react with ____3____, water and ____4____. There is a ____5____ table of how strongly metals react. It is called a ____6____ series.

Reactivity to order

Alkali metals are the most reactive of all the metals. They occupy the top places in the reactivity series.

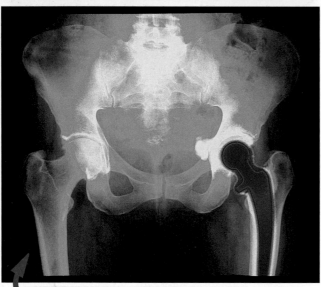

Figure 1 Titanium is an important metal. It's expensive, but is very strong and only half the weight of steel. It's used in aeroplane parts, particularly high-performance military jets and modern airliners. However, those are not its only uses. Its resistance to corrosion and its lightness make it the ideal material for replacement hip joints.

Titanium metal is made in the following reaction. It works because sodium is more reactive than titanium.

titanium tetrachloride + sodium metal → titanium metal + sodium chloride

These are the steps in the process:

- Sodium metal is melted.
- Titanium tetrachloride is put in a container filled with argon (an inert gas).

- Exactly the right amount of molten sodium is stirred in, a little at a time.
- Huge amounts of heat are released as the sodium displaces the titanium.
- The mixture is allowed to solidify.
- A small explosion is used to break it into lumps.
- The sodium chloride is dissolved using dilute hydrochloric acid.
- The acid is neutralised and passed out into the sea.

Questions

1 Why is titanium used in aeroplanes?

2 Why is titanium used in replacement hip joints?

3 Write a balanced symbol equation for the titanium displacement reaction. (*Hint*: tetra means four.)

4 Why is an inert gas used to fill the reaction container?

5 Why is heat released in the reaction?

6 Why is the acid neutralised before being diluted in the sea?

Alkali metals are **caustic** – they will attack and damage flesh. Alkali metals react with oxygen in water molecules or oxygen in the air to make **oxides**. These oxides dissolve in water to make compounds called **hydroxides**. These hydroxides are strong alkalis. They make slimy soap out of your flesh and they do it very quickly. So beware of any contact with alkali metals or the hydroxides they form. The damage they cause is painful and particularly dangerous to the eyes.

Sodium hydroxide's common name is caustic soda. It is used for cleaning ovens and unblocking drains. It turns the muck blocking the drain into slime that can be washed away.

The alkali metals

The alkali metals are: lithium, sodium, potassium, rubidium, caesium, francium (this one is very rare and radioactive).

This is a really spectacular set of elements. They are the most reactive of all the metals. They react rapidly with the oxygen in the air – so rapidly that they must be stored in oil.

Figure 2 Lithium reacts rapidly with water, producing hydrogen gas. The lithium dissolves and becomes lithium hydroxide solution.

Figure 3 Sodium gets melted by the heat released as it reacts with the water. The molten blob races round the surface on a cushion of hydrogen gas.

Figure 4 Potassium reacts so rapidly that it bursts into flame when it is in contact with water. The material burning is the hydrogen gas produced by the reaction. The lilac colour is caused by potassium particles getting heated in the flame.

Figure 5 Rubidium reacts so rapidly that the heat from the burning hydrogen makes the metal explode and fly about the room. Rubidium is very caustic, so this is far too dangerous to do in a school laboratory. People would be blinded.

Figure 6 WOW!! The reaction between caesium and water is even more explosive.

Questions

7 Why are alkali metals dangerous?

8 Write a word equation for sodium reacting with water.

9 Why doesn't the hydrogen produced in the lithium/water reaction catch fire?

10 Look at the alkali metal reactions and put the metals in order of reactivity.

11 Look at the place of the alkali metals in the Periodic Table. What connection is there between position on the table and reactivity?

Remember

Draw up a new safety sign warning about the dangers of the alkali metals. Use images and not words – be creative!

Unspoilt Antarctic

Metals will compete with each other. The ones that are more strongly reactive will win.

Figure 1 Bingham Canyon, Utah. This hole in the ground is nearly 1000 metres deep. It used to be a mountain, but it was found to be a rich source of copper ore.

Metals are precious resources. It is always a problem to find more sources of metal ores. One place where there are large amounts is Antarctica. But should this lost and unspoilt continent be mined and its natural resources extracted for the good of mankind? Greenpeace thinks they should not. There are many useful metals there. To get them out of the ground would require a large-scale industry. Metal ore rarely contains more than 1% of useful material, so there is always a great deal of waste material and mess. This would get dumped in the unspoilt Antarctic wilderness. The development of industry could prevent the observation of wildlife and the scientific work done there.

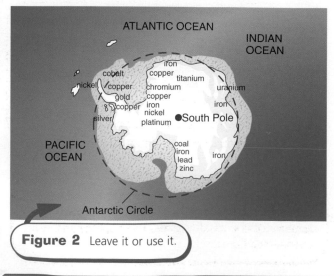

ATLANTIC OCEAN

INDIAN OCEAN

iron
cobalt copper
titanium
nickel copper chromium uranium
gold copper
copper iron
iron
nickel ●South Pole
silver platinum

PACIFIC OCEAN

coal
iron
lead iron
zinc

Antarctic Circle

Figure 2 Leave it or use it.

Questions

1 What metals can be found in the Antarctic?

2 Write a short newspaper article in favour of mining in the Antarctic.

3 Write a letter in reply to the article in Question 2 opposing mining in Antarctica.

4 Produce a poster in support of the opinion in Question 2 or 3.

Reactivity series

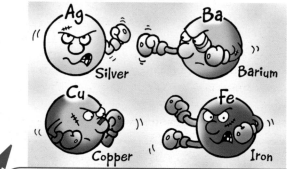

Ag   Ba
Silver   Barium
Cu   Fe
Copper   Iron

Figure 3 Many chemical reactions show the difference in reactivity between metals. Metals don't just compete with each other for oxygen. They will fight each other in any reaction. They compete even more easily in solutions.

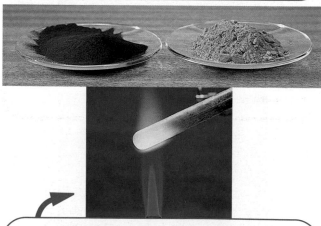

Figure 4 A bit of heat gives the reaction between copper oxide and zinc (top photo) a kick-start. The zinc powder steals the oxygen away from the copper oxide. This makes copper metal. The zinc turns into zinc oxide. As the zinc contains more chemical potential energy than the copper, lots of energy is transferred to the surroundings as heat and light.

Figure 5 Railway workers use a mixture called 'thermit' to weld rails together when they are broken. Thermit is a mixture of iron oxide and fine aluminium powder. A magnesium fuse is used to set the reaction off. When heated, the aluminium steals the oxygen from the less reactive iron. A great deal of energy is released. This melts the iron. The iron metal produced fills the gap between the rails and joins them.

Figure 6 Iron filings and copper sulphate solution before the reaction.

Making metals

Iron

Iron ore is reduced to iron metal by carbon monoxide in a blast furnace. The carbon monoxide steals the oxygen away from the iron.

$$Fe_2O_3 + 3CO \rightarrow 2Fe + 3CO_2$$

Aluminium

Aluminium is much more reactive than iron. The only way it can get reduced to the metal is by using electricity. The electric current pulls the particles apart and turns the aluminium into metal.

$$2Al_2O_3 \xrightarrow{\text{electricity}} 4Al + 3O_2$$

Chromium

They use much cheaper aluminium metal to displace chromium from its ore. Chromium is an expensive metal because it looks so nice.

$$2Al + Cr_2O_3 \rightarrow 2Cr + Al_2O_3$$

Questions

5 Explain how you know that a chemical reaction is happening between copper oxide and zinc metal.

6 Write word equations for the production of iron, aluminium and chromium.

7 Which metals are more reactive than lead?

Remember

Here is a reactivity series written as chemical symbols:

(Most reactive) K – Na – Li – Ca – Mg – Al – Zn – Fe – Cr – Pb – Cu – Ag – Au

Rewrite it as the names of the metals.

Figure 7 Iron is more reactive than copper, so the iron atoms displace the copper from the copper sulphate. The solution becomes iron sulphate and copper metal is left.

Closer

The trial of Sulphur and Sodium

Sulphur (S) and Sodium (Na) are each on trial for elementary crimes. On their own they are stable happy elements, but no real use as materials. When they get out and form compounds – they then cause problems.

> **Sulphur, you are charged with being a major pollutant, causing acid rain and breathing difficulties in humans.**

Defence speech

- Sulphur is used to make rubber hard. Without it we'd have no tyres.
- Hydrogen sulphide is added to natural gas so we can smell leaks and prevent gas explosions.
- Sulphuric acid is used to make detergents. Without it we'd be all be filthy and wear dirty clothes.
- Without sulphuric acid in car and bus batteries we'd all be walking to school.

> **Sodium, you are charged with being a dangerous element that attacks skin and flesh.**

Defence speech

- Without sodium we could not make soap.
- Sodium is used to extract useful metals.
- Most importantly, sodium links up with the poisonous gas chlorine to make table salt. Table salt flavours and preserves our food, and keeps our bodies working properly.

Activity

1 Write a short passage to explain why Sulphur and Sodium are not evil.

2 Make a quiz about the properties of metals. The answers to the questions must form a list of words that goes from A to Z. Work with a partner. When you have finished, swap quizzes with another pair and work out their answers.

3 Make a card for each metal. Include on the card the colour and uses of the metal. Particularly include where the metal is in the reactivity series for metals and how it reacts with oxygen and acids. Keep the cards in reactivity series order.

CHAPTER 3

Energy and electricity

Opener Activity
The human touch

Imagine a world with no humans. It seems likely that the Sun would still blaze and winds would still blow. Sunlight would warm the seas and clouds would still make rain. Plants would still grow. Animals would still walk or fly or swim. There would be many energy transfers going on.

Now add humans to your picture. They could be humans living in small groups, using simple technologies like fire, levers to lift things, and bows and arrows for hunting. Or they could be modern humans living in a global society. Their technologies could include anything from clockwork toys to power stations and aeroplanes.

Questions

1 The text mentions processes and systems that involve energy transfers. How many can you identify? List them.

2 How many of them are non-human energy transfers, and how many involve human technologies?

3 Where does energy come from to run a clockwork toy, a power station or an aeroplane? What about a torch or a digital camera?

4 Humans are amazing. We have created a lot of different technologies to make our lives more comfortable and interesting. We can wonder about the world in ways that no other animal can, as far as we know. So, do you think that humans are good for the world, or bad?

Energy transfer from circuits

Cells and batteries are energy stores that allow circuits to transfer energy to the surroundings. Circuits can transfer energy by heating and by doing work.

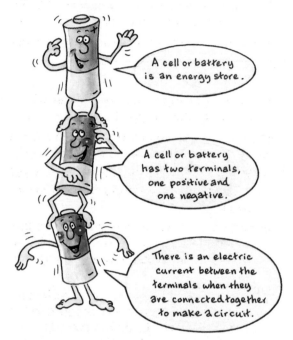

A cell or battery is an energy store.

A cell or battery has two terminals, one positive and one negative.

There is an electric current between the terminals when they are connected together to make a circuit.

The electric circuit in a torch is made of wires and a cell or battery. Some wires transfer energy to the environment when there is an electric **current** in them. They can provide heating or lighting or make motors move. The energy comes from the cell or battery.

Energy transfer by heating

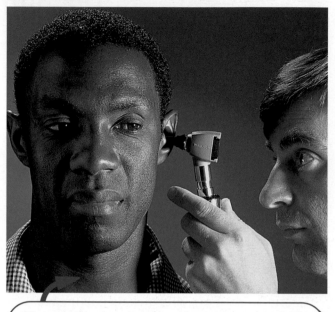

Figure 2 To see inside a patient's ear, the doctor uses a torch with a white hot wire in it.

The wire in the bulb of a torch gets hot – very hot. It transfers energy to the surroundings. The battery in the torch is the source of the energy.

Once the energy has spread into the surroundings, we can't take advantage of it any more. We say that the energy has **dissipated**.

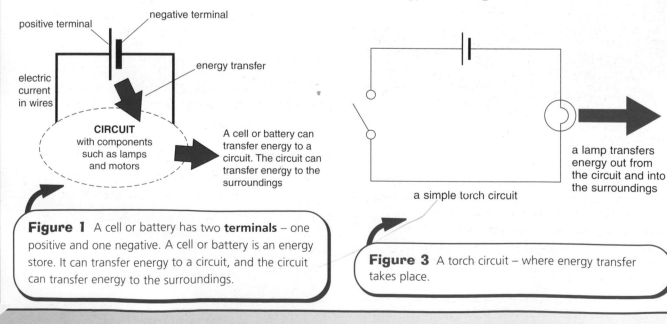

positive terminal

negative terminal

electric current in wires

energy transfer

CIRCUIT with components such as lamps and motors

A cell or battery can transfer energy to a circuit. The circuit can transfer energy to the surroundings

Figure 1 A cell or battery has two **terminals** – one positive and one negative. A cell or battery is an energy store. It can transfer energy to a circuit, and the circuit can transfer energy to the surroundings.

a simple torch circuit

a lamp transfers energy out from the circuit and into the surroundings

Figure 3 A torch circuit – where energy transfer takes place.

Energy transfer by working

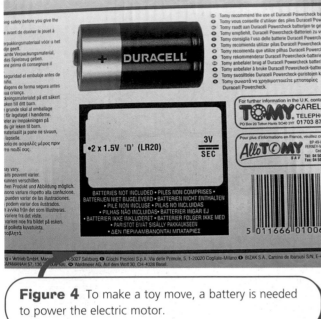

Figure 4 To make a toy move, a battery is needed to power the electric motor.

An electric toy needs a battery (or a similar energy supply). The motor turns and transfers energy to other things around it. It exerts a force which makes the toy travel. The motor does **work**. The battery is the source of energy that allows this to happen. The battery is a good energy store – you can keep the battery for a long time, and use it whenever you want to.

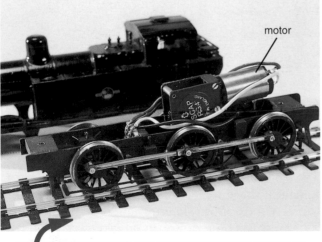

motor

Figure 5 A motor like this contains two or more magnets. Some might be ordinary 'permanent magnets', such as bar magnets. At least one will be an **electromagnet**. That's a coil that becomes magnetic when there is a current in it. The force between this electromagnet and the other magnets is what makes the motor go around.

While the motor is working energy spreads into the surroundings. The motor gets warm and heats the surroundings. The movement of the toy makes the air move. Friction of the wheels on the surface below causes a little bit of heating. The energy becomes dissipated.

Questions

1   What are the processes by which an electric circuit transfers energy to its surroundings?

2   An electric circuit can make a motor go round.
   a) What is needed, apart from the circuit, to make the motor go round?
   b) What has happened to the energy when the motor has stopped?

3   What would you expect to happen in a torch circuit if you added an extra battery?

4   a) When you use an electric drill for several minutes, the motor will get hot. Why do you think this is?
   b) Electrical energy is needed to cause the heating in the motor. Has this electrical energy done useful work in turning the motor?
   c) A motor would only be 100% efficient if it turned all the electrical energy into movement. Why is the electric drill motor not 100% efficient?

Remember

Match the words to the spaces in the paragraph.

**work   heat   stores   from
surroundings   terminals   dissipates
positive   current**

Cells and batteries act as energy _stores_ **1**.
They have _positive_ **2** and negative _current_ **3**.
When a wire is connected to the two terminals,
that makes an electric _current_ **4**.

Energy transfers out _from_ **5** the circuit into
the _terminals surroundings_ **6**. For example, the circuit can
heat **7** the surroundings, or the circuit can
make an electric motor do _work_ **8**.

The energy that the battery makes available
eventually _dissipates_ **9**. It spreads into the
surroundings.

Circuit power

Batteries supply the energy that's needed for current in energy transfer components like lamps and motors. A battery is measured by its voltage. In a series circuit, all of the components have the same current, but they don't have to have the same share of the voltage.

Lottie lives in the mountains, and in the winter there's plenty of snow. Then, she can take a ski-lift to the top of the high slopes and go skiing. She can speed down the slopes and stop at the mountain cafés.

To get up the mountain, Lottie lets the ski-lift do the work. It lifts her higher and higher. It gives her **position energy** or **gravitational potential energy**. Then, on the way down, she has the energy of movement – **kinetic energy**. Friction and air resistance also act on Lottie. She transfers energy to the snow and the air as she skis downhill.

Figure 2 Lottie losing gravitational potential energy and transferring energy to her surroundings.

Figure 3 On her way down the mountain Lottie can rest in the mountain cafés.

The ski-lift lifts Lottie and other skiers to a greater height. If there wasn't a height difference between the two ends of the ski-lift, there'd be no slope for the skiers to come down. In an electric circuit, it's not a ski-lift but a battery that can provide the energy. Instead of a height difference there is a voltage. Another name for voltage here is **potential difference**. It's the difference between the two terminals of a battery that makes the current flow.

Figure 1 Lottie gaining position or gravitational potential energy.

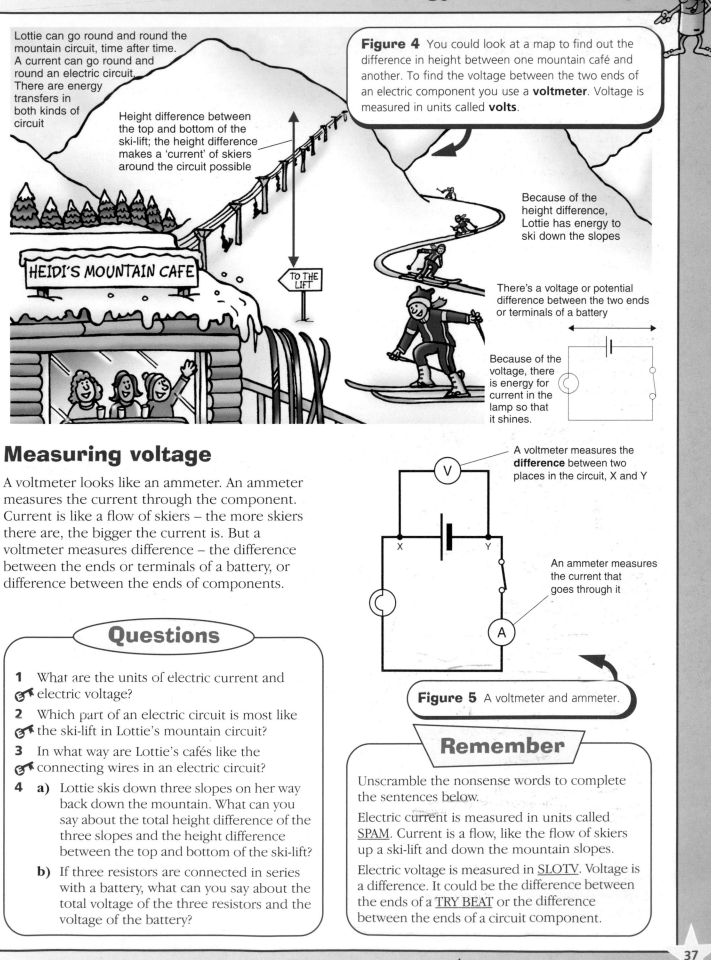

Lottie can go round and round the mountain circuit, time after time. A current can go round and round an electric circuit. There are energy transfers in both kinds of circuit

Height difference between the top and bottom of the ski-lift; the height difference makes a 'current' of skiers around the circuit possible

HEIDI'S MOUNTAIN CAFE

TO THE LIFT

Figure 4 You could look at a map to find out the difference in height between one mountain café and another. To find the voltage between the two ends of an electric component you use a **voltmeter**. Voltage is measured in units called **volts**.

Because of the height difference, Lottie has energy to ski down the slopes

There's a voltage or potential difference between the two ends or terminals of a battery

Because of the voltage, there is energy for current in the lamp so that it shines.

Measuring voltage

A voltmeter looks like an ammeter. An ammeter measures the current through the component. Current is like a flow of skiers – the more skiers there are, the bigger the current is. But a voltmeter measures difference – the difference between the ends or terminals of a battery, or difference between the ends of components.

A voltmeter measures the **difference** between two places in the circuit, X and Y

An ammeter measures the current that goes through it

Figure 5 A voltmeter and ammeter.

Questions

1 What are the units of electric current and electric voltage?

2 Which part of an electric circuit is most like the ski-lift in Lottie's mountain circuit?

3 In what way are Lottie's cafés like the connecting wires in an electric circuit?

4 a) Lottie skis down three slopes on her way back down the mountain. What can you say about the total height difference of the three slopes and the height difference between the top and bottom of the ski-lift?

b) If three resistors are connected in series with a battery, what can you say about the total voltage of the three resistors and the voltage of the battery?

Remember

Unscramble the nonsense words to complete the sentences below.

Electric current is measured in units called <u>SPAM</u>. Current is a flow, like the flow of skiers up a ski-lift and down the mountain slopes.

Electric voltage is measured in <u>SLOTV</u>. Voltage is a difference. It could be the difference between the ends of a <u>TRY BEAT</u> or the difference between the ends of a circuit component.

Meeting the demand

A power station turbine transfers energy from hot steam to a generator and then to the electric cables that are connected to our homes, schools, shops and factories.

In most power stations, it is hot steam that transfers energy to turbine blades. The blades are connected to the generator, and they make it turn at very high speed. The energy then transfers through electric cables to the places where people want energy supplies.

A generator makes its own current. It needs a source of energy from outside the circuit so it can do it.

Figure 1 The steam turns turbine blades (shown above, being fixed) which make the generator turn.

Quick – the adverts are on

Power stations generate electricity at the time it's needed. So if millions of people put their kettles on at the same time, the power stations have to try to respond straight away by generating electricity to meet the demand. That happens during the adverts when a popular TV programme is on.

To help them to solve this problem, the electricity companies use some **pumped storage** power stations. These have generators like any other power stations, but the turbines are not driven by jets of hot steam. Instead, they're driven by flowing water – just like an old water mill but much, much faster. Using flowing water in this way is called **hydroelectric** generation. Since the water has to be flowing fast, hydroelectric power stations have to be in mountainous places.

Pumped storage power stations are hydroelectric. But the big advantage is that they can be put 'into reverse'. They can pump water back up the mountain to a reservoir. That takes energy, but it can be done when the demand for electricity is low, and other power stations have got energy to spare. Then, when *EastEnders* finishes and all those kettles go on, the water can be allowed to

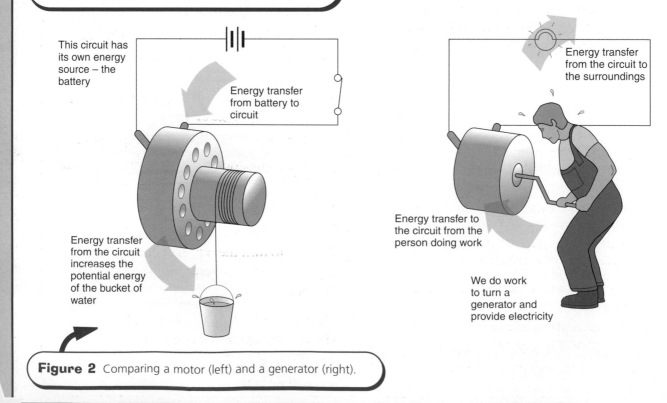

This circuit has its own energy source – the battery

Energy transfer from battery to circuit

Energy transfer from the circuit increases the potential energy of the bucket of water

Energy transfer from the circuit to the surroundings

Energy transfer to the circuit from the person doing work

We do work to turn a generator and provide electricity

Figure 2 Comparing a motor (left) and a generator (right).

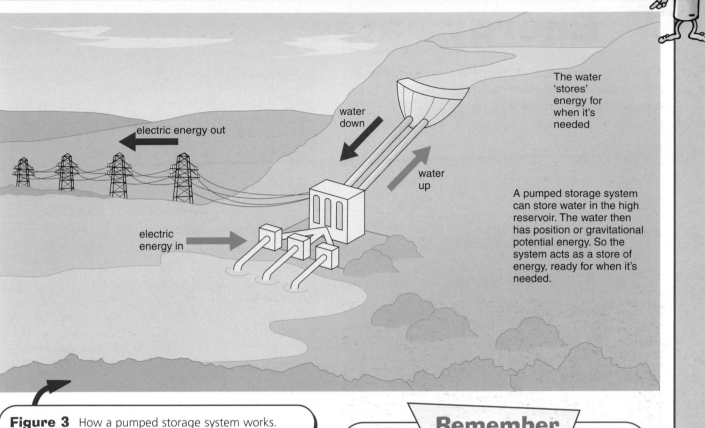

water down

water up

The water 'stores' energy for when it's needed

electric energy out

electric energy in

A pumped storage system can store water in the high reservoir. The water then has position or gravitational potential energy. So the system acts as a store of energy, ready for when it's needed.

Figure 3 How a pumped storage system works.

come tumbling down the pipes from the mountain reservoir to generate electricity to meet the demand.

Pumped storage power stations have very quick start-up times, unlike oil- or gas-fired power stations. All the operator needs to do is open a valve to let the water flow down through the turbine.

Questions

1   Explain the differences between a motor and a generator.

2   **a)** Why does demand for electricity change, depending on the time of day?

    b) Why is this a problem for the electricity companies?

    c) What can they do about it?

3   Does hydroelectric power generation use a renewable or non-renewable energy resource?

Remember

These sentences are all cut into halves. Match up the best halves.

a)   An electric circuit provides energy . . .

b)   A motor can transfer energy, for example by lifting up objects . . .

c)   A supply of energy is needed to keep . . .

d)   People's demand for electricity changes from summer to winter . . .

e)   One way to meet the demand is to use pumped storage systems . . .

f)   They use spare energy to pump water . . .

g)   Then when demand is high, the water can flow back down the mountain pipes . . .

i)   . . . an electric generator turning.

ii)   . . . and from one time of day to another.

iii)   . . . to turn the power station turbines.

iv)   . . . and giving them more position or potential energy.

v)   . . . to a motor to make it turn.

vi)   . . . to high places when demand is low.

vii)   . . . that can work either as pumps or generators.

Energy rates

Different appliances at home transfer energy at different rates. Appliances that transfer energy quickly are expensive to run.

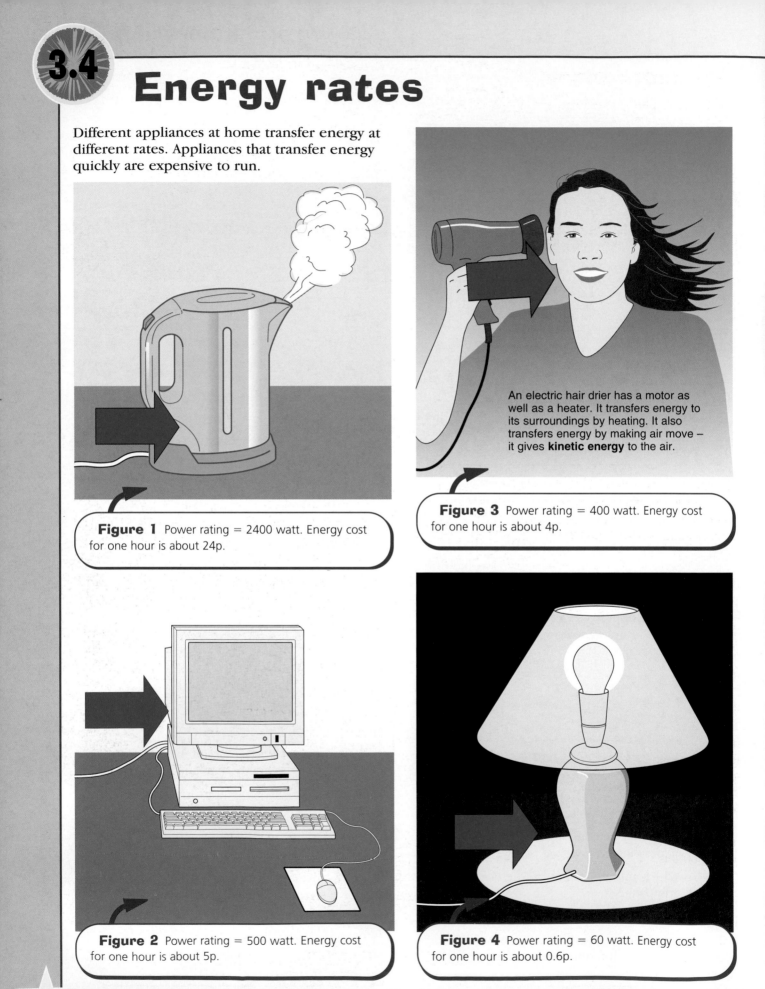

Figure 1 Power rating = 2400 watt. Energy cost for one hour is about 24p.

An electric hair drier has a motor as well as a heater. It transfers energy to its surroundings by heating. It also transfers energy by making air move – it gives **kinetic energy** to the air.

Figure 3 Power rating = 400 watt. Energy cost for one hour is about 4p.

Figure 2 Power rating = 500 watt. Energy cost for one hour is about 5p.

Figure 4 Power rating = 60 watt. Energy cost for one hour is about 0.6p.

How much it costs

Different appliances have different **power** ratings. They transfer energy at different rates. A kettle, for example, has a high power rating and transfers energy quickly. It has a strong heating effect.

Notice that you can find out the *approximate* hourly cost of running an appliance by dividing its power rating by 100. So the energy supply for a 500 watt computer costs about 5p per hour. A 100 watt lamp would cost about 1p per hour.

$$\text{Approximate cost in pence to run an appliance for 1 hour} = \text{the power rating of the appliance (in watts)} \div 100$$

Dissipation

All appliances transfer energy usefully. A kettle heats, a lamp shines, a radio produces sounds. But the energy spreads into the environment. Hot water from the kettle cools down. Light from the lamp is absorbed by surfaces (and makes them just a little bit warmer). Surfaces also absorb sound from the radio. Energy that is spread in this way is no longer useful to us. We say that it has dissipated.

All of the energy that we pay for dissipates. If only we could somehow save it and store it, we'd save a lot of money. Unfortunately this is just not possible.

Wastage

We want a device such as a vacuum cleaner to do work. We don't want it to heat the room. But the motor does get warm. The energy that the motor transfers by heating is not useful. It is wasted. We can compare the useful energy transfer with the 'wasted' energy transfer by talking about **efficiency**. If the vacuum cleaner is 40% efficient then only 40% of the energy that is given to it by the electricity supply is transferred usefully. The other 60% is transferred by useless heating.

Questions

1   Sketch a 400 watt hi-fi and a 1000 watt electric heater. Add arrows to show the flow of energy through the appliances. Show the sizes of the rates of transfer (power) by the sizes (widths) of the arrows you draw.

2   Using this equation, work out the cost of electricity in each of the examples:

Cost of electricity = power in watts × time in hours ÷ 100

   a)   running a 440 W hi-fi for 6 hours

   b)   running a 1000 W heater for 6 hours

   c)   running a 3000 W cooker for 1 hour

   d)   running a 250 W TV for 8 hours

   e)   running a 10 W personal stereo for 200 hours

3   A kettle supplies energy to water to make it hot. If the water cools down again, where has the energy gone to?

4   How does a hair drier transfer energy to its surroundings?

5   How does your body transfer energy to your surroundings?

Remember

Match the anagrams with the list of words.

APPLIANCES, WATTS, KINETIC ENERGY, DISSIPATED, ONE HUNDRED, POWER RATINGS

Motors, such as those in hair driers, have ICE TINNY GREEK. The energy then spreads out and we say that it has ID SIT SPADE.

All electric PAIN PLACES dissipate energy, though we have to pay for the energy just the same. Different appliances have different OR SPIN WET RAG. This is measured in units called STAWT. The cost of the energy to run an appliance for each hour is roughly equal to its power rating in watts divided by H UNDERDONE.

Future homes

For the sake of the planet, we have to think hard about how we use energy resources.

At the Centre for Alternative Technology they've built 'energy-efficient' houses that are designed for careful use of energy resources. Energy cannot be created from nothing and it cannot be destroyed, but it can transfer from place to place. When it transfers and spreads out so that we can no longer have the benefit of it, we say that the energy has been dissipated. To keep warm, we need to take control of these energy transfers as much as we can. This will also save us money.

Renewables and non-renewables

The scientists at the Centre are trying to find ways to reduce use of energy resources. **Non-renewable** energy resources – like oil, coal and gas – will run out. They also cause pollution. We need to use them as little as possible.

One answer to energy problems is to use **renewable** energy resources, like the sunlight that drives solar panels. Solar panels generate electricity.

Figure 1 An energy-efficient house at the Centre for Alternative Technology at Machynlleth in mid-Wales where they try out different ways of dealing with modern living.

Figure 2 At the Centre, the sewage doesn't go to a normal sewage works and into the river. It goes to a reed bed where bacteria slowly work to rot the sewage. The muck that's left over is safe to use as a fertiliser.

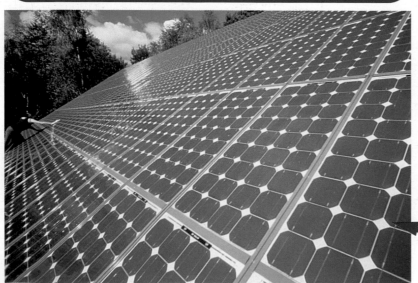

Figure 3 Solar panels on a house at the Centre for Alternative Technology.

Insulation

Another answer is to transfer less energy in our homes. We could transfer much less energy in our homes if we didn't heat them, but we need to keep warm. So we can try to stop energy transferring outwards from our houses. Energy transfers out through the windows, walls, roof and floor. We can reduce this by **insulating** our houses. Double-glazing is one kind of insulation.

Figure 4 Houses are well insulated at the Centre for Alternative Technology.

Efficient appliances

We could transfer less energy in our homes by using appliances, like fridge-freezers, that have high **efficiency**. That means that they can provide us with the same benefits but transfer less energy in the process.

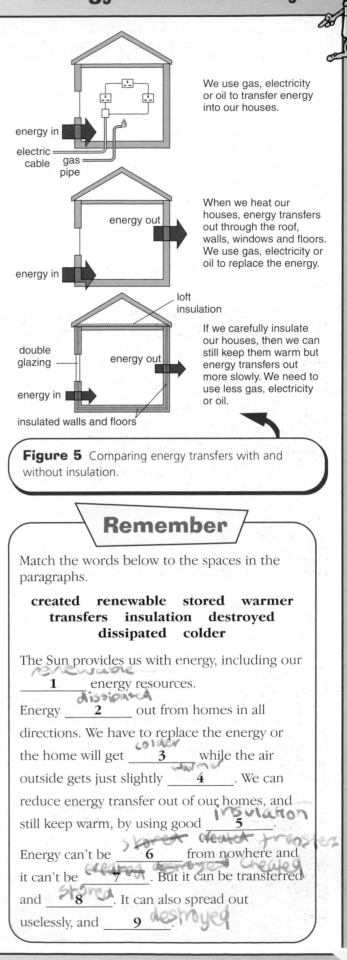

We use gas, electricity or oil to transfer energy into our houses.

energy in
electric cable gas pipe

When we heat our houses, energy transfers out through the roof, walls, windows and floors. We use gas, electricity or oil to replace the energy.

energy out
energy in

loft insulation

If we carefully insulate our houses, then we can still keep them warm but energy transfers out more slowly. We need to use less gas, electricity or oil.

double glazing
energy out
energy in
insulated walls and floors

Figure 5 Comparing energy transfers with and without insulation.

Questions

1 a) Name two design features that make houses 'energy efficient'.

   b) Name two ways in which houses can be designed to make maximum use of renewable energy resources.

2 Do you think that you should have solar panels at home? Explain your answer.

3 Do you think that you should use an energy efficient fridge-freezer at home? Explain your answer.

Remember

Match the words below to the spaces in the paragraphs.

created   renewable   stored   warmer transfers   insulation   destroyed dissipated   colder

The Sun provides us with energy, including our _____1_____ energy resources.

Energy _____2_____ out from homes in all directions. We have to replace the energy or the home will get _____3_____ while the air outside gets just slightly _____4_____. We can reduce energy transfer out of our homes, and still keep warm, by using good _____5_____.

Energy can't be _____6_____ from nowhere and it can't be _____7_____. But it can be transferred and _____8_____. It can also spread out uselessly, and _____9_____.

43

Closer

Lincoln and Lightning

The Green family grow all their own food in their back garden. They generate their own electricity using solar panels and a small wind generator. They don't have a car. As Lincoln says:

The Flash family buy everything from the supermarket. They use mains electricity and have all the latest gadgets. They have an outdoor heater so they can sit in the garden. They have two big cars and a motor boat. They fly to exciting places as often as they can. As Lightning says:

The planet is in trouble because of change. Some places will become wetter and some will have more droughts. Most places will get hotter but some could get a lot colder.

Lincoln Green

You can't spend your life worrying about the future. Enjoy yourself!

Lightning Flash

Questions

1   Where do you get your food from?

2   Where do you get electricity from?

3   What kinds of transport do you use?

4   Are you more like the Green family or the Flash family in the way you live?

5   Which attitude makes most sense to you, Lincoln's or Lightning's?

6   **a)** These are some words relating to energy and electricity. Make your own basic thinklinks chart using the words. Decide on your own layout. The important thing is that it makes sense for you. Use a whole page and leave plenty of space between each item on the chart.

   - electric current
   - energy transfer
   - generator

   - heating
   - lamp
   - motor
   - working

   b) Now fit these words onto your chart, to show how they are linked to the words above.

   - appliance
   - dissipation
   - insulation
   - kinetic energy
   - potential difference (voltage)
   - potential energy
   - power rating
   - power station
   - watt
   - turbine

CHAPTER 4

Fit and healthy

Opener Activity
Junk food

Activity

1. How many adverts can you think of for junk food?

2. In small groups or pairs write down as many as you can think of.

3. Now think about adverts for healthy food or eating. Write down as many as you can think of.

Eating well means having a balanced diet, eating enough of each of the food groups and not having too much fat, sugar or salt. Is the food in the photo junk food or not? If you only ate fast food like burgers it could make you very unhealthy. But even burgers contain some essential food groups.

Activity

Work in groups of three or four and think about the following.

1. Would you ban advertising for junk food and would it work?

2. If you had to give evidence to a government committee on whether or not to ban adverts for junk food, what would you say?

3. In your groups think of points for and against banning adverts for junk food.

4. If you have Internet access find out about Jamie Oliver's school food campaign. What did Jamie's campaign do for school dinners?

Questions

1. If junk food adverts were banned from TV what effect do you think this would have on the diet of young people?

2. Would having more adverts for healthy foods have an effect on the diets of young people?

3. Do you think that your school canteen serves a healthy selection of foods?

4. How might your school encourage more healthy eating?

Healthy systems

There are three main organ systems that have to work together or interact to keep us fit and healthy, the respiratory, digestive and circulatory systems. Another two systems, the skeletal and muscle systems, are essential for support and movement.

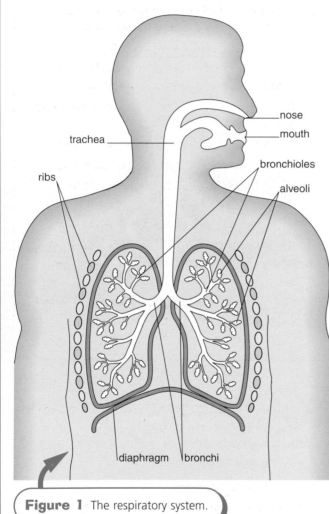

Figure 1 The respiratory system.

The **respiratory system** includes the air passages, such as the **trachea** and **bronchi**, the lungs, including the **bronchioles** and **alveoli**, and the muscles that control breathing, such as the **intercostal muscles** (the muscles between the ribs) and the **diaphragm**.

The **digestive system** is the group of organs that breaks down food into its basic chemical parts, so that the body can absorb them and use them for energy and for growth. This system includes the mouth, the oesophagus or gullet, the stomach, the ileum and colon, the gall bladder, the pancreas, the liver and the rectum.

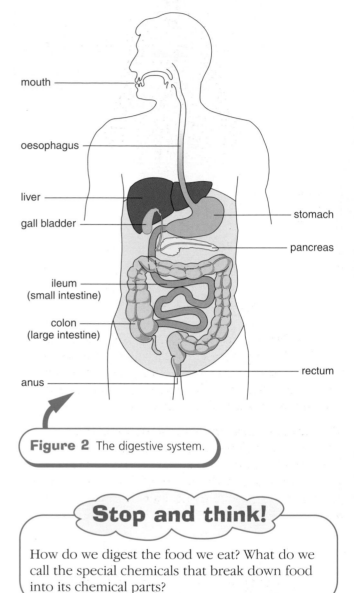

Figure 2 The digestive system.

Stop and think!

How do we digest the food we eat? What do we call the special chemicals that break down food into its chemical parts?

The **circulatory system** is made up of the heart and blood vessels that provide a continuous flow of blood around the body, providing all our tissues with oxygen and nutrients and taking away any waste products.

Stop and think!

Can you remember how blood circulates through the body? What type of blood mainly travels through arteries and what type travels mainly through veins? Where in the body is this different?

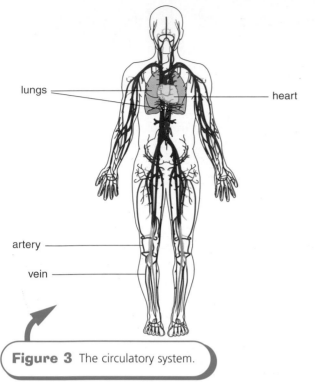

Figure 3 The circulatory system.

The **skeletal system** gives us a body shape and works with our muscles to allow us to move or lift things. Our arms and legs act like levers. The skeletal system is made up of the bones of the skeleton and the different types of joints between the bones.

The **muscle system** is made up of all of the muscles of the body and the **tendons** that attach the muscles to the bones, or to each other. **Ligaments** are made of tough elastic tissue. They bind together the ends of bones and help prevent excessive movements of the joints during exercise.

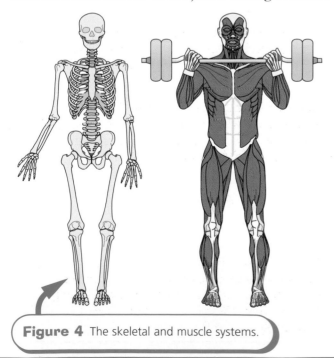

Figure 4 The skeletal and muscle systems.

Questions

For the questions below, use the following phrases to describe what happens to your breathing rate and/or your heart rate during the activities listed.

a) increases slightly
b) increases a lot
c) slows down
d) increases quickly then slows down quickly
e) increases but takes time to slow down

1 When I go to sleep, my breathing rate . . .

2 When I suddenly run for a bus and run 20 metres to the bus stop, my breathing rate . . .

3 When I play football, both my breathing rate and heart rate . . .

4 When I get a sudden fright, my heart rate . . .

5 When I do a lot of exercise, my heart rate . . .

6 When I sit down quietly in front of the television, my heart rate . . .

7 When I go for a brisk walk, my heart rate . . .

8 When I go for a brisk walk, my breathing rate . . .

9 When I am in a swimming race, my heart rate . . .

10 When I play an exciting computer game and I think I can win it, my heart rate . . .

Remember

The three main organ systems that work together to keep us fit and healthy are:

- the respiratory system
- the digestive system
- the circulatory system

Two other systems are essential for support and movement:

- the skeletal system
- the muscle system

Copy the table into your exercise book and put the words listed below into the correct columns.

diaphragm, trachea, heart, small intestine, bronchi, large intestine, bronchioles, veins, intercostal muscles, arteries, oxygen, tissues, oesophagus, stomach, lungs

Respiratory system	Digestive system	Circulatory system

4.2

Diet, exercise and fitness

Getting fit is not just about training and exercise. Fitness is about how we eat, look after ourselves and keep the organs and organ systems in tip-top condition. If we are going to remain fit and healthy, we must eat a balanced diet, do a reasonable amount of exercise, not drink excess alcohol or smoke, and not take drugs other than those prescribed for us.

Different people have different dietary needs. Very active people, such as athletes and those with physical jobs, need lots of energy from food. People who are less active or who have sedentary jobs (jobs that don't require them to move around a lot, like office work) need less energy. Men usually need more energy than women and adults need more than children.

The requirements for different nutrients also differ at different ages and stages. For example, during your teenage years and for women during pregnancy, extra protein and minerals are needed. When it comes to vitamins, however, the daily requirements vary less between individuals.

A top class athlete has their diet carefully worked out for them. They make sure that they have a diet that will provide all the energy they need. But even athletes' diets will vary. There is no one diet that will suit everyone. The more energy you need, the more energy-giving foods you have to eat. So an athlete's diet may be rich in these types of foods (carbohydrates). An office worker who ate the same diet as a weightlifter would soon put on lots of extra weight, and much of the food's energy would be turned into fat. This could lead to major health problems including heart disease. Fitness is not just for athletes. Everyone should have a diet and exercise routine that keeps them fit and healthy.

A pregnant woman or a woman planning a pregnancy may also need to pay special attention to her diet. She should, for example, make sure that she has enough folic acid in her diet. Folic acid is one of the vitamin B nutrients and helps to protect developing babies from brain and spinal cord defects or problems.

Stop and think!

Can you recall what the different food groups are? What makes up a balanced diet? What types of food groups should we not have too much of? What are the other things that we need for a healthy diet?

Proper training prevents injuries

Exercise is important in helping us keep fit and healthy, but any exercise must be done properly. It is easy to injure yourself if you don't know what you are doing or how your skeleton and muscles work. The most common type of injury through exercise is damage to the joints, such as the elbow, ankle, shoulder, knee, back or neck. Our joints work in different ways. Figure 1 shows the two main types of joints that we have. A **hinge joint** allows our arms and legs to bend, and a **ball and socket joint** allows our arms to circle at the shoulder and our legs to circle at the hips. The hinge joints and muscles work as levers.

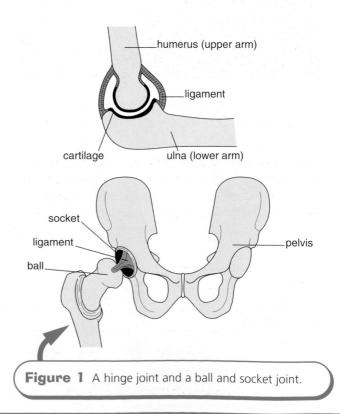

Figure 1 A hinge joint and a ball and socket joint.

Very often an injury will happen when a muscle is stretched too far (a pulled muscle) or a joint is over extended (pushed further than it should go). Another common injury happens when the ligaments are stretched too far (a pulled ligament). If a muscle or ligament has been pulled or a joint injured, it needs to be rested so that the body has time to repair the damage. Sometimes, if the damage is too great, the body cannot repair the muscle or joint.

Not all injuries and joint problems are caused by exercise. Sometimes the joints literally wear out. This happens in people who suffer from **arthritis**. It commonly happens to hip joints. Fortunately we are now able to replace hip joints by surgery.

Figure 2 Replacement joints like this are fitted into the bones to replace the worn out or damaged parts.

Different sports exercise different muscles and body systems. Regular exercise is important even if you don't want to be a sportsperson. The table below shows the benefits of doing different sports.

Questions

1 What are the six different food groups needed to maintain a balanced diet?

2 Which two food groups give us nearly all of our energy and, of these, which one gives us most energy?

3 What do you think would happen if a normal person ate the weightlifter's diet, but didn't do any weightlifting?

4 Why does a growing baby need more protein in order to keep it healthy?

5 Why do most athletes and teams have trainers? What else might the trainer do apart from advise them on exercise?

6 Which would be the best sport to take up if you wanted to improve the fitness of your heart and lungs, the suppleness of your joints and your muscle power?

Remember

Rearrange the sentences below into a sensible paragraph and copy it into your book.

- We must also make sure that we have vitamins and minerals to keep the body's organ systems working properly.

- We must eat enough energy-giving foods for the sports we do.

- We must make sure that we eat a balanced diet.

- Regular exercise is needed even if you don't want to play in a team or be a sportsperson.

- Being fit and healthy means looking after lots of different systems in the body.

- One of the best ways to keep fit and healthy with some exercise is to go swimming regularly.

	Heart and lungs	Joints	Muscles
Golf	*	**	*
Swimming	****	****	****
Jogging	****	**	**
Brisk walking	**	*	**
Football	***	***	***
Tennis	***	***	**

Table 1 Comparing the effects of different sports. (* = poor, **** = excellent)

Smoking and health

Smoking can cause serious health problems. Often the problems don't appear for many years, leading some young people to think that smoking is not harmful. The truth is that smoking can lead to all sorts of health problems and can seriously affect your fitness.

Why is tobacco harmful?

Figure 1 Cigarettes are commonly smoked by young people who may then become addicted and suffer ill health later in life.

There are three chemicals that can be harmful in tobacco smoke. They are nicotine, carbon monoxide and tar.

Nicotine is a powerful chemical that is **addictive** – that is, our body comes to depend on it. At first the amount of nicotine the body becomes addicted to is quite small, but the longer someone smokes, the more nicotine they need and the more difficult it is to live without a daily dose of nicotine. Some people smoke because they say that smoking calms them down in a stressful situation. This happens because nicotine is a stimulant that behaves like a **tranquilliser**. Tranquillisers are drugs used to calm people down if they are suffering from stress. Usually tranquillisers are only prescribed by a doctor because some of them can be addictive too.

Carbon monoxide is a gas. It is similar to carbon dioxide, but is very dangerous. The gas is colourless, odourless and poisonous, and in large amounts can kill. Gas fires that are not properly serviced can give off carbon monoxide. People have been killed by a build up of this gas in unventilated rooms. People who smoke only take in small amounts of carbon monoxide, but over a long period of time it decreases the amount of oxygen that reaches the tissues in the body and can lead to a build up of fatty deposits in the arteries.

Figure 2 Cigarette companies have to put health warnings on all packets of cigarettes.

The **tar** in cigarettes and cigarette smoke irritates the lungs and respiratory system and deposits a layer of chemicals on the respiratory tract (the trachea, bronchi, bronchioles and alveoli). This can lead to difficulty in breathing. Because the layer of tar shouldn't be present in the lungs, the body tries to get rid of it by producing more mucus and trying to cough it up. This is what causes the famous smoker's cough. The longer you smoke, the worse it will get. The tar also contains chemicals that can cause cancer. Smokers suffer from higher rates of mouth cancer, cheek cell cancer and lung cancer than non-smokers.

Figure 3 The smoker's lung on the right is less efficient and the tissue has become hardened and blackened by the effects of tobacco smoke.

Smoking and cancer

Ninety percent of lung cancer deaths are linked to smoking, and 30% of all cancer-related deaths are caused by tobacco. Lung cancer is not the only type of cancer associated with smoking. There are also links with mouth cancer, lip cancer, bladder cancer and in women, cervical cancer (the cervix is the entrance to the womb).

Some smokers smoke pipes and cigars because they believe that they are less dangerous. It is true that there are fewer cases of lung cancer in pipe and cigar smokers, but there are more cases of lip, mouth and throat cancer.

Smoking and other diseases

Many people do not know that there are other diseases, apart from cancer, that are linked to tobacco and smoking. Tobacco smoke causes the tiny air sacs in the lungs – the alveoli – to become less elastic and to fuse together. This makes them less efficient and reduces the surface area of the lungs that can let oxygen into the bloodstream and carbon dioxide out. This results in people finding it very difficult to breathe and gasping for air, and can lead to a disease known as **emphysema**. Many heavy smokers die from this.

Figure 4 Emphysema means that not enough oxygen is reaching the tissues. This photo shows a lung from a smoker with emphysema.

Smokers are also more likely to suffer from blocked and diseased arteries. This reduces the blood flow around the heart and can result in chest pains or **angina**.

Strokes are more common in smokers than non-smokers. This is where part of the brain is damaged by a lack of blood supply. **Heart attacks**, where the heart muscle is deprived of blood, are also found more often in smokers.

Women who smoke while they are pregnant risk harming their unborn baby. The chemicals in the tobacco smoke pass into the mother's bloodstream and are transferred across the placenta into the unborn baby's bloodstream. Because the baby is so much smaller, the effects of small amounts of chemicals are greater than on the adult mother.

Passive smoking

When you inhale the tobacco smoke of other people but do not smoke yourself it is called **passive smoking**. Passive smokers may still be at risk from some of the diseases linked with smoking. The children of smokers often have more chest and ear infections than the children of non-smokers, and non-smokers who work in smoke-filled areas like pubs and bars are at risk from tobacco-related cancers.

Questions

1. What is the name of the addictive chemical found in tobacco smoke?

2. Although low tar cigarettes are better than high tar ones, why are the cigarettes still unhealthy?

3. If there were 36 276 deaths from lung cancer in a year, how many of these could be linked to tobacco?

4. If there were 118 000 deaths from all types of cancer in a year, how many would be linked to tobacco?

5. People who are ill need to be treated by the health service. Some people have private health care but most are treated by the National Health Service (NHS). How does persuading people to give up smoking help the NHS?

6. What is the effect of nicotine on the arteries? Would they get narrower or wider? What happens to the blood supply?

Remember

Using the information on the problems and diseases linked to smoking, produce a leaflet on the dangers of smoking that would be suitable for this year's new intake of Year 7 pupils.

Alcohol and health

The effects of alcohol on people's health are more difficult to assess than the effects of tobacco, but alcohol is still a dangerous drug if too much is consumed too quickly or for too long.

How much is too much?

To measure how much alcohol people drink, a system was developed based on units of alcohol. It was decided that one unit of alcohol equalled ½ pint of ordinary beer or lager, one glass of wine or one pub measure of a spirit, such as whisky or vodka. The problem is that some drinks have an increased level of alcohol, so drinking them means that you are actually having more than one unit in a measure. Some drinks manufacturers now label their bottled drinks with the number of units they contain to help people measure how much they are drinking. People who drink at home often give themselves and their guests more than a pub measure. Another problem happens when young people drink alcohol. The number of units that are recommended as safe limits are set for normal healthy adults. The effect that alcohol has on children and especially babies is more extreme.

Stop and think!

Can you recall what the major organs in the body do and where they are found?

Drinking and health

Alcohol can affect many different cells, tissues and organs in your body. The organ most at risk is the **liver**. Heavy drinking destroys liver cells and eventually the liver can stop working.

Figure 1 A badly damaged liver (top) compared with a healthy liver (below). The cause of the damage is alcohol.

Number of units a week for an adult male over 18 years of age	Too much or not?	Number of units a week for an adult female over 18 years of age
Up to 21	These are generally safe limits for healthy normal adults if spread over the week.	Up to 14
22–35	This level of drinking may not damage your health long term, but if you drink all of this in two or three sessions it will cause damage.	15–21
36–49	Regularly drinking this much in a week will cause long-term damage to your health.	22–35
50 or more	Drinking this much regularly will definitely cause serious damage to your health and you may even become dependent on alcohol – this means it will be difficult for you to cut down or give up.	36 or more

Table 1 Guidelines for safe drinking.

Scientists have found that for adults, small amounts of alcohol – no more than two units a day – can lower the risk of heart disease, but drinking more than that each day increases the risk of heart disease. Heavy drinkers can also suffer from stomach problems, including stomach cancer, ulcers (where the lining of the stomach is being eaten away by the stomach acid), cancers of the mouth, tongue, throat and oesophagus. Heavy drinking also leads to damage of the brain tissue.

Just as with smoking, women who drink while they are pregnant are risking their unborn baby's health. The alcohol enters the bloodstream and is passed along the umbilical cord into the baby's bloodstream. Because the baby is so much smaller and its cells, tissues and organs are still developing, the alcohol can affect the baby's health quite dramatically.

Alcohol and behaviour

Alcohol is often the cause of silly or violent behaviour. Drinking alcohol can have different effects on different people. Some people feel drowsy and just want to fall asleep. In lots of situations this is not a problem, but it could be if people have a few drinks at lunchtime and then have to operate machines in factories after lunch. Other people get aggressive after drinking and this can often lead to fights and people being seriously injured. In many cases, fights will break out over something very trivial, such as accidentally banging into someone or misunderstanding something someone has said.

Alcohol actually slows down our reactions, though people who drink often think it speeds up their reactions! Drinking and driving is not acceptable. To drive cars, motorbikes or scooters, you must be alert and ready to react to other traffic and pedestrians quickly. Scientists have shown that even drinking small amounts of alcohol can affect how safely you can control a vehicle. The only safe way to drink and drive is to drink non-alcoholic drinks.

Questions

1 For a normal healthy adult, what is the recommended safe number of units they can drink over a week and how many pints of beer or glasses of wine would this be?

2 When someone is thought to be alcohol dependent, what does this mean?

3 Many fights and arguments take place in town centres. When are they most likely to take place?

4 Alcohol must not be drunk in football grounds when there is a football match in progress. Why do you think that this law has been introduced?

5 Why is drinking alcohol and driving or operating machines dangerous?

Remember

Using the information on this page, produce a leaflet for sixth formers telling them about alcohol and its effects.

Figure 2 The driver of this car had been drinking alcohol. The driver lost control of the car and killed the motorcyclist in the crash.

Drugs and health

Drugs are chemicals that alter how our bodies work. They can be divided into three groups: recreational, medicinal and illegal. All drugs can be dangerous if they are used in the wrong way.

If you mention the word drug, many people think of illegal drugs such as heroin, ecstasy or cannabis. The word drug is used for any chemical that changes how organs in the body work or that changes how a disease affects us. Drugs include any medicines prescribed to us by doctors or those that can be bought 'over the counter' at a chemist shop. Many drugs are manufactured legally by drug companies, but others can be found naturally. Drugs can be placed into three groups: **recreational**, **medicinal** and **illegal**.

Recreational drugs

Figure 1 Recreational drugs

Tea and coffee contain a drug that affects how our body works. The drug is called **caffeine**. This is found naturally in coffee beans, tea leaves and cocoa beans. It is also put into some soft drinks artificially, such as cola. Caffeine increases the nerve activity in the brain. Normally when you drink a cup of coffee or tea, it has the effect of 'waking you up'. If you take large amounts of caffeine, it can cause your hands to tremble and it feels like your heart is racing. People who regularly drink large amounts of coffee or tea can suffer from withdrawal symptoms if they do not get enough caffeine in a day. Did you know that caffeine is on the banned list of drugs for athletes, as it can help them to perform better?

Other recreational drugs are not as harmless, but they are still legal for adults to buy. These include **nicotine**, found in tobacco, and **alcohol**, found in many different types of drinks.

Medicinal drugs

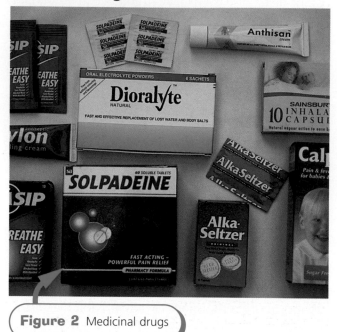

Figure 2 Medicinal drugs

Many drugs can be bought over the counter at a chemist shop. This does not mean that you do not have to be careful when you take them. All medicines should only be taken according to the instructions and only when you really need them. Paracetamol, a common painkiller, could kill you if you take too many at once or don't follow the instructions carefully. The problem is that the drug can damage your liver, and once this happens, it often cannot be reversed and you could easily become very ill or die. You should always ask your parents or guardians before taking any type of drug or medicine.

Many of the drugs prescribed by your doctor are also dangerous and must be taken how and when the doctor says. Some prescribed drugs are just as addictive and dangerous as the illegal drugs, but doctors know how much to give and can keep a check on patients to make sure that the drug is not causing any problems, but is actually making the person better. All prescription and over-the-counter drugs have been tested before they were released. The final stage in testing the drugs has been testing on groups of people to see what, if any, **side effects** a drug has. Drugs and medicines prescribed for someone should never be taken by anyone else and any drugs left over should either be flushed down the toilet or handed back to a chemist to prevent accidents.

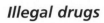

Illegal drugs

There are many different types of illegal drugs but they all have something in common – they all change the way a person feels or thinks they feel. Many illegal drugs were first developed to try and help or cure people. LSD, or acid, was actually discovered by accident by a Swiss chemist in 1943. Heroin was developed as a non-addictive painkiller in 1874. It failed completely as it is very addictive and can easily kill rather than stop pain. Some everyday plants, such as a type of mushroom, contain chemicals that can make you **hallucinate** – see things that aren't really there.

There are many different types of illegal drugs, including cocaine, heroin, cannabis, acid and ecstasy. They all have street names and some have more than one like cocaine which can be called charlie, coke, snow, white and sniff.

Who's your best friend?

Many young people say that the first time they take a drug they are pressurised by a 'friend'. They say that they feel as if they should join in with the rest of their friends and do what they do. This is what we call **peer pressure**. Your peers are simply those others just like you. All of your classmates are your peers. So why is it so difficult to say no to your peers? Are all of your peers good friends?

If you ask an eight-year-old 'what is a friend?', they may say something like: 'A good friend is someone who enjoys the same games that I do and who is fun to be around.' 11-year-olds may say that a friend is someone who likes the same things, someone who shares the same ideas about what is good or bad, fun or boring, right or wrong.

Are the people who put pressure on you to drink or smoke or take drugs friends at all?

Think about the following tips that parents might use to help you discuss the issues surrounding drugs. In small groups or on your own, think about how you would like your teachers and your parents to talk to you about serious issues such as alcohol, drugs, smoking and sexual relationships. Which of the tips are good ones and which ones wouldn't work for you?

In your exercise book you could write your own top ten tips for parents and/or teachers on how to help you deal with serious issues like drugs and drug abuse.

Top Ten Tips for Parents

1 Listen to your children when they want to talk to you about their feelings on a subject.

2 Don't try to scare your children into staying away from drugs with lies.

3 Talk openly about what really happens if you take a particular drug.

4 Encourage your children to make informed choices about what they do and how they behave.

5 Make sure that your children have correct information that is written specifically for them by experts.

6 Be a good example to your children.

7 Discuss what a good friend is and support children who find it difficult to deal with peer pressure.

8 If you think there is a problem, talk to your children first before you ask for help from others.

9 If there is a problem, ask for help.

10 Don't ignore the subject if it comes up in conversation; make time to talk about it with your children.

Questions

1 How many groups can we put drugs into and what are they?

2 Which recreational drug(s) is it legal for you to buy and which recreational drugs is it illegal for you to buy?

3 If some prescription drugs can be as dangerous as illegal drugs, how does a doctor try to make sure that their patient isn't harmed by the drug?

4 What has to happen to any drug before it can be sold or prescribed?

5 Many illegal drugs are known as 'mind-altering'. What do you think this means?

Remember

Using the information above on the problems linked to drugs, produce a leaflet that would be suitable for pupils in your school or a neighbouring school.

Closer

Complementary therapies

Many people try alternative or complementary therapies to treat illnesses. Some doctors think that this could be dangerous.

Acupuncture

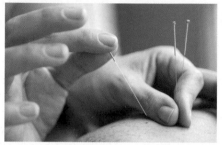

Acupuncture is a system of healing practised in China and the Far East for over 4000 years. Fine, stainless steel disposable needles are inserted into specific points on your body. Acupuncture is used to treat anxiety and back pain. Many doctors recommend it.

Colour therapy

Colour therapists believe that colour can affect our physical and emotional health.

The brain 'sees' the visible wavelengths of light as colour. Each colour wavelength is said to vibrate at a particular frequency. Colour therapists believe that this vibrates particles in our cells.

Chinese herbal medicine

In herbal medicine, illnesses are treated using combinations of herbs. Every herb is classified as either hot, cold, damp or dry, and is also classified by taste as sweet, sour, bitter, salty or pungent.

Chinese medicine is most commonly used to treat skin diseases, allergies, digestive complaints, pain, psychological problems, children's diseases and addiction.

Reflexology

A reflexologist puts pressure on specific areas on your feet or hands that represent parts of the body. Massaging these areas is said to affect organs and systems. Because the big toe represents the head and neck, working in this area relieves migraines or headaches.

Questions

1 What does the word complementary mean and what other, nearly identical word is it often confused with?

2 Why might some doctors think that complementary therapies are dangerous?

3 Why are disposable needles used in acupuncture rather than reusable ones?

4 Many people believe that colours can change our mood; red makes you angrier, green is calming. Does this prove that colour therapy works?

5 How may areas of the foot or hand be connected to other parts of the body? (*Hint*: think about the various systems in your body.)

Chemistry and the environment

Opener Activity
The London smog disaster of 1952

Early on 5 December 1952 the London sky was clear and cold. As a result, the people of London were burning large amounts of coal, so smoke and soot billowed from the chimneys. The absence of wind led to the formation of fog.

When night came the fog thickened and visibility dropped to a few metres. The fog became smog. Smog is fog that has soot in it.

That day, hanging in the air were thousands of tonnes of black soot, sticky particles of tar and gaseous sulphur dioxide. Most of this had come from coal burnt in domestic fireplaces. Smoke particles trapped in the fog gave it a yellow-black colour. The sulphur dioxide reacted inside these foggy, sooty droplets to form sulphuric acid, creating a very intense form of acid rain.

This 'pea soup' smog remained until 10 December. Road, rail and air transport was brought to a standstill. Theatres had to be closed when smog in the auditorium made conditions intolerable. But, most importantly the smoke laden fog that shrouded the capital brought the premature death of an estimated 12 000 people, and illness to many others.

Questions

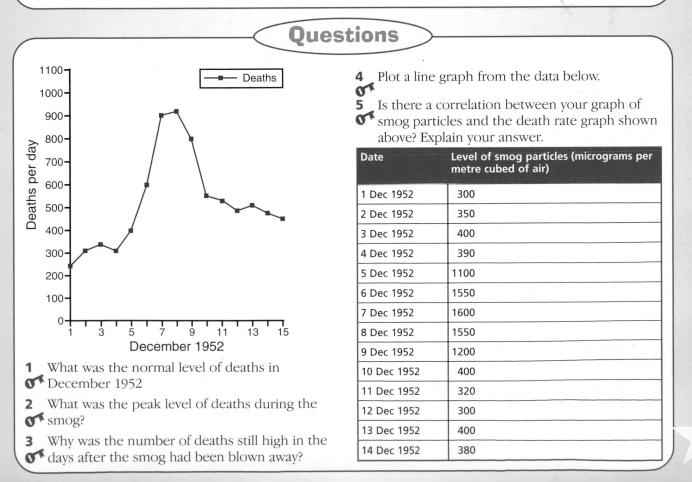

1 What was the normal level of deaths in December 1952

2 What was the peak level of deaths during the smog?

3 Why was the number of deaths still high in the days after the smog had been blown away?

4 Plot a line graph from the data below.

5 Is there a correlation between your graph of smog particles and the death rate graph shown above? Explain your answer.

Date	Level of smog particles (micrograms per metre cubed of air)
1 Dec 1952	300
2 Dec 1952	350
3 Dec 1952	400
4 Dec 1952	390
5 Dec 1952	1100
6 Dec 1952	1550
7 Dec 1952	1600
8 Dec 1952	1550
9 Dec 1952	1200
10 Dec 1952	400
11 Dec 1952	320
12 Dec 1952	300
13 Dec 1952	400
14 Dec 1952	380

5.1 Acids in the air

Oxides of sulphur and nitrogen increase the normal acidity of the rain. This makes the rain damage the environment where it falls.

Figure 1 Lime spraying is used to counteract acid rain because it is alkaline in solution. Lime is the compound calcium oxide.

One rainstorm that hit Pitlochry, Scotland broke a record, not for size but for acidity. The rain was pH 3.0 and turned Universal Indicator solution pink. The rain was more acidic than vinegar!

Rain is naturally acidic. It always has been. The rain that fell on the people who lived in Iron Age huts had dissolved some carbon dioxide from the atmosphere to make it weakly acidic. The acid in normal rain is carbonic acid. The first Iron Age brooch went rusty quickly because the acid in rain reacted with it. The limestone wall of the hut slowly dissolved away because the rain reacted with calcium carbonate.

During the last 200 years the problem has got much worse. Pollutants from lots of industrial and domestic processes have made rainfall more strongly acidic. Acid rain attacks marble and decorative stonework. Worse still, it kills vegetation and runs off into rivers and lakes where it kills the water life.

When coal and oil get burnt to produce electricity, the sulphur atoms in the fuels react with oxygen from the air to become sulphur dioxide. Sulphur can also be released into the atmosphere by volcanic eruptions. Sulphur dioxide dissolves in rain to make sulphuric acid.

A sad story

I am a sad Swedish tree.

My friends around me look in an awful state.

We are not growing, we are dying.

The weather is killing us.

The rain used to be good for us. Now it is poison.

It is full of acid.

The acid gases in the air dissolve in the rain. Then the rain falls on us.

The acid gases come from burning coal and oil to make electricity.

The acid kills my leaves.

The acid poisons the fish in the lakes.

Just so people can watch television and use the microwave.

In a country called Britain.

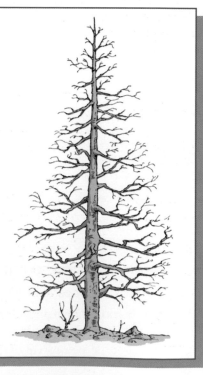

The pH scale

Acids are substances that produce hydrogen ions when they dissolve in water. The strength of an acid solution is given by measuring the concentration of these hydrogen ion particles.

Normal, pure water has one hydrogen ion for every $10\,000\,000$ (10^7) molecules. On the pH scale this is 7.0. pH 7.0 means a neutral solution.

Acid solutions have a pH number of less than 7.0. Alkali solutions have a pH of more than 7.0.

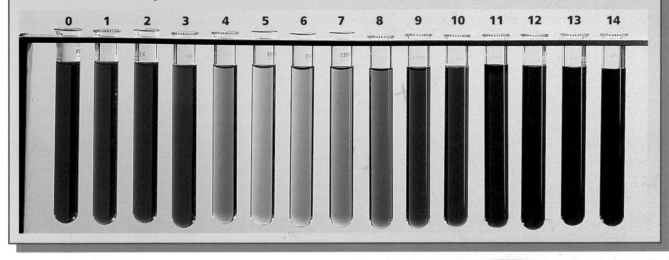

Petrol and diesel fuel is burnt in cars to make them go. The reaction is carried out at high pressures and also produces various oxides of nitrogen. These oxides are often called 'NO_x'. They dissolve in rain to make nitric acid.

These stronger acids dissolve in rain, giving it a much lower pH than normal. The acid rain never falls in the places that produce the pollution. It falls on places downwind from there.

Remember

Complete the paragraph using information from the text.

_____**1**_____ is produced when pollution gets dissolved in clouds.

This pollution is caused when ____**2**____ of non-metals are released into the ____**3**____.

Non-metal oxides tend to be ____**4**____ and ____**5**____ oxides are bases. Some metal oxides ____**6**____ in water to make ____**7**____.

Questions

1 What is Universal Indicator solution?

2 What colour is Universal Indicator solution in pure water and in strong acid?

3 What acid is present in normal rain?

4 Is it formed from a metal oxide or a non-metal oxide?

5 What acids are present in acid rain?

6 Are they formed from metal oxides or non-metal oxides?

7 Calcium oxide is a typical metal oxide. Is it acidic or alkaline?

8 What does this tell you about metal oxides and non-metal oxides?

9 Draw a diagram to show where the pollution in acid rain comes from.

10 Write word equations for the formation of the acid rain compounds.

11 Catalytic converters on cars turn NO_x back into nitrogen gas. Explain why this reduces acid rain.

12 Create an illustration to explain the effects of acid rain to a non-reader.

Plants and rock

Plants grow and die in the soil. Rocks are worn down, broken up and join the rock cycle. All these changes affect our environment.

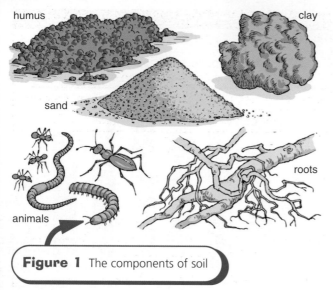

Figure 1 The components of soil

From an early age, we know about soil or 'earth' from digging in it. We imagine that the soil goes deep down, but in fact it's really only a layer about 10 m thick.

Acidity and pH

Different soils have a different pH. The pH of the soil affects which plants can grow in that soil. Some plants can only grow in soil that is acidic and some can only grow when soil is alkaline. Most soils have a pH of between 6.0 and 7.0. This means that soil is weakly acidic. This is because roots absorb nutrients such as potassium, magnesium and calcium ions from the soil and then transfer hydrogen ions back to the soil to preserve a balance. If the soil is too acid, it stops the bacteria releasing nutrients into the soil.

Soil pH	How to fix it
Less than 4.0	Badly polluted. Add lots of lime and give time to recover
4.0 to 6.0	Add lime (calcium oxide)
6.0 to 7.0	NORMAL SOIL
7.0 to 9.0	Add gypsum (magnesium sulphate)
Above 9.0	Badly polluted. Add lots of gypsum and sulphur powder

Table 1 How to treat soils of different pH.

Questions

1. What is pH and how is it measured?
2. What are the components you would find in a good healthy soil?
3. What is humus and what does it add to soil?
4. Why is it important for air to get into soil?
5. Why is soil normally slightly acidic?
6. What do you do to a soil if it is *too* acidic?
7. What do you do to a soil if it is *too* alkaline?
8. Cabbages like alkaline soil. What would you do to a normal field if you wanted to grow a crop of cabbages?

Rock wear

Figure 2 What has caused these rocks to look this way?

Buildings are made from smooth hard rock because it looks very beautiful, and also because rocks wear away very slowly. You don't notice any change over a week, or a month or a year. After ten years, however, you may see the surface begin to become pitted. When this happens, moss and small plants can get a toe-hold and begin the destruction of the rock. The little pits get widened and deepened by the roots. Water fills up the little holes and makes them into cracks when it freezes and thaws in the winter.

Expansion of the outer layer of the rock as it is heated by the Sun causes stresses that make it flake away from the cold rock underneath. Small fragments of rock will then break off and be carried away by the rain. Eventually the beautiful smooth rock becomes rough, worn and damaged.

What can wear away solid rock?

- **The Sun** – heating, expansion and contraction causes rock to flake.

- **Frost** – gets into cracks, and then expands the water in them as it turns to ice. This splits the rock up.

- **Plants** – their roots continue the damage caused by frost.

- **The rain** – makes streams that gradually beat at it and wear it away by washing fragments downstream.

- But most of all **chemicals** in the environment react with the minerals in the rocks.

Remember

Rocks can be a mixture of many different minerals, but minerals are pure substances.

Acids and rocks

Acids get at rocks from everywhere!

- **Roots**: put acid particles in the soil.

- **Rain**: contains dissolved carbon dioxide which makes it weakly acidic.

- **Pollution**: adds considerably to acidity in the atmosphere. Nitric acid from car exhausts and sulphuric acid from burning fossil fuels are the major sources.

Rocks contain many 'basic' minerals in their mixture of materials. A 'base' in chemistry is a material that neutralises an acid. The acids in the environment dissolve the grains of the 'basic' minerals out of the rock, leaving the rock weakened and more easily eroded. This can be a significant problem when the rock is used for building materials or for decoration.

Rocks and 'basic' minerals	
Granite contains salts of	Calcium, Potassium, Sodium
Gabbro contains salts of	Iron, Magnesium
Dolomite contains salts of	Magnesium, Calcium
Limestone contains salts of	Calcium

Table 2 The salts found in some common rocks.

Questions

9 Name six things that can damage rocks.

10 Name three ways that acids get into the environment.

11 Why are acids so harmful to rocks?

12 Why should a bridge over a polluted river *not* be built of limestone?

13 Why do you often find flakes of broken rock at the bottom of an exposed rock surface?

14 Why is acid rain harmful to rocks like granite that are normally weathered very slowly?

Remember

Use the words below to complete the sentences

minerals   different   6.0   soil   weakens   rocks   7.0   wrong

Both ____1____ and rocks suffer if the pH is ____2____. Some plants like soils with a ____3____ pH, but normal soil has a pH of between ____4____ and ____5____.

If acidic water gets onto ____6____ then it dissolves some of the ____7____. This ____8____ the rock.

Global greenhouse

Certain gases in the atmosphere trap energy from the Earth's surface. Increased amounts of these gases are causing global warming. This means the average temperature of the Earth's surface is increasing.

The Earth's atmosphere acts like a kind of greenhouse. It traps energy and keeps the Earth warm. It makes the Earth's surface 33°C warmer than it would be otherwise. Without the atmosphere, the Earth would be a frozen planet with no life.

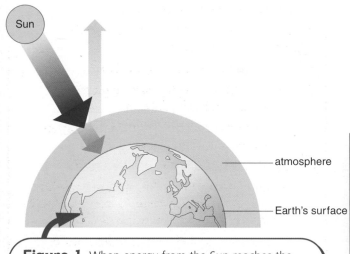

atmosphere

Earth's surface

Figure 1 When energy from the Sun reaches the Earth, 30% is reflected back into space, 20% is absorbed by the atmosphere and 50% is absorbed by the surface of the Earth.

The Earth in turn radiates this energy out into space again as infrared rays. Some of these rays are absorbed as they pass through the gases of the atmosphere, causing it to heat up. This traps extra energy in the atmosphere, just like what happens in a greenhouse. Not all the gases in the atmosphere absorb energy. Oxygen, nitrogen and the noble gases absorb very little of the infrared energy.

Figure 2 The most significant greenhouse gas is carbon dioxide. Natural and industrial processes both put carbon dioxide into the atmosphere and take it out. Slash and burn of rainforests (top) and volcanic eruptions (bottom) both add carbon dioxide to the atmospere.

Greenhouse gas	Amount in atmosphere (parts per million)	Greenhouse factor
CO_2 (carbon dioxide)	355	1
CH_4 (methane from rotting and from animals' digestion)	2	11
CFCs (chlorofluorocarbons)	0.001	34 000
NO_x (nitrogen oxides)	0.3	270

Table 1 The 'greenhouse factor' is a measure of how well each gas traps energy by heating.

Chemistry and the environment

Puts carbon dioxide into the atmosphere	Takes carbon dioxide out of the atmosphere
Burning fossil fuels	Photosynthesis and growth in forests and jungles
Animal respiration	Photosynthesis and growth of sea plankton
Rotting vegetation	
Burning forests to create farmland	
Volcanic eruptions	

Table 2 Inputs and outputs of carbon dioxide.

So the problem is that 'human activity' is increasing the amount of carbon dioxide in the atmosphere. This is causing more energy to be trapped which results in changes to the Earth's climate.

By our actions, we are disturbing the natural balance of the planet. The Earth's environment may be able to cope in the long run, but there will be severe problems caused by the extra energy.

Global warming will cause:

- higher temperatures (2° to 5°C higher) during the next century
- melting of ice masses at the North and South poles
- a rise in sea level (of between 20 and 30 cm)
- more flooding of low-lying land
- more violent weather
- more cloud cover and heavy rain
- changes in sea currents
- deserts to move further north
- more storms, hurricanes and floods causing human suffering
- changing crop patterns
- changes in food webs and possible extinction of some species.

Remember

Look at the list of effects that global warming will cause.

Draw several illustrations to show some of these effects. Combine the drawings into a collage warning about the consequences of global warming.

Questions

1. What causes the greenhouse effect?
2. How cold would the Earth be if there was no greenhouse effect?
3. What happens to the Sun's energy as it is reflected back from the Earth?
4. Name two gases that contribute to the greenhouse effect.
5. Where do these gases come from?
6. How is human activity making global warming more of a problem?
7. What are the effects of global warming on human life?
8. Use this information to plot two graphs.

   Graph A should be of the amount of carbon dioxide in the atmosphere (y-axis) against the number of thousands of years ago (x-axis).

   Graph B should be average temperature (y-axis) against the number of thousands of years ago (x-axis).

Thousands of years ago	CO_2 in atmosphere (parts per million)	Temperature compared with now (°C)
160	200	−9
140	300	0
120	280	−2
100	240	−5
80	230	−5
60	220	−7
40	200	−8
20	200	−9
0	355	0

a) Do both the graphs show the same trend?
b) What is the relationship between the amount of CO_2 in the atmosphere and the average temperature?

63

A tale of two ozones

Ozone is a form of oxygen that absorbs harmful ultraviolet light but is poisonous to our bodies. Ozone is pure oxygen, but it is not 'O_2'. In ozone, three oxygen atoms form a triangle-shaped molecule with the formula O_3.

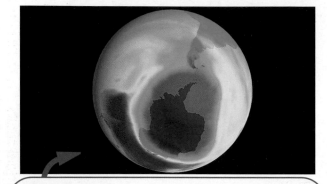

Figure 1 The thinning of the ozone layer is particularly bad over the Antarctic.

Figure 2 Bright sun and traffic add up to poison.

The high atmosphere

Manufactured chemicals, particularly chlorofluorocarbons (CFCs) from fridges and aerosol sprays, drift up to the stratosphere (between 20 and 50 km above the Earth) and react with the ozone molecules there. Up in the stratosphere, the ozone molecules do a useful job absorbing harmful ultraviolet (UV) radiation. Because of the CFCs and other chemicals, there is less ozone up there, so more harmful radiation gets through.

Without the ozone layer, life may never have evolved as we know it now.

Skin colour determines how we are affected by ultraviolet radiation. All skins produce a dark coloured pigment – **melanin** – when exposed to ultraviolet radiation. Melanin absorbs the radiation and stops it penetrating to the tissue below. Dark-skinned people have a lot of this pigment in their skin so are harmed less by UV radiation.

Streetcar poisoning: ozone at ground level

For many years, car engines were produced cheaply to run on cheap fuel and provide convenient mass transport. No-one predicted how many problems cars would cause in the environment. Their ability to cause ozone gas at ground level was never thought about. This is a complicated reaction that involves strong sunlight.

	Ultraviolet A (longest wavelength)	Ultraviolet B (medium wavelength)	Ultraviolet C (shortest wavelength)
Harm rating	Least harmful	Does considerable damage	Lethal
Effect	Tans skin. Can cause damage if skin is exposed for too long.	Burns and ages skin. Causes skin cancers and eye damage (cataracts). Kills plankton in the seas.	Kills small organisms. Damages DNA rapidly; causes skin cancer and eye damage.
Absorption by atmosphere	Gets through ozone layer and oxygen easily.	Absorbed by ozone – not affected by oxygen	Mostly absorbed by oxygen and remaining ozone in the air.
Precautions	Not a problem, use suntan cream.	Use total sunblock and cover up with long-sleeved clothes.	Not yet a problem.

Table 1 Types of ultraviolet radiation.

Chemistry and the environment

UV radiation and skin

- Skin is 3 mm thick and UV radiation penetrates through it
- UV light makes skin lose its elasticity
- then it makes skin furrowed and lumpy
- then UV radiation can damage the skin DNA
- this causes cancers
- these cancers have to be cut out leaving scars
- there were 40 000 cases of skin cancer in the UK last year
- the number of skin cancer cases doubles every 10 years as ozone layer damage gets worse
- if left untreated, skin cancer can kill.

So make sure you wear high factor suntan creams and sunglasses.

Motor fuel and pollution

- Car engines burn fuel at high pressures.
- Because of this, the exhaust gases contain carbon monoxide, unburnt hydrocarbon fuel (petrol or diesel) and oxides of nitrogen (NO_x).
- Oxygen (O_2) in the air gets changed into ozone (O_3) when it is combined with the unburnt hydrocarbon and oxides of nitrogen (NO_x) and there is strong sunlight.
- The reaction is rather slow and often the reacting air mass has drifted away from the town centre into residential areas.
- If people breathe in the ozone that is produced, it reacts with the blood and prevents it from carrying oxygen.
- Because of this, people's brains don't get enough oxygen. Your brain uses up one-fifth of the oxygen you breathe in.
- It is also very bad for people with asthma and breathing problems.

Questions

1 What is the formula for an ozone molecule?
2 What does ozone do to blood?
3 What chemicals destroy ozone?
4 What radiation does ozone absorb?
5 What does this radiation do to our skin?
6 Why do dark-skinned people have more protection from damage by this radiation?
7 How should you protect your skin from this sort of radiation damage?
8 What chemicals in traffic fumes cause the ozone problem in cities?
9 The ozone reaction only happens in bright sunlight. Why do you think this is so?
10 Why is city centre pollution a problem for areas downwind of the city centre?
11 Write a short paragraph for a leaflet that would advise an asthmatic how to avoid both types of ozone-related problems.

Remember

Use the words below to complete the sentences.

**breathing traffic radiation damage
cream chemicals layer stratosphere
ultraviolet ozone air**

The ozone ___1___ in the ___2___ is getting thinner due to ___3___ destroying the ozone.

This lets in ultraviolet ___4___. This ___5___ radiation can ___6___ skin and cause nasty cancers if you do not use suntan ___7___ on your skin.

___8___ gas can cause ___9___ problems when it is produced by ___10___ reacting with ___11___ fumes.

Sustainable development

Air that you can't breathe without getting ill, water that fish can't live in, land so poisoned from industrial use that you can't safely build houses on it – it has to stop! We can't go on treating the environment as a dustbin – the bin is nearly full.

Sustainable development is becoming a rapidly growing industry. It means living life without spoiling the environment for the future. It also means designing and engineering things with sustainable development in mind. What it does NOT mean is giving up our useful technology to go back to horses and carts.

Cars

Cars are very wasteful and even the most modern cars pollute the environment. What is a shiny, new and very useful machine at the start of its life, eventually becomes a useless lump of mixed materials.

Possible action to be taken

Every car should have two additional taxes added to its price. One to pay the cost of all the pollution. The second to pay for recycling the car. But this costs money.

Fuels: carbon tax

Most fuels contain carbon. This burns in air to make carbon dioxide which adds to the greenhouse gases in the atmosphere. The global warming and climate change caused by the increasing amounts of greenhouse gases is very costly.

Possible action to be taken

There should be an extra tax on every litre of motor fuel and every unit of gas or electricity. But this costs money.

Forestry

Trees and the wood they produce are essential raw materials. They are a valuable money earner when cut down. But trees absorb carbon dioxide from the air to grow and help to balance the amount of oxygen and carbon dioxide in the air.

Possible action to be taken

For every tree cut down and sold, there must be a new one planted. But this costs money.

Biodiversity

There is a huge variety of habitats in every country. Forests, hedgerows, meadows, wetlands, mountainside gorse and sand dunes all exist in the UK, but only farmland – grassy meadows for grazing and cultivated fields – makes a lot of money.

We spend much of our time clearing forest, ripping up hedgerows and draining wetlands to turn them into farmland. When we do this we endanger and destroy the species of plants and animals that live in these habitats. We are reducing rapidly the variety of living organisms in our environment.

Possible action to be taken

Keep track of the diversity of living organisms. Protect endangered habitats such as wetlands. But this costs money.

Transport

Personal means of transport, such as cars, are usually only used by one or two people at a time. They are very wasteful in terms of the amount of space they occupy and the amount of fuel they use. Public transport makes much better use of fuels and space on roads and in cities. In addition, public transport is much less polluting than lots of small cars running everywhere.

Possible action to be taken

- Pollution-free electronic cars and trams in towns
- High-speed rail networks instead of motorways
- Offshore airports to cut noise pollution

But this costs money and can be inconvenient.

Renewable energy

Some of the major polluters of the environment are the energy industries.

Coal and oil burnt to make electricity are the major causes of acid rain. Oil tankers regularly pollute the seas. The industrial sites of oil refineries and gas works are so polluted that they can't be used for other purposes. Motor fuel causes city centre smoke and ozone pollution as well as adding nitrogen oxides (NO_x) to acid rain.

Elsewhere in these books there are references to renewable methods of generating electricity and providing for energy needs. These are less polluting, but they all still damage habitats for biodiversity.

Possible action to be taken

Power companies could set up wind farms and hydroelectric dams. Encourage builders to install solar cells to generate electricity on new buildings.

Design schools and shops that use lots of natural light rather than burning electricity. But this costs money.

Recycling

Why should a fridge or washing machine get dumped for the council to take away? Someone has had a lot of use from it, then it just gets dumped with the rest of the rubbish. Rubbish needs to be sorted into what can and cannot be recycled.

Possible action to be taken

When you buy a fridge you should also pay the cost of getting it recycled safely. Waste disposal systems at home should sort out waste and send all the glass, paper, card, metal and rubber for recycling. This sorting should be done by the people who make the waste *before* it is collected. But this costs people time and money.

Scientists

Prof. Kathy Sykes

Kathy is a professor of public understanding of science. Her field is science communication. She is talking here about the *Rough Science* TV programmes.

I did a PhD in physics on a biodegradable plastic. After that I worked at a new hands-on science centre, where I spent about five years coming up with ideas for wild things to show scientific principles. Since then I've been communicating science in different ways.

I think it's really important to try to have a holistic approach to science. One of the problems in science today is people are in narrow fields. On *Rough Science* different kinds of scientists solve problems by bringing several subjects together.

The *Rough Science* programmes show how science can be really fun. For example, they show how you can enjoy looking at a beautiful rainbow and then understand how that rainbow was formed.

Activity

1   Other areas of concern could be health care, agriculture and chemicals, nuclear power, space rubbish and air pollution. Find out about one of these and write a paragraph with possible action to be taken.

2   All the proposed action for the seven areas of concern above cost money. The benefit will be for the people who have less mess in the future, but not so much for the people who live now.

Design parts of an advertising campaign to persuade people that this is a benefit to their lives.

Produce slogans, leaflets, posters, radio adverts, storyboards for TV adverts or videos for the campaign.

There will need to be a 'scientific' argument in your adverts or people will not see the sense in it.

Pollution control

1 During the Industrial Revolution, the coal burning factories were built with tall chimneys. The tall chimneys prevented soot and fumes from affecting the houses nearby. But the tall chimneys did not prevent acid rain. Explain both these ideas.

2 Copy and complete the following sentences:

When coal burns it produces an acidic gas called sulphur dioxide. This is because coal contains quantities of _____ .

The sulphur dioxide dissolves in the _____ _____ in the air to form _____ acid. This falls as acid rain.

3 Petrol and diesel fuel contain little or no sulphur. Explain how this helps the environment.

4 In the 1960s, the number of fish in lakes and rivers in Europe fell sharply. When the water in the lakes was tested it was found to be so acidic that the fish were dying. One solution to this was to put large quantities of limestone (calcium carbonate) in the lakes and into the rivers leading to the lakes.

a) Explain why adding limestone to the water helped solve the problem of the lakes and rivers being too acidic.

b) Why was adding limestone NOT a permanent solution to the problem?

Activity

Make a snakes and ladders game about sources of pollution (the snakes) and how people can prevent the pollution happening (ladders).

Instructions

- Draw an 8×8 grid like a chessboard on a piece of A3 paper.

- Use these eight 'snake' ideas
  ⇒ acid rain
  ⇒ global warming
  ⇒ greenhouse gases
  ⇒ 2 × effects of climate change
  ⇒ ozone layer damage
  ⇒ UV radiation
  ⇒ NO_x in city centres

- Make eight snakes of different lengths to fit on your board game.

- Each snake should have an explanation.

- Make eight ladders that are the solution to the eight snake problems, these should have an explanation as well.

- Fit your snakes and ladders on to your grid to make the game.

- Get a dice and two player tokens. Play the game with a partner.

CHAPTER 6

Gravity and space

Opener Activity
Balancing gravity

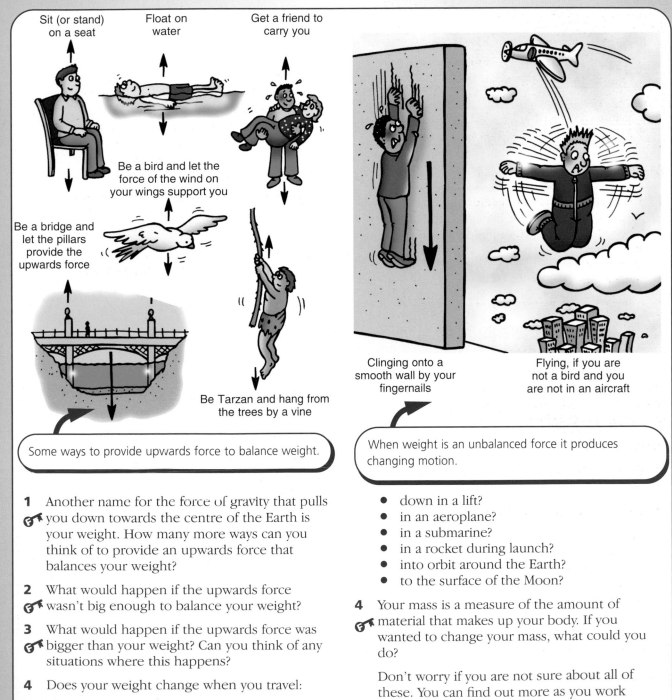

Sit (or stand) on a seat

Float on water

Get a friend to carry you

Be a bird and let the force of the wind on your wings support you

Be a bridge and let the pillars provide the upwards force

Be Tarzan and hang from the trees by a vine

Clinging onto a smooth wall by your fingernails

Flying, if you are not a bird and you are not in an aircraft

Some ways to provide upwards force to balance weight.

When weight is an unbalanced force it produces changing motion.

1 Another name for the force of gravity that pulls you down towards the centre of the Earth is your weight. How many more ways can you think of to provide an upwards force that balances your weight?

2 What would happen if the upwards force wasn't big enough to balance your weight?

3 What would happen if the upwards force was bigger than your weight? Can you think of any situations where this happens?

4 Does your weight change when you travel:

• up in a lift?
• down in a lift?
• in an aeroplane?
• in a submarine?
• in a rocket during launch?
• into orbit around the Earth?
• to the surface of the Moon?

4 Your mass is a measure of the amount of material that makes up your body. If you wanted to change your mass, what could you do?

Don't worry if you are not sure about all of these. You can find out more as you work through the chapter.

Parachuting on the Moon

Balanced and unbalanced forces have the same effects on motion wherever you are.

Figure 1 The force of gravity can make the parachutist accelerate downwards – but there's also the force of air resistance that acts upwards. When these forces are in balance, parachutists drift to the ground at a constant speed. They fall but they don't accelerate.

The Moon is smaller than the Earth so its gravitational pull is weaker, but it is still strong enough to make you accelerate towards the surface.

Nobody has ever tried parachuting on the Moon. It wouldn't work. Parachutes rely on air resistance. The Moon has no air. On the Moon there'd be no force of air resistance to exert an upwards force. The jumper and the parachute would accelerate together towards the ground, and go on accelerating until they hit the surface. Parachuting from high up above the Moon is dangerous!

Figure 2 On Earth, we know that air resistance will have a big effect on the motion of a feather. But a feather and hammer accelerate to the Moon's surface together. Astronauts on the Moon have tried this to prove that it is true.

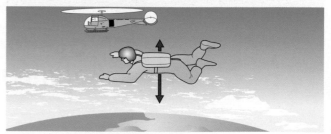

High above the Earth, near the start of a jump, gravitational force is pulling down. The force of air resistance acts in the opposite direction. But the jumper is still only moving slowly, so the force of air resistance is small. The forces are unbalanced. Motion changes. The jumper accelerates towards the ground.

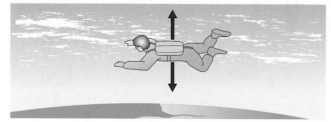

The jumper has accelerated. In fact she has gained so much speed that air resistance has grown as big as the force of gravity. The forces are in balance. Motion is not changing any more. The jumper falls at a steady speed, her terminal velocity.

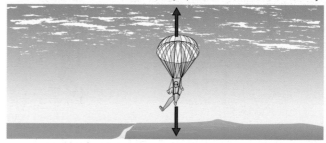

With the parachute open, air resistance can balance the force of gravity while the jumper falls quite slowly and steadily.

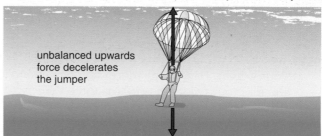

unbalanced upwards force decelerates the jumper

As she lands, the surface of the Earth exerts a large but bearable upwards force. Forces on the jumper are unbalanced, and motion changes. The parachutist decelerates. Speed changes and becomes zero.

Figure 3 A parachutist descending to Earth.

High above the Moon, near the start of a jump gravitational force is pulling down. There is no force of air resistance acting in the opposite direction. The jumper is experiencing unbalanced force. Motion changes, and the jumper accelerates downwards towards the surface.

The jumper has accelerated. There is no air resistance to balance the force of gravity. The jumper goes on accelerating.

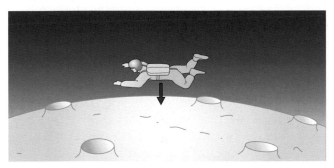

An unbalanced force keeps our jumper accelerating ... moving faster and faster towards the Moon's rocky surface.

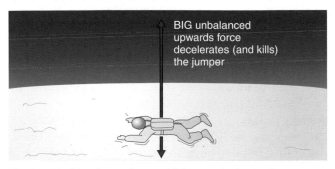

BIG unbalanced upwards force decelerates (and kills) the jumper

The jumper hits the surface at high speed. The surface exerts a large upwards force which very quickly changes the speed of the jumper to zero. The force is so big that the jumper's body can't withstand it.

Figure 4 A parachutist descending to the Moon.

The steady motion of the parachutist towards the surface of the Earth is called **terminal velocity**. We can think of terminal velocity as the parachutist's maximum speed.

Parachutists on the Moon have no terminal velocity. They would accelerate down faster and faster until they hit the surface.

Average speed – worked example

If a parachutist falls 60 metres in 8 seconds, what is their average speed?

average speed = distance ÷ time
= 60 metres ÷ 8 seconds
= 7.5 metres per second

Questions

1 When does the Earth parachutist stop accelerating downwards?

2 Why can the forces acting on the Moon parachutist never become balanced during the fall?

3 When do both parachutists experience an unbalanced upwards force?

4 Why wouldn't a helicopter work on the Moon?

5 What is the average speed, in metres per second, of a jumper who falls 390 metres in one minute? (One minute = 60 seconds)

Remember

Unscramble the anagrams to complete the sentences below.

Average speed = <u>ITS DANCE</u> ÷ time. When distance is measured in metres and time is measured in <u>SON DECS</u>, then speed is measured in <u>REST ME</u> per second.

The movement of a body stays the same when the forces acting on it are <u>DANCE LAB</u>, but always changes when the forces are <u>BUNDLE A CAN</u>.

Air resistance and friction provide forces that act in the <u>O SPOT PIE</u> direction to the <u>MEMO VENT</u>. For a <u>GILL FAN</u> object, the force of air resistance acts <u>WARP SUD</u>.

Houston, we have a problem

The further away you go from the Earth or from any other planet or Moon, the weaker the force of gravity it exerts. The force of gravity acting on an object is called its weight, measured in newtons. Weight is different from mass, which is measured in kilograms.

The astronauts of the Apollo 13 space mission very nearly didn't make it back safely to Earth. Getting humans from space and back down to the Earth's surface is not easy. People have bodies, and bodies have **mass**. We can measure the mass of a human body, or any kind of body, in **kilograms**. (We could also use **grams** for small bodies – a kilogram is a thousand grams. Or we could use **tonnes** for large bodies – a tonne is a thousand kilograms.)

Figure 1 Film actor Tom Hanks plays Jim Lovell in the movie of the real Apollo 13 space mission.

Whether an astronaut is in space or walking on the Moon, they have exactly the same body. There is no more or less of it. It isn't any bigger or smaller in one place than another. It has the same mass wherever it goes. But the force of gravity on a body is NOT the same wherever it goes. An astronaut on the Moon experiences a smaller force than on Earth. And when floating freely in space, the astronaut experiences no force at all. The force of gravity acting on a body is also called its **weight**. Weight, unlike mass, changes depending on where you are. Since weight is a force it is measured in **newtons**.

Newtons? We have a problem

If you spend your whole life on Earth and you're not too worried about what happens in space then there is no problem. You don't have to bother about the difference between mass and weight, or between kilograms and newtons. But scientists care about space. Science has to tell the truth about what happens on the Moon, and anywhere else, as well as on the Earth.

So for our everyday life it's acceptable to most people to talk about our weight and to measure it in kilograms. We just need to remember that we need to be more careful with what we say when we talk about space. Then we MUST measure weight in newtons and mass in kilograms.

Weightlessness in deep space

If you go on a diet, you're hoping that there will be less of you. You want to lose mass (measured in kilograms). If there is less of you, the Earth doesn't pull you so hard. If you lose mass then you also lose weight. You don't press so hard on the spring inside the bathroom scales.

But you can also lose weight without losing any mass at all. You can eat all the chocolates and cake you like. If you are floating freely in deep space, a long way from any big object (like the Earth or Moon) and its gravitational pull, then you still have mass. There is no force of gravity acting on you. You don't have any weight. You are **weightless**.

'Weightlessness' in Earth orbit

The strength of the force that a large object like the Earth or Moon can exert on your body depends on how far away you are. The further you go away from it, the weaker the force and the less you weigh. Astronauts in a space station in orbit above the Earth are far enough away from the Earth for the force of gravity to be a bit less than it would be on the ground. But only a little bit. The Earth is still pulling on their bodies. The force changes their motion, so they keep turning. If they have the right speed at the right height then the 'size' of this 'turning' matches the shape of the Earth below. They travel in circular motion. Their spacecraft travels in the same circle. The walls and floor of the spacecraft don't exert any force on the astronauts (unless they crash into them). The astronauts feel exactly as they would if they were in deep space a long, long way from the Earth. They *feel* weightless.

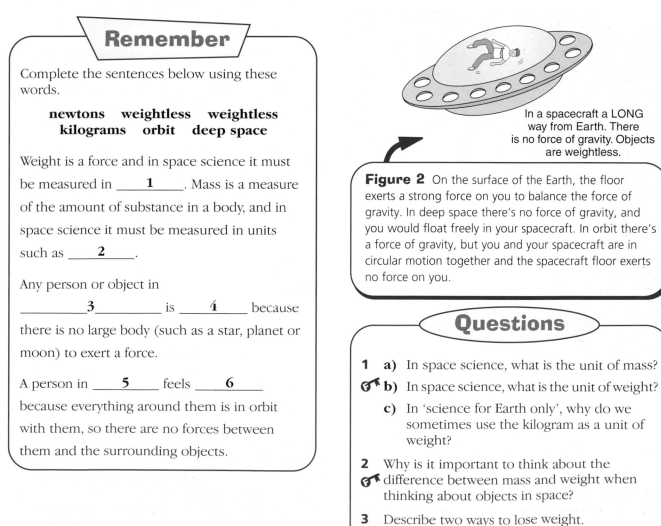

upwards force exerted by the floor

On Earth. Upwards and downwards force in balance.

weight

In a spacecraft in orbit. There's no upwards force to balance weight. The result of this is the curved pathway of orbit.

high velocity

future pathway (orbit)

weight

In a spacecraft a LONG way from Earth. There is no force of gravity. Objects are weightless.

Figure 2 On the surface of the Earth, the floor exerts a strong force on you to balance the force of gravity. In deep space there's no force of gravity, and you would float freely in your spacecraft. In orbit there's a force of gravity, but you and your spacecraft are in circular motion together and the spacecraft floor exerts no force on you.

Remember

Complete the sentences below using these words.

**newtons   weightless   weightless
kilograms   orbit   deep space**

Weight is a force and in space science it must be measured in ____**1**____. Mass is a measure of the amount of substance in a body, and in space science it must be measured in units such as ____**2**____.

Any person or object in _____**3**_____ is ____**4**____ because there is no large body (such as a star, planet or moon) to exert a force.

A person in ____**5**____ feels ____**6**____ because everything around them is in orbit with them, so there are no forces between them and the surrounding objects.

Questions

1   a)   In space science, what is the unit of mass?

☞ b)   In space science, what is the unit of weight?

   c)   In 'science for Earth only', why do we sometimes use the kilogram as a unit of weight?

2   Why is it important to think about the
☞ difference between mass and weight when thinking about objects in space?

3   Describe two ways to lose weight.
☞

The Isaac Newton story

Gravitational force keeps the motion of planets in constant change.

Galileo was an Italian who died in the year that Isaac Newton was born. One of Galileo's original ideas was that moving objects keep on moving when they are left to themselves.

Isaac Newton was born on a farm in Lincolnshire on Christmas Day, 1642. His father died, and Isaac's mother got married again. Unfortunately, Isaac's new stepfather didn't have much time for children. Poor Isaac was sent to live with his grandparents. He had a lonely childhood.

Isaac had a strong curiosity. As a young man he put his finger between his eyeball and the bone around it – just to try to find out what was there. He was ill for several days, and was lucky not to go blind.

Figure 1 The story of Isaac Newton.

Isaac Newton developed ideas about force. We often think that the natural thing for moving objects to do is to slow down and stop. But Newton worked on Galileo's idea that the natural thing for moving objects to do is to keep on moving at the same speed. It takes a **force** to change the motion.

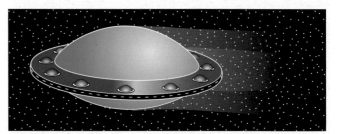

Air resistance and friction provide forces, so sometimes we make the mistake of thinking that moving objects always slow down and stop. Now that we can picture spacecraft moving where there is no air to slow them down, it's easier for us to see that steady motion IS what happens naturally.

Unbalanced forces change the speed and/or the direction of moving objects. This is a version of **Newton's First Law**. When there is no force or when forces are balanced, motion does not change.

Newton's other great achievement was to say that the everyday force that makes apples fall off trees is the SAME kind of force as the force that keeps the Moon in orbit around the Earth and keeps the planets in orbit around the Sun. This is the force of **gravity**.

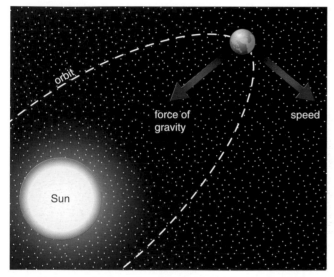

Isaac Newton said that the natural thing for planets and moons to do is to travel in straight lines at steady speed. He said that it was the continuous force of gravity acting on them that made their motion change, so they travel in curved paths and not straight lines. They stay in orbit because of the combination of their speed and the force of gravity.

Telescopes and rainbows

Isaac Newton was not only interested in forces and gravity.

- He explained the refraction of light by lenses.

- He invented ways of making better lenses.

- He developed a better telescope.

- He investigated the dispersion of white light into colours by a prism.

- He explained how rainbows are formed.

- He was director of the Royal Mint and a Member of Parliament.

Questions

1   Think about some moving objects such as a bag sliding across the floor, a rolling ball, a skater and a spacecraft.

   a) What does your 'common sense' tell you about what is more natural – steady motion or slowing down and stopping?

   b) Do you think that the ideas of Galileo and Newton agree or disagree with your 'common sense'?

   c) Is 'common sense' always a reliable way of understanding how the world behaves?

2 a) Why doesn't a satellite in orbit around the Earth slow down?

   b) In what way is the satellite's motion changing all the time?

3   What forces do the passengers feel in these situations:

   a) When a lift starts moving?

   b) When a lift is rising steadily?

   c) When a train starts moving?

   d) When a train is moving along at a steady speed?

   e) When a car goes round a sharp corner at a steady speed?

   f) When a car stops quickly?

Remember

Match the words below to the spaces in the paragraph.

**resistance   gravity   directions
movement   planets   orbit   force
same**

Isaac Newton developed two very important new ideas. He said that ____**1**____ is what makes ____**2**____ change, and that the gravity that we feel here on Earth is the ____**3**____ as the gravity that keeps the planets in ____**4**____ around the Sun. The planets' ____**5**____ change all of the time as they follow their curved paths. It is the force of ____**6**____ that produces this change. In space, there is no air ____**7**____ acting on a spacecraft. There is no resistance to the movement of ____**8**____.

Stories of the Solar System

People have followed the movements of the Sun and the Moon and of stars and planets for thousands of years. The idea that we live on one of a family of nine planets is an idea that is not so old.

If you follow the movement of the Sun or the Moon across the sky, it's easy to think that they travel around us. In the past, many people believed that the Earth was at the centre of everything – the centre of the Universe. The idea that the Earth is at the centre of everything is called the **geocentric Universe**.

The Sun at the centre

If you follow the tracks of the planets, month by month, they move backwards and forwards. That's hard to explain if everything goes around the Earth. So a Polish monk called Copernicus said that there was another way of looking at it. We can imagine that the Sun is at the centre and that we are moving (along with the other planets) around the Sun. That provides a different explanation of the movements of the planets in the sky. The idea was so new that nobody took much notice for a while – but then a few brave people realised that there might be something in the monk's idea.

The idea that the Sun is at the centre of the Solar System is called the **heliocentric** idea.

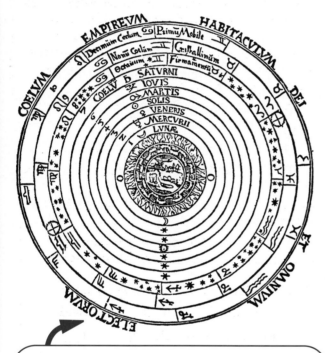

Figure 1 The geocentric model of the Universe. This picture was produced in 1539. It shows the Earth in the centre, and the Moon, Sun, planets and all the stars moving around us.

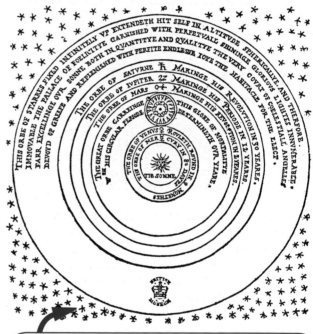

Figure 2 The heliocentric model of the Universe. This picture was produced in 1576.

Figure 3 At first sight it seems to make sense to say that the Sun goes around the Earth, once every day. But careful observations of the motions of the planets show that they, including the Earth, all go around the Sun. It takes us a year for a complete round trip. In the meantime our planet spins. It is this spin that makes it look as if the Sun moves across the sky each day.

Figure 3 Johannes Kepler worked with detailed measurements of the motions of the planets. He realised that they don't move in perfect circles. This meant that Copernicus' suggestion fitted exactly with the motions of the planets that people could see.

Figure 5 In Galileo's time, 400 years ago, people only knew of the Earth and five other planets – Mercury, Venus, Mars, Jupiter and Saturn. But one by one, people discovered Uranus, Neptune and Pluto. And thanks to scientists like Isaac Newton, we know that it is the strong gravity of the huge Sun that holds the planets in their orbits. This picture of Uranus was taken by the Hubble Space Telescope.

Figure 4 Galileo Galilei used a new technology – the telescope. With this he saw shadows of mountains on the Moon, and moons in orbit around Jupiter. He saw with his own eyes that everything did NOT go around the Earth. This was still too new for many people, and Galileo was arrested for his ideas.

Remember

Complete the gaps in the sentences using the words below.

**Galileo   telescopes   geocentric
Newton   heliocentric   Copernicus**

There are different ways to try to explain how we see the Sun, the Moon, the planets and stars moving across our sky. The ____1____ explanation says that the Earth is the centre of all movement.

A Polish monk called ____2____ suggested a new idea with the Sun at the centre. This is called the ____3____ idea.

____4____ supported the new idea. He claimed that his observations with ____5____ provided evidence for the heliocentric idea.

____6____ provided the concept of gravity acting across space. This provides a force that holds planets, including the Earth, in orbit around the Sun.

Questions

1 **a)** What's the difference between the geocentric idea and the heliocentric idea of the Solar System?

   b) Which idea do you prefer?

2 What new technology did Galileo use to observe objects in space?

3 What evidence did Galileo have that not everything in the Universe goes around the Earth?

4 Why is space scary?

Energy searches by satellite

Satellites are held in orbit by the Earth's gravity. We can use satellites to help us to look for energy resources and to find our way around. They can also help us to look for signs that we are harming the Earth.

Figure 1 A satellite in orbit above the Earth's atmosphere.

Figure 2 A satellite picture of a weather system over the Atlantic Ocean.

Satellites can be launched into space by rocket. They go around the Earth, in **orbit** above our **atmosphere**. It takes a lot of energy to lift an object so high. Once a satellite is in orbit, its speed keeps it there. If a satellite stopped, it would crash straight to Earth. But it has high orbital speed so it falls in a curve. It falls but it keeps missing the Earth!

The atmosphere is the layer of air around the Earth. Energy from the Sun heats the atmosphere. It heats it more in some places than in others and that creates wind. Automatic cameras, on satellites high above the Earth, take pictures of the Earth below, like the one in Figure 2. We can use the pictures to see where the wind is blowing and to make weather forecasts. Satellites can also be used

to search for different rock features. This helps people find out where there might be fossil fuels or other resources under the ground.

Infrared and radio

Satellite cameras often use the same kind of light that our eyes use to make pictures. But some cameras use 'invisible light', such as infrared light. Our eyes can't see this kind of light, though our skin can detect the warming effect of infrared if it is strong enough.

Satellites can be used for communication as well as for taking pictures. We can send TV pictures and telephone signals around the world. You may have a receiver of satellite signals on the side of your house. The signals are carried by radio waves. Radio waves are another form of 'invisible light'.

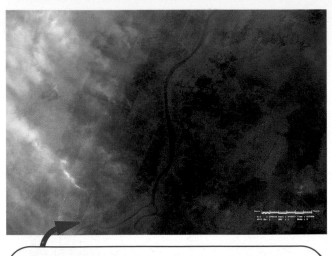

Figure 3 This satellite picture shows forest fires burning in Indonesia in South East Asia. The pale blue colour is the smoke. The picture uses 'false colour' to help us see different features. Crops are shown in red and forest is dark green.

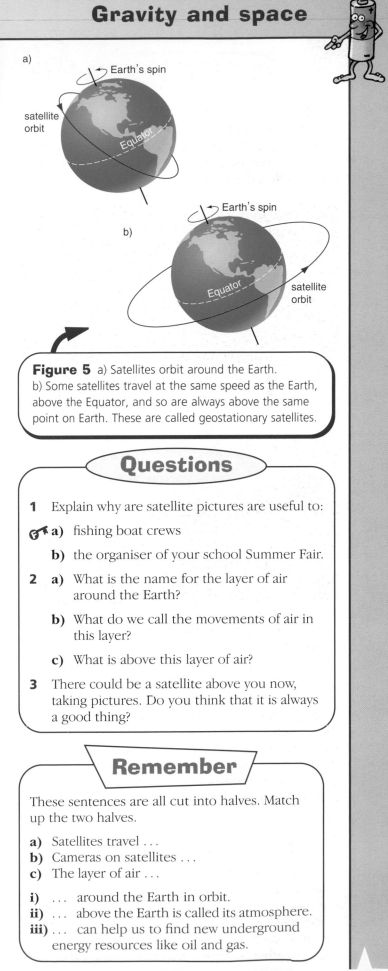

Figure 5 a) Satellites orbit around the Earth.
b) Some satellites travel at the same speed as the Earth, above the Equator, and so are always above the same point on Earth. These are called geostationary satellites.

Questions

1 Explain why are satellite pictures are useful to:

🗝 **a)** fishing boat crews

b) the organiser of your school Summer Fair.

2 a) What is the name for the layer of air around the Earth?

b) What do we call the movements of air in this layer?

c) What is above this layer of air?

3 There could be a satellite above you now, taking pictures. Do you think that it is always a good thing?

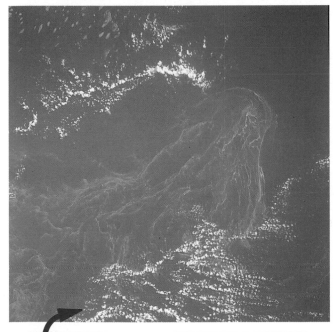

Figure 4 A sensitive camera on a satellite also produced this picture. It shows a huge patch of sea that's brimming with tiny living things called plankton. Many of the living things get their energy from the light of the Sun. Animals like fish and whales eat plankton. Satellite pictures can help fishing boats to find the best places to search for fish. When we eat the fish, we eat the energy resource that the plankton made using the sunlight.

Remember

These sentences are all cut into halves. Match up the two halves.

a) Satellites travel . . .
b) Cameras on satellites . . .
c) The layer of air . . .

i) . . . around the Earth in orbit.
ii) . . . above the Earth is called its atmosphere.
iii) . . . can help us to find new underground energy resources like oil and gas.

Closer

The Space Race

In the 1950s and 1960s, Russia and the USA competed fiercely to explore what exists above the Earth's atmosphere. Their competition was called 'the Space Race'. The Russians went into the lead. In 1957 they launched Sputnik, the very first artificial satellite. Then in 1961 they sent the first person into space, Yuri Gagarin. Not long later, others such as Valentina Tereshkova followed. But then the Americans started the Apollo programme. The objective was to send people to the Moon. Neil Armstrong stepped on to the Moon in 1969.

The first man and woman in space, Yuri Gagarin and Valentina Tereshkova.

Now there are hundreds of artificial satellites. Some are sent up by governments to do scientific research, providing information about the Earth's atmosphere and climate. Others are sent by TV companies to beam 'satellite TV' signals back down to Earth. Others are made by telephone companies, for worldwide communication.

International communication by telephone.

Activity

1 Choose one item from the list below and use the Internet to research it. Choose one, two or three images. Write a short explanation about them. You could present your images and explanations as a small poster.

- Sputnik
- Telstar
- Yuri Gagarin
- Valentina Tereshkova
- John Glen
- Apollo 11
- Neil Armstrong
- Space shuttle
- Yang Liwei
- Meteosat
- Galileo satellites
- Indian Space Program (or you can try other countries instcad of India)

2 Do you think that countries should compete with each other or work together for space missions and exploration?

3 Who owns space? Should private companies be allowed to send satellites into orbit? What benefits would we lose if they were not?

4 Create a word puzzle using the ten most important words from this chapter. First you will need to decide what these are. Don't make a simple wordsearch, but make a puzzle that requires the puzzler to know what the words mean. A crossword would be one good idea. When you have finished, let your neighbour try your puzzle, and you can try theirs.

CHAPTER 7

Plants, photosynthesis and food

Opener Activity
Veggie power!

- When you went to bed last night you were probably sleeping on sheets made from cotton.
- When you took your shower or washed your face this morning you used soap that contained oil from corn, soya beans or cotton and fats from cattle.
- The milk, toast, cereal, juice or other breakfast foods you ate were grown on a farm.
- The paper bag you packed your lunch in and the paper you did your homework on were made from trees.

Plants are very important. One plant, the soya plant, provides soya beans, an important food source. It is a versatile plant that is used in making lots of everyday items.

Soya beans and two pods.

Activity

1 Look at the list of products below. Which of these can be made from soya and which cannot? Discuss this in small groups.

- Flour
- Milk
- Resins
- Electrical circuits
- Fuel for cars
- Glass
- Face cream
- Perfume
- Crayons
- Solvents
- Soap
- Printing ink
- Meat substitute for vegetarians

- Knife blades
- Plastic

2 Now try and think of an alternative source for making each item on the list.

3 How many things are you wearing that might have come from plants?

4 How many things have you eaten in the past 24 hours that were plants or parts of plants?

5 If plants were to die out what effect could this have on our lives?

6 Plants take carbon dioxide out of the atmosphere and provide oxygen. Can life exist if plants were to die out?

Living on fresh air

Plants make their own food by a process called photosynthesis. Four things are needed for photosynthesis to occur: sunlight, carbon dioxide, chlorophyll and water. The speed of photosynthesis also depends on the temperature.

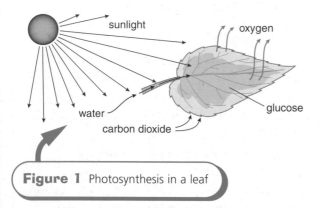

Figure 1 Photosynthesis in a leaf

Plants make their own food using energy from **sunlight** to join together **water** and the gas **carbon dioxide** from the air. The plant makes a type of sugar called **glucose** and produces the gas **oxygen** as a waste product. This process is known as **photosynthesis**. The word photosynthesis describes what the plant does – *photo* means light and *synthesis* means making, so plants make food using light. We can use a **word formula** to show this chemical process. (*Hint*: you will need to learn this equation.)

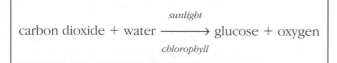

$$\text{carbon dioxide} + \text{water} \xrightarrow[\text{chlorophyll}]{\text{sunlight}} \text{glucose} + \text{oxygen}$$

The carbon dioxide enters the leaf through tiny holes called **stomata**. (Stomata is used for lots of holes. One hole is called a **stoma**.) The oxygen that is made or produced goes back into the air through the same holes. Any part of a plant that is green can photosynthesise, but it mainly happens in the leaves. Most of the stomata are on the underside of the leaf, but there are some on the top of the leaf and on the stem. Plants cannot use all of the sugar that they make straight away and so they have to store some of it. To do this, they have to join units of sugar together to make starch. They store the starch in their leaves for use when they cannot make food, for example in the dark.

Can you remember how we break up starch molecules when we digest our food? Do you remember how we drew starch and sugar molecules to show that the starch is a long branching chain?

When plants photosynthesise, they get bigger and heavier. This is called the plant's **biomass**. It is amazing to think that the wood that makes up a tree has come mainly from the gases in the air and the water from the soil.

If a plant is going to photosynthesise, it must have four things:

1   Sunlight
2   Water
3   Carbon dioxide
4   Chlorophyll

Figure 2 This plant has everything it needs to photosynthesise.

Three of these things – sunlight, water and carbon dioxide – will affect how much food a plant can make and how quickly it can make it. There is another factor that will affect how quickly and how much a plant will photosynthesise and that is the surrounding temperature. Just like animals, plants work best when the surrounding temperature is not too hot and not too cold.

Look at the three graphs below in Figure 3. They show what happens when the factors that affect photosynthesis in plants are changed.

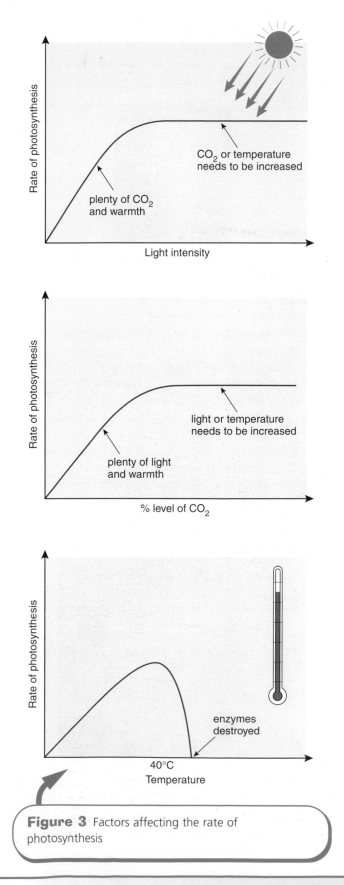

Figure 3 Factors affecting the rate of photosynthesis

For Questions 1–6, explain how the shape of the graph helps you find the answer.

1 What is the best temperature for plants to be kept at if you want them to photosynthesise?

2 What happens to the rate of photosynthesis after about 40°C?

3 Describe what happens to the rate of photosynthesis if you increase the level of carbon dioxide.

4 Can you just keep increasing the amount of light to make the plant photosynthesise more?

5 If a plant is given plenty of carbon dioxide, will it just keep on making more and more sugar?

6 Describe what happens when the light intensity increases.

7 As well as making sugar, the plant also stores food as starch. Where is this food stored

    a) in potato plants?

    b) in wheat plants?

    c) in cabbage plants?

8 A cactus is a plant with no leaves. Where does a cactus make its food and where does it store its supplies of food and water? (*Hint*: what part of the plant do the spikes protect?)

Remember

Choose the correct word from each pair of words to make a summary paragraph that you can write in your exercise book.

Plants make their own FOOD/WASTE by a process known as PHOTOSYNTHESIS/RESPIRATION. In this process, NITROGEN DIOXIDE/CARBON DIOXIDE from the air is joined with MINERALS/WATER taken from the soil to make the sugar CELLULOSE/GLUCOSE. Using the energy from WIND/SUNLIGHT, the green chemical HAEMOGLOBIN/CHLOROPHYLL joins the chemicals together. The gas OXYGEN/HYDROGEN is produced and is put back into the atmosphere. Plants increase their biomass when they photosynthesise. Plants need the right amount of water, carbon dioxide and the right TEMPERATURE/SOIL in order to photosynthesise well.

Discovering photosynthesis

It took hundreds of years for the whole of the process of photosynthesis to be understood. Some of the main figures in the story are outlined below.

As long ago as the 1640s, people were thinking about how plants lived and got their nutrients. In those days, nearly everybody thought that the soil provided plants with everything they needed to grow and that the plant's biomass came from the soil. Then a Flemish (now Belgium) scientist called Joannes Baptista van Helmont (1579–1644) carried out an experiment that proved that the soil didn't give plants very much in the way of nutrients and couldn't provide much of the biomass of a plant.

Figure 1 Joannes Baptista van Helmont

His experiment was very simple but took him 5 years to complete. He took 90 kg of dried soil, planted a small willow tree, weighing 2.5 kg, in the soil and looked after it. He watered it and let it grow for 5 years. Then he dried and re-weighed the soil and the tree. Van Helmont knew that no more soil had been added and that he only gave the tree water. He found that after starting with 90 kg of soil, he only lost 0.5 kg. The tree however had gained nearly 77 kg. Somehow the tree had gained a different amount of mass than the soil had lost. He concluded that the extra mass must come from the water – a good idea but not quite the full picture. Van Helmont didn't know about the gas carbon dioxide.

How plants transported water from the roots to the shoots was looked at by the English clergyman Stephen Hales (1677–1761). One of his best known experiments measured the water vapour given off by plants – now known as **transpiration**. Like van Helmont, Hales grew a plant in a closed

container and saw that the volume of air above the surface of the water went down by about 14%. He thought that this was because the plant was using up the air. He also showed by experiments that sap flows upwards in plants. His work was published in 1727.

Figure 2 Rev. Stephen Hales

Nearly 50 years later, a British scientist called Joseph Priestley (1733–1804) added another piece to the puzzle. In 1772 he suggested that plants must produce oxygen. He put a shoot from a plant into water and covered it with a jar to stop air getting to the plant. He then burned a candle in the jar until it went out. Later he was able to re-burn the candle in the same jar. He concluded that the candle went out because there was no oxygen left in the jar. As no more air was let into the jar, Priestley concluded that the plant must have produced more oxygen, allowing the candle to be re-lit and burn.

Figure 3 Joseph Priestley

Several years after Priestley's work, the last piece of the puzzle was discovered by the Dutch scientist Jan Ingenhousz (1730–1799). He showed

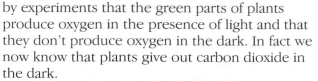

by experiments that the green parts of plants produce oxygen in the presence of light and that they don't produce oxygen in the dark. In fact we now know that plants give out carbon dioxide in the dark.

Figure 4 Jan Ingenhousz

But the story doesn't end there. An American scientist, Melvin Calvin (1911–1997) worked out the chemistry of photosynthesis that happens in the plant cells – a very complicated process that we now call the Calvin cycle. Calvin also worked on plant oils and discovered that some plants from the Amazon forests produce oils that can be used as a substitute for diesel oil. Calvin's work earned him the Nobel Prize for Chemistry in 1961.

Figure 5 Melvin Calvin

It has taken us over 350 years to really understand how plants make their own food and to discover that the mass of a plant, its biomass, is made up from the gases in the air that we breathe and the water the plant takes from the soil. Without photosynthesis there wouldn't be any life on Earth and certainly no animals on the land. Photosynthesis means that plants can produce their own food, glucose, and store what they don't immediately need in the form of starch. The plants use some of the glucose for respiration in their

cells, like animals do, which is why carbon dioxide is released at night. The products of photosynthesis are useful to us as well as to the plant, giving us wood, oils, vegetable proteins and perfumes.

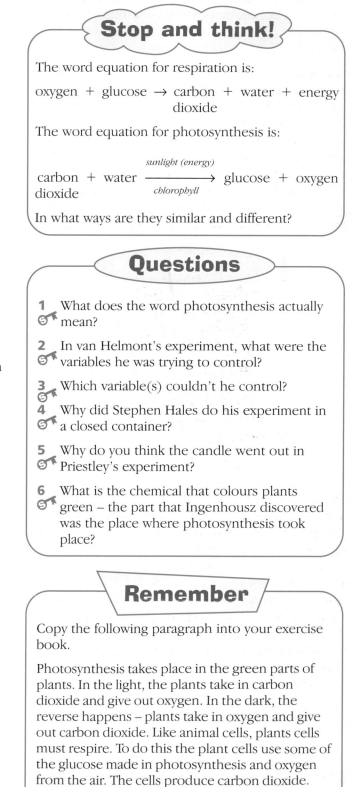

Stop and think!

The word equation for respiration is:

oxygen + glucose → carbon + water + energy
dioxide

The word equation for photosynthesis is:

$$\text{carbon dioxide} + \text{water} \xrightarrow[\text{chlorophyll}]{\text{sunlight (energy)}} \text{glucose} + \text{oxygen}$$

In what ways are they similar and different?

Questions

1 What does the word photosynthesis actually mean?

2 In van Helmont's experiment, what were the variables he was trying to control?

3 Which variable(s) couldn't he control?

4 Why did Stephen Hales do his experiment in a closed container?

5 Why do you think the candle went out in Priestley's experiment?

6 What is the chemical that colours plants green – the part that Ingenhousz discovered was the place where photosynthesis took place?

Remember

Copy the following paragraph into your exercise book.

Photosynthesis takes place in the green parts of plants. In the light, the plants take in carbon dioxide and give out oxygen. In the dark, the reverse happens – plants take in oxygen and give out carbon dioxide. Like animal cells, plants cells must respire. To do this the plant cells use some of the glucose made in photosynthesis and oxygen from the air. The cells produce carbon dioxide. Plants produce many useful products such as wood, oils, vegetable proteins and perfumes as well as chemicals that can be used as medicines.

Roots

Roots are as important to a plant as its leaves. They have a number of roles, including taking water and minerals from the soil into the plant, and helping to anchor the plant in the ground.

When we grow plants, we don't often see the roots – they remain hidden underground. If you've ever dug up a plant or watched someone re-pot a houseplant, you might have seen what gardeners call the root ball. Some plants, even fairly small houseplants, can have a large network of roots that spreads out in the soil.

Figure 1 The roots of this plant have nearly filled the flowerpot so it's time to re-pot the plant to give the roots some more space.

Roots are very simple structures, but they are vital to plants. A root doesn't just help the plant, it also helps to maintain the soil and can break up rocks. The root's main job is to absorb water from the soil for the plant to use in photosynthesis. In Figure 2 you can see how the structure of the root helps the plant to take up water.

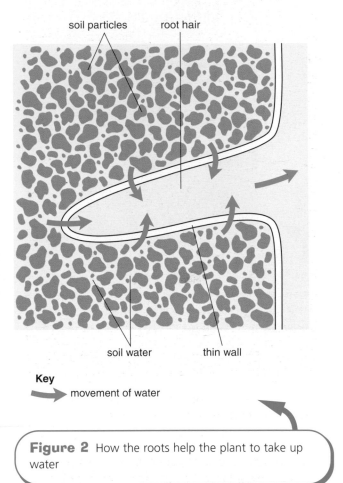

soil particles   root hair

soil water   thin wall

Key
→ movement of water

Figure 2 How the roots help the plant to take up water

The job of the root doesn't end there though. Roots have other jobs or functions. The root will anchor the plant in the soil and stop it from being blown down in the wind or easily uprooted when animals walk through it.

Roots come in two main types – **tap roots** and **fibrous roots**.

A tap root is a thick root that is quite long and just extends down into the soil. This sort of root is useful if the soil dries out and the plant has to go deeper to find water. Trees have tap roots and these sorts of roots stop them from being blown down easily, but they can be uprooted more easily than plants that have fibrous roots.

Fibrous roots are the ones that you see on many garden plants. They are thin and there are lots of them that spread out from the plant but do not go down into the soil a long way. These roots are good at stopping plants from being uprooted by animals but they cannot grow deep into the soil to search for water.

tap root   *fibrous roots.*

Figure 3 The tap root on the left is thick and long. The fibrous roots are thin and widespread.

Just as humans need water to live, so do plants. The roots are adapted to gather water as efficiently as possible. If you look at the photograph of a root, you will see that they are long, thin branching structures. This means that the roots will cover a large surface area. Because they are thin it means that the water does not have to travel far to get into the plant and can easily be moved from the roots up to the stem and leaves. Plants lose water from their leaves and this process is known as **transpiration**. If we look at the root hair cell in Figure 2, we can see how it is adapted to take in water.

Stop and think!

Grass has fibrous roots and no tap roots. How does having a fibrous root system help the grass in fields of sheep and cows?

How can a tap root help trees in hot countries such as Greece where they have little to no rain and strong winds called the meltemi during July and August?

For plants to grow, they also need **minerals**. It's a bit like us having a balanced diet. The minerals are dissolved in the water in the soil and taken in through the roots. Plants need a balanced diet of minerals and other chemical salts for healthy growth. For example, magnesium is needed for the plant to make the chemical chlorophyll. Nitrates and potassium, that the plant gets from fertilisers added to the soil by farmers and gardeners, are essential for the plant to make plant proteins.

Questions

tap roots, fibrous roots

1. What two main types of roots do plants have?
2. If a large, heavy, tall tree had a fibrous root system instead of a tap root, what problems or advantages might it have in the following situations? *in water supply*
   a) a long dry summer,
   b) a winter with lots of rain,
   c) a sudden period of gale force winds.
3. When trees are uprooted in gales they will die. Why might the tree die even if it is lifted up and planted back into the soil?
4. Why might a deciduous tree (one that loses its leaves in autumn) have more problems with high winds in the summer than in the winter?
5. Where do plants get their minerals from?
6. Why are minerals needed in plants?
7. How is the root system of a plant able to cover a large surface area?
8. Which of the two main root types is most likely to cover the largest surface area in two plants of the same size?

Remember

Copy the following into your exercise book.

Roots are essential for taking in water from the soil. Roots will also take in minerals that are dissolved in the water. The water is essential for plants to photosynthesise, while the minerals are needed for making proteins, for example. Roots increase their surface area by branching and dividing many times and have small projections called root hairs. The thin walls make it easier for water to enter the cell.

There are two types of roots, fibrous and tap roots. Tap roots grow deep into the soil to search out water, and fibrous roots help small plants anchor themselves.

Plants for food and plant nutrients

We eat different parts of the different plants we eat – leaves, shoots, roots, fruits and seeds. Plants need three main minerals to stay healthy – nitrogen, phosphorus and potassium. These three minerals are found in fertilisers in different proportions, depending on the type of plant that they are to fertilise.

Which parts of a plant do we normally eat? Different plants provide different parts that we can eat. In some plants it's the fruit, in others it's the seeds, though it can just as easily be the shoots, roots or leaves. In short, all parts of plants can provide us with food, but not all of the parts are nice, or in some cases, safe to eat. In order to grow healthy plants that we can harvest and eat, we must provide plants with the right nutrients.

If you get into small groups, you can probably think of many other plant foods that we eat in addition to the ones in Figure 1. Make a table in your exercise book like Table 1 below and use the plants in the photograph and ones that you think about in class to fill in the first column then tick which parts of the plant we commonly eat.

Figure 1 We can eat all the plants in this photo. They can form part of a food chain for humans, though the food web that we are part of can be very complex.

> ## Stop and think!
>
> Take a typical meal, say one you had last Sunday, and draw out a food web for the various different types of foods you ate. How many producers did you eat? How many primary or secondary consumers did you eat? Why wouldn't a vegetarian like to eat any secondary consumers?

Very often, the part of the plant that we eat is the part that contains the plant's stored energy – that is the starch made from the glucose the plant can't use immediately.

Nutrients for plants

Gardeners and farmers know that if they are going to grow plants successfully, they need to add fertiliser to the soil. This provides the plants with all of the nutrients they need for healthy growth. The three most important nutrients are **nitrogen**, **phosphorus** and **potassium** (known as N, P, K). Fertilisers often show the percentages of these three minerals on the front label of the bag like the one in Figure 2. Gardeners and farmers know that the minerals are always listed in the order N then P then K.

- Nitrogen (N) is the main nutrient needed by plants for new, green plant growth. Plants that are mainly leaves (such as grass) need plenty of nitrogen, so the first number is very high in fertilisers for lawns.

- Phosphorus (P) helps the plant grow roots. It also increases the numbers of flowers on flowering plants. Lots of phosphorus is very useful for plants that have bulbs and for newly-planted trees and shrubs. Fertilisers for these plants often have high middle numbers.

Parts of the plant that we eat					
Name of plant	Leaves	Stem	Roots/bulbs	Fruits	Seeds
Carrot	✗	✗	✓	✗	✗

Table 1

Figure 2 The percentages of N, P and K in this bag of fertiliser are shown on the bag.

- Potassium (K) is good for the overall health of plants. It helps them withstand very hot or cold weather and helps to defend them against diseases. Most soils already have some potassium, so the third number in the fertiliser can be smaller than the other two.

Plants also need small amounts of other minerals for healthy growth, such as **calcium (Ca)** to improve the growth of young roots and shoots and **magnesium (Mg)** to help seed formation. Magnesium is also an important part of the chemical chlorophyll. Finally **sulphur (S)** and **iron (Fe)** help the plant to maintain a dark green colour.

Minerals and nutrients are not the only factors that affect the growth of plants. Some plants are affected by the pH of the soil they grow in (see section 8.2).

Questions

1 Looking at your table of plants that we eat, what is the most commonly eaten part of the plant?

2 Why do the seeds from a plant, such as broad beans, need to have a store of starch?

3 Why would some roots, like carrots and potatoes, need a store of starch?

4 Why are the letters N, P, K used for fertilisers?

5 If groundkeepers in a sports stadium want to feed the grass, which of the following fertilisers should they buy?

   a) Low nitrogen fertilisers

   b) High phosphorus fertilisers

   c) High nitrogen fertilisers

   d) Fertilisers with equal amounts of all three nutrients

6 If a houseplant was growing healthily but the normally green leaves were developing patches where the green colour was much lighter or missing, which mineral might the plant be missing in its soil?

7 What mineral should a gardener use if they want to get more flowers on their plants?

8 What mineral needs to be added to soil if the gardener wants a good crop of seeds?

Remember

Look at the list of words below and discuss in small groups which ones should be used to fill the spaces in the paragraph; not all of the words will be used!

minerals, tap roots, leaves, nitrogen, calcium, phosphorus, iron, bulbs, flowers, berries, warmth, fertilisers, stems, onion, potassium, oxygen

Many different plants provide us with food. Sometimes we will eat the _leaves **1**_ , for example a lettuce, or we may eat ___ **2** tap roots__ such as carrots and __bulbs **3** stems__ such as _onion **4**_ . Not all parts of the plant can be eaten. Some may produce _**5**_ that are harmless to birds, but poisonous to humans.

For plants to grow well we often need to provide them with _**6**_ . They will contain _nitrogen **7**_ to help growth, especially in leafy plants, _phos **8**_ for the roots and _**9** potassium_ to help the plant survive in difficult weather conditions. Small amounts of other _**10** minerals_ are also needed for healthy plant growth.

Killing weeds

Just like animals, plants compete for natural resources, such as space, light, water and nutrients. Farmers and gardeners have to deal with the problems of weeds competing with their plants or crops. Herbicides have been developed to combat this problem.

If you've ever been on a crowded train or bus, you will know how difficult it is to move, and even sometimes to breathe. We all need room to live, and just because plants don't move around, it doesn't mean they don't need room as well. More importantly, the plants have to compete for sunlight and for the nutrients they get from the soil.

When plants are grown, they all have to compete for space, light, water and nutrients. If you look at the packets of seeds you can buy, the instructions normally tell you how far apart the seeds should be planted. This makes sure that when the plants are fully-grown, they are not competing for valuable resources. Farmers have to plant their crops very carefully to make sure that the crop they grow gives the biggest harvest and the healthiest plants.

Weeds

Weeds are a common problem for farmers and gardeners. Simply put, a weed is any plant that grows where we don't want it. Weeds are a serious threat to our food crops and whilst many **herbicides** (weedkillers) are available to farmers, there are limits to how effective they can be. For example, **non-selective** herbicides – which kill a wide range of plants – can only be used before the crop starts to grow. Once the crop appears above the surface of the soil, **selective** herbicides that only kill certain types of plants have to be used.

Herbicides can be used to control weeds. Farmers use a variety of methods, depending on how, where, when and what type of weed is growing. There are two main ways in which herbicides affect the plants they are applied to. Some herbicides kill parts of the plant that they come into contact with, other herbicides are absorbed either by the roots or leaves of the plant and then move within the plant slowly killing it.

Figure 1 Plants competing with each other

Figure 2 The three main methods of applying herbicides to weeds. a) Crop sprayers are a common sight in the countryside. b) Town and city council workers often use the spot method to control weeds along roadside grass verges. c) The wiper method can be used to attack different weeds at different heights.

Stop and think!

In Figure 1 you can see that plants are competing for space above the ground. What are the plants doing to try and get more sunlight? What do you think the plants are competing for below ground?

1 General herbicide application

This method uses a crop sprayer to spray the whole of a field or an area of it. The crop sprayer may be a large self-propelled machine with a wide boom carrying the spray nozzles, a tractor-mounted machine, or a sprayer mounted on an 'all terrain vehicle' (ATV or quad bike). The spray will be a selective herbicide.

2 Spot application

This method uses a small sprayer carried on the person's back, with a hand pump. Individual weeds or patches of weeds, such as thistles or docks, may be sprayed by this method. The benefits of this method are that it may be suitable for controlling the occasional small patch of weeds.

3 The weed wiper

This method uses a wick soaked in herbicide, mounted on a short boom trailed behind a tractor or ATV. The height of the boom is controlled to only allow taller plants to come into contact with the wick. This can be particularly useful for controlling tall weeds such as thistles, docks and nettles. The benefits of this method are that the costs will be considerably cheaper than general application.

It is really only in the last 50 years that we have used herbicides to control weeds. Before this, we either had to pull out the weeds by hand, plough them into the soil or sort out the seeds to prevent the weeds being planted with the crops. Herbicides are also used extensively on industrial sites, roadsides, ditches, banks and recreational areas.

Questions

1 The word herbicide means 'to kill plants'. The first part of the word, herb-, means plant and the ending, -cide, means to kill. The letter 'i' is used to join the two together to make the complete word. What words do you think are used to describe chemicals that kill the following:

   a) insects?

   b) pests?

   c) fungus?

   d) worms? (*Hint*: the word used to describe something that is a worm or that is worm-like is verm, like the pasta called vermicelli – 'worm-like' pasta.)

2 If a farmer were growing a crop of soya beans, say which method of applying herbicides he or she might use in the following situations and say why you chose that method.

   a) When the crop has begun to grow but lots of fast-growing thistles are competing for space.

   b) After a field has been ploughed and the seeds planted, but before they have started to grow.

3 Weeds are plants and may be part of a food web. What might be the effect of killing all of the flowering weeds in a field to grow non-flowering plants?

4 One method of controlling weeds used to be to plough all of the plants into a field and leave it as bare earth. A better method used today is to let grass grow on the field until the farmer wants to grow a crop there. How might these methods affect local food webs?

5 When council workmen are spraying herbicides along the roadside, what safety precautions should they take to prevent the chemicals from harming them?

Remember

In small groups, discuss the following sentences and put them into a sensible order. Copy them into your exercise book.

- Killing the weeds can also affect other plants and animals in the food web.
- These chemicals are called herbicides.
- Just like animals, plants have to compete for natural resources, such as light, water, nutrients and space.
- Weeds, like all other plants, are often part of a food web.
- Some herbicides are general and will kill any plants that grow in a field.
- Farmers need to control weeds to make sure that the crops they grow are not competing for resources with the weeds.
- Farmers and gardeners often use chemicals to control the growth of weeds.
- Plants that grow where they are not wanted are called weeds.
- Other herbicides are selective and kill just the weeds.

Pves

There are different ways of dealing with the problem of pests, including chemicals or organic methods. The use of chemicals has affected bird populations in this country.

I'm sure that at some time you've been called a pest. The word is used in everyday language quite a lot. You could be a pest, or perhaps you've pestered your parents to buy you something. In biology, a pest is any animal that will destroy crops. Anything from field mice to cabbage white butterflies to aphids, slugs and snails are pests. Farmers and gardeners need to control them in much the same way as they need to control weeds, though there are more options available. Since the 1970s, farmers have been using more and more herbicides, pesticides and fungicides to control the damage that pests do to their crops, rather than using organic methods. Organic methods of pest control include the use of other insects as predators that feed off the pests and not the crops. The use of chemicals has affected the populations of birds that rely on those same pests and plants as food.

Stop and think!

Can you remember how one chemical pesticide called DDT affected the populations of herons? Think back to work you have done previously on food chains and webs and how this chemical affected the herons that live around rivers and farmland where the chemical was used.

The article on the next page gives information on how the bird population in the United Kingdom has gone down in the last 25 years. Read it carefully and in small groups think about the answers to the questions at the bottom of the page. Write down your answers in your exercise book.

(c)

(a)

(b)

(d)

Figure 1 Some of the British bird species that are declining in number. (a) Starling, (b) lapwing, (c) bullfinch and (d) grey partridge.

Sharp decline in UK bird populations

A recent report by the Royal Society for the Protection of Birds (RSPB) has described a dramatic decline in bird populations in many parts of the UK over the last 25 years. The report links the declining populations in a number of bird species with use of pesticides in the country. It says that the problem is not direct poisoning from pesticides, but destruction of the birds' food sources.

The decline may also be related to changes in farming methods, such as making silage instead of hay, and so removing food and shelter for populations of birds and insects earlier in the season. The practice of winter cropping, in which farmers use general herbicides to 'clean' fields, may also be a factor in the decline.

The report describes the three ways by which pesticides can reduce birds' food sources:

– Insecticides can reduce the numbers of invertebrates, which are an important food source for birds during their breeding season.
– Herbicides may reduce the number of plants which host invertebrate species, thus reducing the numbers of invertebrates that live and feed on them.
– Herbicides may also reduce the number of weeds and seeds that supply birds with food in the winter months and which feed some bird species during breeding.

The bird species that show the most serious decline in population numbers between 1969 and 1994 are listed below. The number in brackets shows the percentage decline in the species.

tree sparrow	(89%)
grey partridge	(82%)
turtle dove	(77%)
bullfinch	(76%)
song thrush	(73%)
lapwing	(62%)
reed bunting	(61%)
skylark	(58%)
linnet	(52%)
swallow	(43%)
blackbird	(42%)
starling	(23%)

The report showed that insects such as butterflies, moths, beetles and grasshoppers were more prominent in the diets of bird species that were declining, while species with populations that were stable or increasing had diets consisting mainly of woodland type plants.

Use of pesticides in the UK has been increasing steadily since the early 1970s. Figures from the Ministry of Agriculture show that cereal crops are now sprayed with six times as many fungicides and twice as many herbicides as they were in the 1970s. In the past 25 years, the number of pesticide applications on cereal crops has nearly tripled.

The RSPB report makes a number of recommendations for changes in agricultural methods, including that farmers be encouraged to adopt organic practices and that targets should be set for reducing pesticide use. The report also recommends that there should be better monitoring of how pesticides affect invertebrate and plant species, more research on the ecology and behaviour of individual bird species and widespread experimental studies to assess the effects of pesticides and other farming practices on wildlife.

Questions

1 What is the main reason for the decline in bird populations?

2 How do herbicides affect the bird populations?

3 How do insecticides affect the bird populations?

4 How might pesticides affect the bird populations?

5 Why are the pesticides, herbicides and insecticides used?

6 What could be done to protect the populations of birds?

7 In what way is the decline in the numbers of birds detailed in this report different to the killing of herons by DDT?

8 Should pesticides be used to produce more food for humans at the expense of other animals?

Remember

Write a report for your school newsletter or for a local newspaper explaining why the RSPB report on the decline of bird populations is so worrying.

Use these phrases to start the paragraphs of the report:

A recent survey by the RSPB reports that …

There are three reasons given, these are …

The worst affected birds are …

Other animals affected are …

The report suggests we should change …

Other action we need to take is …

Closer

Leylandii

When you need some privacy in your garden and decide to plant a hedge, you need a fast growing tree. A type of conifer called *leylandii* is a very fast growing tree. It can grow up to 5 feet per year. It has been blamed for taking the goodness out of the soil and for making bright sunny gardens gloomy and dark. But this tree is not an old established tree from nature. It was in fact an accident.

Cupressocyparis leylandii, its proper scientific name, was 'born' in South Wales in 1888, the unplanned offspring of a Monterey Cypress and Alaskan Cedar tree. The parent tree is at Leighton Hall in Powys. Six small trees were sent in 1892 to Mr Leyland's estate in Haggerston Castle near Berwick, where all six still stand today among caravan holiday homes. It was given its name, *leylandii,* after Mr Leyland.

No permission is needed to plant a hedge, but if a hedge overhangs a boundary the owners of the adjoining property have the right to cut back branches and roots to the boundary line.

New laws are coming in to stop neighbours arguing over the height of hedges. Oversized *leylandii* have led to more than 10 000 un-neighbourly disputes. Some have ended in court cases, violence, and in one case murder followed by suicide.

Activity

Imagine you have the task of making rules about the height of hedges on boundaries between neighbours. In small groups discuss the problems of neighbour disputes.

1   What common sense rules can you come up with about what your neighbour is allowed to do with your hedge?

Think about:

- the height

- blocking of views

- if your neighbour can cut the trees back or cut them at all.

2   In small groups discuss whether or not the government should make laws telling people what they can do in their own gardens. Share your group's thoughts with other groups. Do you all agree?

CHAPTER 8

Using chemistry

Opener Activity
Pyrotechnics

- Firework science is called pyrotechnics.
- Pyrotechnics is chemistry dressed up in flashy clothing.
- Every firework contains a mixture of chemicals. When the firework is lit, the chemicals react, and the bonds between the atoms that make up the chemicals shatter and rearrange themselves to form new substances.
- In firework reactions, this rearranging releases energy as movement, light and sound.

Activity

Jai Li is a leading fire fighter. She has to brief her watch about fireworks. She looked back to the notes she made when she took her firefighter exams, but there is more information there than she needs.

It is your job to cut out the irrelevant information, and put what is left in order of importance. Keep it short, Jai Li may have to brief her watch very rapidly.

Jai Li's notes

• Fire triangle rules: to put out a fire remove either the source of fuel, the heat or the oxygen.	• The oxidiser in gunpowder releases oxygen that makes the other materials burn.	• Reactions that give out energy are called exothermic reactions.
• Sulphur produces a mildly acidic gas that makes you cough.	• Fireworks defeat the fire triangle. They have their own source of oxygen mixed with the fuel. Once burning, a firework cannot be put out.	• Gunpowder contains sulphur, carbon and potassium nitrate.
• Substances such as potassium nitrate and potassium chlorate release oxygen when heated.	• Just a small glow or spark provides enough energy to start gunpowder burning.	• All the atoms in the firework chemicals are still there after the reaction, they've been rearranged into new substances, and some are in the air.
• When gunpowder is contained in a thick paper shell, the burning gas builds up and then bursts the shell open with a bang.	• Bonfires obey the normal fire triangle rules.	• Gunpowder burns very very quickly, releasing lots of gas that can be used to throw the firework into the air.
• You can smother a firework on the ground with soil or sand.	• Different metal salts cause different colours copper salts – blue magnesium salts – white strontium salts – red barium salts – green sodium salts – gold lithium salts – red	

The rules of the game

Chemistry has a set of rules, just like any other science. The rules of chemistry explain how particles react with each other to make new substances. These rules are our best explanation of how things happen.

1 Energy and temperature

All matter is made of particles. These particles can be atoms, molecules or ions. The particles in matter are moving all the time. As matter get hotter, the particles have more energy, so they move faster and faster. At **absolute zero** (−273°C), the particles would be motionless.

The motion of particles makes smells spread.

Figure 2 Do you remember the carnival model of states of matter?

Figure 1 Francis often had smelly cheese for lunch, which made him very unpopular!

PONG!

2 States of matter

In solids, particles are neatly arranged and are vibrating. You can only get at the outermost particles.

In liquids, the particles are a milling, mixing, close-packed crowd.

In gases, the particles are all flying about separately past each other, and are easy to get at.

3 Energy transfers

Energy is *taken in* when chemical bonds are broken apart. Energy is *released* when chemical bonds are remade.

When fuels burn, more energy is released than is taken in. The extra energy heats up the surroundings.

4 How chemical reactions work

All atoms, apart from the noble gases, will form compounds. When they form compounds, it's all to do with electrons. They try to make a full shell of electrons on the outside of the atom. There are two ways that atoms can do this easily:

- **Metal with non-metal**. Metal atoms have few outer electrons. When they form compounds, they try to get rid of these electrons. The outer shells of non-metals are nearly full. They grab the electrons from metals to complete their outer shells.

Figure 3 Oxygen and magnesium atoms.

- **Non-metal with non-metal**. All non-metal atoms have outer shells that are nearly full. They will **share** electrons with each other to get enough electrons to have a full shell. The electrons have to orbit both atoms, so this holds the atoms together in a little group. This is a **molecule**.

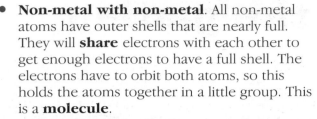

Figure 4 Happy ever after?

5 Conservation of mass

Figure 5 What's happened here?

Matter cannot be created or destroyed (except in the sort of nuclear reaction that takes place in the Sun). All chemistry is a way of using energy to rearrange the atoms into new and more useful materials.

Charcoal burns away on a barbecue, so that only a scrap of ash is left. But the atoms of carbon that make up the charcoal have not ceased to exist – they have become carbon dioxide in the air. When the tree next to the barbecue grows bigger, it's not creating atoms out of nothing. It uses the carbon from the carbon dioxide in the air. Of course this takes years, not minutes. . .

Questions

1 What is absolute zero?

2 Write a few sentences to explain the idea of 'movement and temperature' to a junior school pupil. Use only words that a nine year old would understand.

3 Draw a series of diagrams to show how the particles in two liquids mix together.

4 What happens to the movement of the particles when a solid melts?

5 Why does burning hydrogen gas in oxygen transfer energy and cause heating?

6 To start a Bunsen flame, you have to put heat in. Explain why.

7 Metals cannot form compounds with other metals. Explain why this is so.

8 a) Chlorine has seven electrons in its outer shell, and needs eight. How many bonds does this form?

   b) Oxygen has six electrons in its outer shell, and needs eight. How many bonds will it form?

9 When copper reacts with air, black copper oxide forms. Explain why its mass increases.

10 If a gas dissolves in water, does the water get heavier or lighter? Explain your answer.

Remember

Learn and practise these rules. Draw a thinklinks chart linking these ideas together.

Poison gas, combustion and explosions

Burning is a chemical reaction that needs a supply of oxygen. Usually the source of oxygen is the air. But in matches and explosives, the oxygen atoms are combined in the chemical itself.

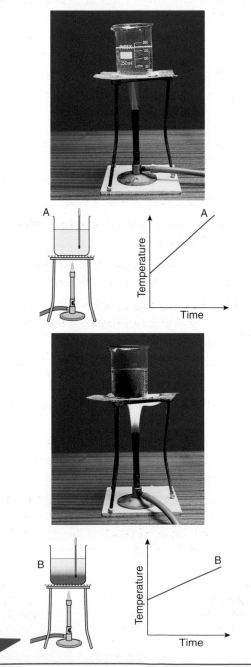

Figure 1 Burner A has a clean blue flame. Burner B has a yellow flame made by glowing soot particles. The beaker has become all sooty.

Burner A is producing more heat per second than burner B. This is because burner A has the correct air/methane mixture.

Burner B has too little air to completely burn the gas, so less energy is transferred. Some is left in the unburned soot particles.

Burner A

$$CH_4 + 2O_2 \rightarrow CO_2 + 2H_2O$$
methane   oxygen   carbon dioxide   water

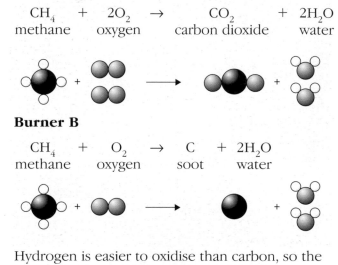

Burner B

$$CH_4 + O_2 \rightarrow C + 2H_2O$$
methane   oxygen   soot   water

Hydrogen is easier to oxidise than carbon, so the water gets formed first in the combustion reaction.

Fact box

Hydrogen gas is a fuel for the future.

1 It can be made easily by passing electricity through water.

2 Oxygen is one of the by-products of the process.

3 It burns to give water vapour so is non-polluting.

BUT hydrogen gas is dangerously explosive.

Danger – poison gas

Sometimes when there is too little air, **carbon monoxide** (CO) gets formed in the combustion reaction. Carbon monoxide is a poisonous gas and kills people. Every year people die in accidents due to using gas heaters in badly-ventilated rooms or by running a car engine in a closed garage.

Fireworks

Explosives are materials that have the oxygen they need to burn built into their compounds, rather than relying on the air to provide it.

The constituents of gunpowder are:

- charcoal, which burns to give lots of heat
- sulphur, which burns to give lots of heat
- saltpetre (potassium nitrate), a salt that contains lots of oxygen atoms.

When gunpowder burns, lots of heat is released quickly. The gases produced expand rapidly, making an explosion.

Figure 2 Explosives in action

Fireworks are just compressed gunpowder burning very, very fast. The gunpowder is compressed into a tube to make the fireworks burn longer. Explosive 'bangers' are made from uncompressed gunpowder.

Matches

A match is like a mini controlled firework. Its head contains:

- carbon, to burn rapidly
- sulphur, to burn rapidly
- potassium chlorate, to provide the oxygen.

The equation for the reaction is:

Questions

1 Write a word equation for methane burning in a good supply of air.

2 What makes the yellow colour in a yellow Bunsen flame?

3 Why is energy released during combustion?

4 Why is water formed instead of carbon dioxide when methane burns in a limited supply of air?

5 What is the poisonous gas that can be formed when fuels burn in a poorly-ventilated place?

6 What are the constituents of gunpowder?

7 What are fireworks made of?

8 What substances make up the head of a match?

9 Why can a match 'flare up' even if there is very little oxygen left in the air?

10 What is the acid gas you can smell when a match has been lit?

11 Why do 'banger' fireworks explode and others just burn with a whoosh?

12 Explain how a firework rocket shoots up in the air. (*Hint*: gases expanding/forces.)

Remember

Combustion is burning fuels with oxygen to release energy.

If there is not enough oxygen the fuel is not completely burnt, and there can be unwanted waste products.

Explosives have oxygen atoms combined in their fuel. They burn fast and release all their energy at once. A match head is like a tiny piece of explosive.

potassium chlorate	+	sulphur	+	carbon	→	potassium chloride	+	sulphur dioxide	+	carbon dioxide
$KClO_4$	+	S	+	C	→	KCl	+	SO_2	+	CO_2

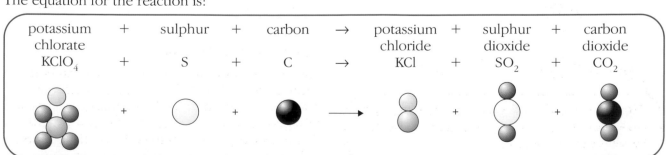

Hot food and cold relief

All changes – chemical and physical – involve energy transfers, otherwise they would not happen. Some chemical changes give out heat. But there are changes that need to take in heat to make them work.

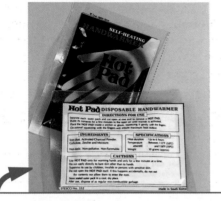

Figure 1 This handwarmer contains chemicals which, when shaken together, react to give out heat. This is called an **exothermic reaction**.

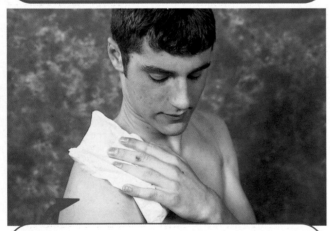

Figure 2 Twist the pack and it gets cold enough to numb the pain of a sporting injury. Injuries such as sprains or bruises hurt because of the swelling. Cold helps to reduce the swelling. The chemicals combine to take in energy, so the pack gets cold. This is called an **endothermic reaction**.

Making cold

Chemical changes can produce cold. To do this they take in energy. As the particles are separated, energy is taken in. Most cooking reactions are endothermic – they need heat to keep them going.

100 g of water + 10 g sodium thiosulphate crystals

Before mixing	After dissolving
20°C	6°C

Making heat

Many chemical changes make heat. For example, acid particles combine with alkali particles to make water molecules. This is putting particles together, so it gives out energy as heat.

25 cm³ of acid solution + 25 cm³ of alkali solution

Before mixing	After mixing
20°C	29°C

All fuels have a strongly exothermic reaction with oxygen in the air.

Questions

To turn clay into ceramic material a lot of heat has to be put into a kiln.

Cooking food is a chemical change that needs heat. After being heated, the molecules in the food become easier to digest.

Electrical energy is put in to change the aluminium oxide into aluminium metal and oxygen.

1 Like the self-heating 'hot pad', self-heating cans of food have been produced. Suggest when or where this would be a useful product.

2 Lime (calcium oxide) reacts with water to produce calcium hydroxide and lots of heat. Write a word equation for this reaction.

3 Which injuries are treated with cold packs?

4 Freon is the liquid used in fridges. Inside the freezer compartment, the liquid freon is allowed to evaporate. Explain why this cools the fridge. *heat energy to evaporate into Freon uses the a gas*

5 Copy and complete this table: *down*

Chemical change	Endothermic or exothermic?
Sodium thiosulphate dissolving	En
Acid–alkali reaction	Ex
Firing clay pots	En
Cooking vegetables	En
Making aluminium metal	En

Electricity from metals

Metals burn in oxygen and cause heating. Metals dissolve in acids and cause heating.

Figure 3 This electric cell is made from the reactive metal and the non-reactive carbon (graphite) rod in a conducting solution (salt water).

If the metal is in an electric cell and the cell is connected in a circuit, then the chemical energy stored in the metal can be transferred as electricity. Metals that are high up the reactivity series release more energy than those which are lower down in the series. This is like the difference in energy transferred when burning magnesium ribbon and copper foil.

In Figure 3, the reactive metal wants to get rid of electrons. The electrons are pushed through the circuit by the energy from the metal. The voltage of the cell measures how much energy the electrons are carrying.

Metal	Symbol	Voltage measured in the electric cell	
Aluminium	Al	−1.66	7
Copper	Cu	+0.34	2
Iron	Fe	−0.44	5
Lead	Pb	−0.13	4
Magnesium	Mg	−2.37	8
Nickel	Ni	+0.23	3
Silver	Ag	+0.80	1
Zinc	Zn	−0.76	6

Table 1 Voltages of some common metals.

Questions

6 Put the metals in the table into their order of reactivity.

Remember

Fill in the gaps in the sentences below using words from the text.

Physical __1__ *work* and __2__ *chemical* changes all need __3__ transfers to make them happen. *energy*

Chemical changes that give out energy are called __4__. *ex*

__5__ burning are exothermic. Those changes that take in energy are __6__. *~~make~~ en*

__7__ food is an endothermic change. *digesting*

Bad air day

Air is a dangerous substance for metals and food. They will react with oxygen in the air if they can to make new substances. These new substances spoil their properties – metals corrode and food goes rotten.

Pie problems

Figure 1 The apple has gone brown.

Lis was annoyed. She had cut up the apple slices for a pie. She then made the pastry. But by the time she finished the pastry, the apple had gone brown. What could she do?

Charlotte came to the rescue. She explained: 'Cutting the apple opens the cells. Apple goes brown because stuff inside the cells reacts with oxygen. It is an **oxidation reaction**. There are enzymes in the apple. These make the oxidation happen faster than normal. You could put the apple in water, but because there is oxygen dissolved in water, the apple will still slowly go brown.

Either put a weak acid like citric acid on the apples – the acid stops the enzyme working and the apples will go brown much more slowly – or put a vitamin C solution on the apples. Vitamin C is called **ascorbic acid**. It is an **antioxidant**. It gobbles up any oxygen on the apples, so they stay a nice colour.

My advice is to use lemon juice on your apples. It contains sour tasting citric acid *and* vitamin C . . . '

That is exactly what Lis did. And her apple pies were perfect.

Questions

1   Why had the apple started to go brown?

2   What makes the reaction with the air faster?

3   Apple goes brown slower in water. Explain why.

4   What does citric acid do to stop the apple going brown?

5   What does vitamin C do to stop the apple going brown?

6   What is the chemical name for vitamin C?

Getting rusty

Figure 2 When water and oxygen get through a small hole in the paint, it reacts with the metal to make flaky rust.

Charlotte knew her car was getting on in years. Lis was helping her to sort out the problem. She said:

'To prevent rust:

- clean off all the flaky rust that lets water in.
- cover the metal with a layer of paint or grease. Then the water and oxygen cannot get to it.
- protect the iron by using a more reactive metal. The metal (usually zinc or magnesium) is put in contact with the iron. This gets corroded away instead of the iron, leaving the iron strong and like new.'

Lis continued to explain. 'If the iron object is going to get banged about, like a bucket or metal dustbin, then it gets dipped in molten zinc metal to protect it. This is called **galvanising** the metal. The zinc isn't like paint, it reacts with the water and air leaving the iron strong and not rusted.'

Making acids and alkalis

Reactive metals combine with oxygen in the air to make alkaline oxides. Non-metals react with oxygen to make acidic oxides. The less reactive metals make insoluble oxides so they have no effect on the indicator solution. These metal oxides are called **bases**. They react with acids to neutralise them. So they fit into the metal oxide pattern.

Figure 3 Colours of some common oxides in Universal Indicator.

Questions

7 What would happen to Charlotte's car if she didn't stop the rusting?

8 What two substances together cause rust?

9 Why does paint protect against rust?

10 Why is galvanising not like painting?

11 Galvanising is called sacrificial corrosion. Explain why.

12 Copy and complete this table. Use ticks to indicate yes.

Oxide	Is it an acid?	Is it an alkali?	Is it a base?
Sodium oxide			
Potassium oxide			
Magnesium oxide			
Iron oxide			
Zinc oxide			
Carbon dioxide			
Phosphorus oxide			
Sulphur dioxide			
Chlorine oxide			

Remember

Use the words listed below to complete the sentences.

**food   reactive   flavour
corrode   air   alkalis
solutions**

Oxygen is a very ____1____ gas. It gets everywhere in the ____2____. It can react with ____3____ to spoil its colour or ____4____.
Oxygen reacts with metals to make them ____5____.

Acids and ____6____ are ____7____ of different oxides.

In control

We control chemical reactions to make less useful chemicals into more useful ones.

We control chemical reactions so that we can transfer the maximum amount of energy from chemical changes.

We control chemical reactions so that we can clean up dirt, waste and pollution, and stop them from harming the environment.

Man-made materials

Polymers

Plastics are all man-made materials called **polymers**. Man-made polymers were invented in the last century, but many natural materials are polymers. Proteins, starch, cellulose and DNA are all polymers.

'*Poly*' means many. A polymer is made from lots of smaller molecules joined together.

'*Mono*' means one. The small molecules that get joined together are the **monomers** that make up the polymer.

Each different type of plastic (or polymer) is made from different monomers.

Polymer	Monomer
Starch	Glucose molecules – starch can be broken down into glucose by digestion
Proteins	Amino acid molecules – proteins can be broken down into amino acids by digestion
Polythene	Ethene (C_2H_4) molecules
Polystyrene	Styrene (C_8H_8) molecules
PVC	Vinyl chloride (C_2H_3Cl) molecules

Table 1

Chemical reactions are used to join the monomer molecules together. A good 'model' for the reaction is putting wagons together to make a train, or putting beads together to make a necklace.

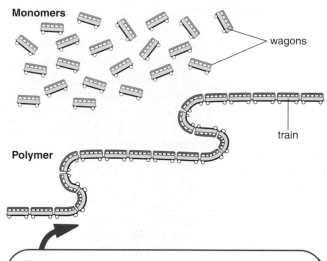

Figure 1 One difference is that thousands of monomer molecules get joined together to make polymer molecules. This would be several kilometres long if it were a train.

Crude oil (petroleum) is a liquid mixture of lots of different hydrocarbons. Because they have different boiling points, they can be separated by **fractional distillation**. In the natural mixture we call crude oil, there are as many 'fuel oil' molecules as 'petrol' molecules, but there is much more demand for petrol (for cars) than for fuel oil (for oil-fired central heating) – even in the winter.

The oil companies make the extra fuel oil into petrol. This is not an easy process:

- **Cracking**: The fuel oil is heated until it is very hot. This makes the molecules break into small fragments.

- **Repolymerisation**: These small fragments are passed over a substance called a **catalyst**. This makes the fragments join together – but in smaller molecules than before.

- **Distillation**: The altered fuel oil is sent back to the fractionating column. The smaller molecules that have been produced come out at the 'petrol' level.

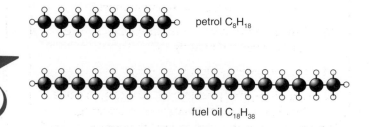

petrol C_8H_{18}

fuel oil $C_{18}H_{38}$

Figure 2 Petrol and fuel oil both come from crude oil.

Better fuels

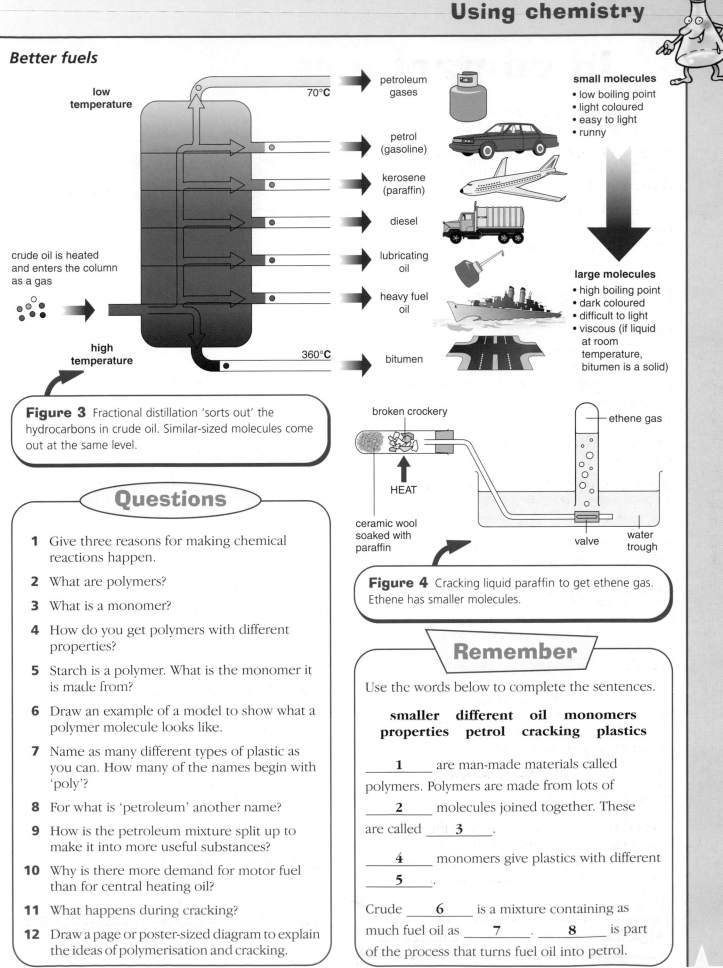

Figure 3 Fractional distillation 'sorts out' the hydrocarbons in crude oil. Similar-sized molecules come out at the same level.

Figure 4 Cracking liquid paraffin to get ethene gas. Ethene has smaller molecules.

Questions

1 Give three reasons for making chemical reactions happen.

2 What are polymers?

3 What is a monomer?

4 How do you get polymers with different properties?

5 Starch is a polymer. What is the monomer it is made from?

6 Draw an example of a model to show what a polymer molecule looks like.

7 Name as many different types of plastic as you can. How many of the names begin with 'poly'?

8 For what is 'petroleum' another name?

9 How is the petroleum mixture split up to make it into more useful substances?

10 Why is there more demand for motor fuel than for central heating oil?

11 What happens during cracking?

12 Draw a page or poster-sized diagram to explain the ideas of polymerisation and cracking.

Remember

Use the words below to complete the sentences.

smaller   different   oil   monomers
properties   petrol   cracking   plastics

___1___ are man-made materials called polymers. Polymers are made from lots of ___2___ molecules joined together. These are called ___3___ .

___4___ monomers give plastics with different ___5___ .

Crude ___6___ is a mixture containing as much fuel oil as ___7___ . ___8___ is part of the process that turns fuel oil into petrol.

Ideal partners

Alkali metals are very reactive metals. The halogens are reactive non-metals. They form very stable compounds together. The best known is common salt – sodium chloride.

Common salt (sodium chloride) has a multitude of uses as well as going on chips. It's a very useful material.

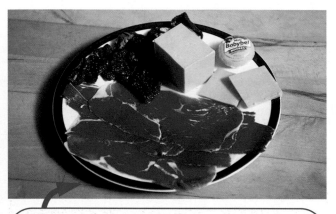

Figure 1 Salt doesn't just bring out the flavour in food. It's used to preserve food as well. The fungi and bacteria that make the food go bad are killed by table salt. The salt draws the water out of their cells by a process called **osmosis**. This kills the organisms that make the food go bad.

Figure 2 Salt makes ice melt at a lower temperature. When it's icy, the council puts salt on roads to keep them free of ice.

Figure 3 Salt is essential for making soap. It is also used to make the alkali called sodium hydroxide. This is used to make paper, rayon, drugs, textiles and in many other industrial processes.

Figure 4 Salt is used to make washing soda. This is added to washing powder. Washing soda is also used to make glass.

Figure 5 Table salt is the starting material to make the bleach that keeps swimming pools free from germs. We use a concentrated form of the same chemical to bleach textiles and clean toilets.

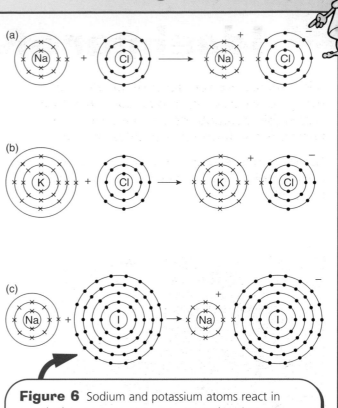

Did you know that the word 'salary' comes from salt? It comes from Ancient Roman times when soldiers used salt to pay for their food. Salt was a commodity that was valued and taxed in the olden days.

A transfer fee?

The alkali metals of Group 1 start every new row of the Periodic Table, so they also start a new **shell** of electrons. All the alkali metals have just one **electron** in their new outermost shell.

The **halogens** of Group 7 are at the other end of the row, just before the noble gases. The halogens have one electron missing from their **outer shell** of electrons.

This explains the similarity between the two groups as 'families' of elements. Like all atoms, the alkali metals seek chemical reactions that give them a full outer shell. They all want to lose their one outer electron, so they react in very similar ways with the same substances. The outer electron gets taken away and they become a completely stable particle in the process. When alkali metals react with halogens, the halogens take this outer electron to complete their outermost shell and become stable.

An alkali metal atom loses one electron when it reacts to form a **positive ion**.

A halogen atom gains one electron when it reacts form a **negative ion**.

Figure 6 Sodium and potassium atoms react in exactly the same way. It's very easy to lose just one electron in this way. That is why the alkali metals are so reactive. It's also very easy to pick up one extra electron. That's why the halogens are so reactive.

Remember

Use words from these pages to fill in the spaces in the sentences below.

Alkali metals (Group 1) have one ____**1**____ in their outer ____**2**____. They lose this to form a ____**3**____ ____**4**____.

____**5**____ (Group 7) have one gap for an ____**6**____ in their ____**7**____ shell. They ____**8**____ an electron to form a negative ____**9**____.

Compounds formed between alkali metals and halogens are very ____**10**____.

Questions

1   How does salt preserve food?

2   Why does salt make roads safer?

3   What is osmosis?

4   Name three materials that use salt in their manufacture.

5   Draw dot and cross diagrams for the formation of
   a) lithium bromide
   b) potassium fluoride.

6   How many electrons are in the outer shell of
   a) a chlorine atom?
   b) a chloride ion?

7   How many electrons are in the outer shell of
   a) an iodine atom?
   b) an iodide ion?

8   How many shells of electrons are there in
   a) a sodium atom?
   b) a sodium ion?

Two men of science

Alfred Nobel, inventor of dynamite

Alfred Nobel was a Swedish chemist. His father was an <u>engineer</u> and inventor who moved to Russia to design torpedoes for the Russian government. While working for his father, Alfred found out about nitroglycerine for the first time. Nitroglycerine is a highly <u>explosive</u> liquid, but it's very hard to handle. If it gets bumped, knocked or dropped, it tends to explode. In those days (1852), <u>gunpowder</u> was used for military devices. Alfred could see that if you could make nitroglycerine easier to handle, it would be much more <u>efficient</u> than gunpowder.

Back at their factory in Stockholm, Alfred, his father and Alfred's younger brother Emil experimented with nitroglycerine in their <u>laboratory</u>. Alfred saw the main use of explosives as being in the <u>mining</u> industry. Sadly, over the years they had several explosions in their laboratory. A big one in 1864 killed Emil and several other people, so the city of Stockholm shut down the laboratory. This did not stop Alfred. He moved his laboratory to a barge on a big lake near Stockholm. He was working full-time on finding a way to transport nitroglycerine safely as well as controlling its <u>detonation</u>. Finally, in 1866, he came up with a solution. He mixed nitroglycerine with an absorbent clay. This turned the liquid into a paste. The paste could be formed and shaped as desired and was safe to transport. It could even be burned if it was in small flakes. To make it explode, he invented a blasting cap (detonator). This contained mercury fulminate and could be set off by lighting a <u>fuse</u>. The product was patented with the name 'dynamite'.

The market for dynamite and detonators grew very rapidly. Soon Alfred was a very rich man. Alfred was a great inventor, and besides dynamite he invented other products such as <u>synthetic</u> rubber, synthetic leather and artificial silk. Alfred was always saddened by the military uses of his invention, dynamite. He was a man who was very interested in literature, poetry and peace-related issues. When he died in 1896 he used his fortune to establish a <u>foundation</u> that awarded yearly Nobel Prizes. Like Alfred's own interests, the Nobel Prizes are awarded for Chemistry, Physics, Physiology, Medicine, Literature and Peace.

Questions

1 Make a list of the 10 words underlined and explain what they mean in this passage.

2 Why did the city of Stockholm close down Alfred's laboratory?

3 Do you think they were right to do this?

4 How do you make dynamite explode?

5 Why was this safer than nitroglycerine?

6 Why do you think Alfred Nobel founded the Nobel Prizes?

To research

1 What happens when someone is awarded a Nobel Prize?

2 What does the Prize consist of?

3 Who won them last year?

Nylon and a troubled inventor

Wallace Hume Carothers was born in 1896 in Iowa in the USA, but did not live to be old. He was the man who was responsible for starting the science of man-made plastics, and was the inventor of nylon and neoprene. He was a brilliant chemist and inventor, but also a troubled soul.

First he studied accounting and then took up science. His field of research was polymers. Polymers are any class of natural or man-made substances composed of very large molecules. These large molecules are made up of lots of smaller chemical units called monomers. The monomer units are joined together like wagons in a train. Polymers make up many of the materials in living organisms, including proteins, cellulose, DNA, natural rubber and real silk. Those made in laboratories have led to important products such as plastics, resins, man-made textiles and synthetic rubber.

Carothers worked for the DuPont company. In 1931 he invented neoprene, the synthetic rubber. It was made using ethyne (sometimes called acetylene) which is a hydrocarbon gas used a lot in welding to produce a very hot flame. Neoprene is made by an addition reaction between the ethyne molecules.

But most of all he wanted to invent a substitute for silk. Silk came from Japan in those days, and Japan and the USA were about to go to war. Carothers made his new material by combining the chemicals hexamethylene diamine and adipic acid to create a very long, very smooth molecule. These monomers joined together by producing a water molecule at each link. The reaction is rather like a neutralisation reaction between an acid and an alkali. The DuPont company decided to call the new material Nylon, because the work on its development had been done in New York and London. In 4000 years of history, textiles had seen only three basic developments: machine weaving, waterproofing materials and synthetic dyes. Nylon was the fourth step forward. Since nylon, many other man-made textiles have been introduced.

Carothers was never a happy man. He suffered from a condition called manic depression. He carried the poison cyanide with him all the time, and could list all the famous scientists who had committed suicide. In April 1937 he committed suicide by taking the cyanide. He had been severely affected by the death of his favourite sister.

Questions

1   What is neoprene?

2   What is nylon used for?

3   What natural material was nylon supposed to be like?

4   What is a polymer?

5   What chemical is used to make neoprene?

6   What two chemicals are used to make nylon?

7   What other molecule is produced when nylon gets made?

8   Why was the new material called nylon?

9   How old was Carothers when he committed suicide?

To research

1   How is nylon made now?

2   What other synthetic fibres are there?

3   Why was nylon used for parachutes?

Closer

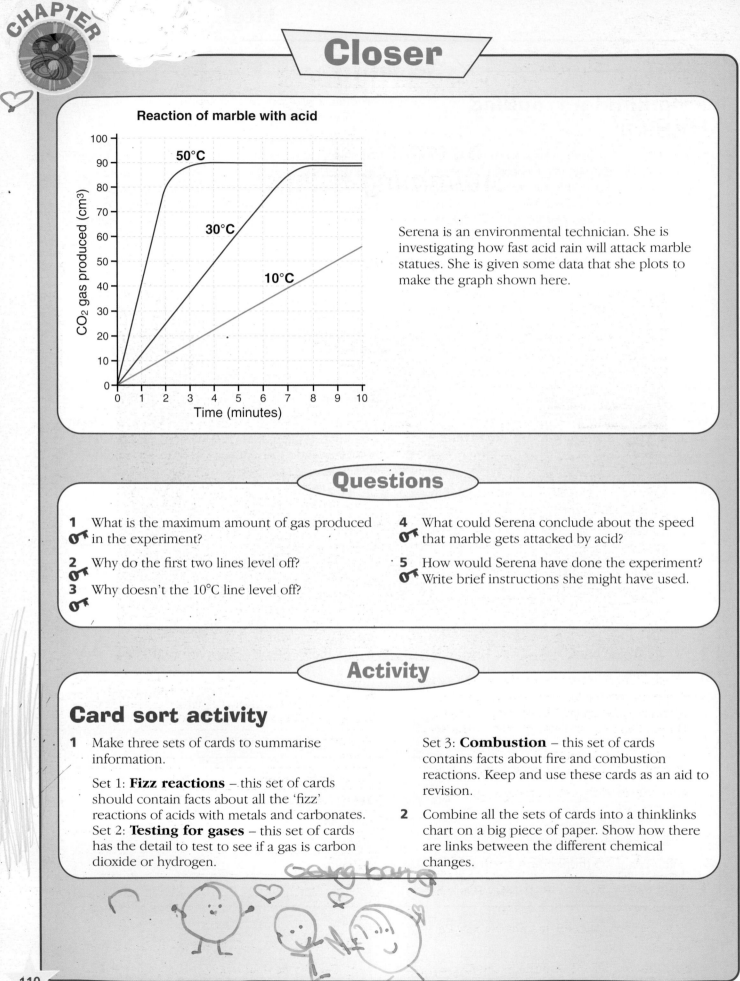

Reaction of marble with acid

Serena is an environmental technician. She is investigating how fast acid rain will attack marble statues. She is given some data that she plots to make the graph shown here.

Questions

1 What is the maximum amount of gas produced in the experiment?

2 Why do the first two lines level off?

3 Why doesn't the 10°C line level off?

4 What could Serena conclude about the speed that marble gets attacked by acid?

5 How would Serena have done the experiment? Write brief instructions she might have used.

Activity

Card sort activity

1 Make three sets of cards to summarise information.

Set 1: Fizz reactions – this set of cards should contain facts about all the 'fizz' reactions of acids with metals and carbonates.

Set 2: Testing for gases – this set of cards has the detail to test to see if a gas is carbon dioxide or hydrogen.

Set 3: Combustion – this set of cards contains facts about fire and combustion reactions. Keep and use these cards as an aid to revision.

2 Combine all the sets of cards into a thinklinks chart on a big piece of paper. Show how there are links between the different chemical changes.

CHAPTER 9

Speeding up

Opener Activity
Swimming trunks

Questions

1   An elephant doesn't seem to be a very good shape for moving fast, on land or in water. What are good shapes for moving on land? Think of animals and also of human transport.

2   Why are modern railway locomotives 'streamlined', but old steam engines are not?

3   What are good shapes for moving through water? Why?

4   What are the best shapes for flying?

5   What different challenges are there in flying through air and in moving through water? Again, think of this in terms of birds and fish, and in terms of aircraft and boats.

6   The table shows some different maximum speeds.

   a) How much faster is a peregrine falcon than a lion?

Moving object	Maximum speed in kilometres per hour
Blackbird military aircraft	3600
Peregrine falcon (bird of prey)	More than 320
Bullet train (Japan)	260
Steam train, 1935	170
Cheetah	110
Lion	80
Ostrich	65
House mouse	12

   b) How far can a Blackbird plane fly in 1 hour?

   c) Predict how far a bullet train or an ostrich could travel in 2 hours and in half an hour.

Space speed

In space there are no drag forces. Spacecraft can travel at very high speeds. They use rockets to exert forces to change their motion.

Figure 1 In space there is no air. There is nothing to resist motion. There are no drag forces. So there is no need for forces of thrust to balance drag. If these space fighters use their rocket motors to produce forces of thrust, they'll accelerate.

Figure 2 Forwards thrust produces forwards acceleration. Sideways force produces sideways acceleration, allowing the fighters to make turns. And with no drag forces, very high speeds are possible.

Figure 3 Jake Spacerunner must protect his planet from the Evil Empire.

The Evil Empire threatens to destroy the peaceful Planet Gaia. Only Jake Spacerunner can save the millions of people who live there. First he must challenge the dreaded Garth Radar, on his space station 10 000 kilometres away. To have any chance, he must get there in less than 500 seconds. What speed will he have to fly at to make it there in time?

$$\text{speed} = \frac{\text{distance}}{\text{time}}$$

$$\text{speed} = \frac{10\,000}{500}$$

$$\text{speed} = 20 \text{ kilometres per second}$$

Figure 4 From the distance and the time available Jake can work out the speed needed to reach the space station.

Questions

1 a) Why doesn't a spacecraft need a thrust force to keep going at steady speed?

b) What happens when a thrust force does act on a spacecraft?

2 Imagine that you are the pilot of a speeding spacecraft. You have rocket motors that can fire forwards, backwards, left or right.

Which way do you move the lever to:

a) accelerate forwards?

b) slow down (or accelerate backwards)?

c) turn left?

d) turn right?

3 Work out the speed that you would need to reach a space station 80 000 kilometres away if you had to get there in 1000 seconds. Write down your calculation like the one on the left.

Remember

Match the half sentences together.

a) In space there is no air resistance . . .

b) In space, force of thrust is not needed . . .

c) The formula for working out average speed is . . .

d) Units for speed include . . .

e) In space, speed can be very high, . . .

i) . . . and so there is no force of drag.

ii) . . . kilometres per hour and metres per second.

iii) . . . so it is sometimes measured in kilometres per second.

iv) . . . to balance drag.

v) . . . average speed = $\frac{\text{distance}}{\text{time}}$

Every 0.01 seconds counts

Sports events are timed with quite high precision. During an event, an athlete's speed often changes from one instant to the next. The athlete also has an average speed for the whole race.

Figure 1 The athletes in this race were timed to the nearest hundredth of a second.

We can compare how quickly athletes run by measuring their time. At athletics events this is done with quite high **precision**. The time is measured to the nearest hundredth of a second. A hundredth of a second is written as 0.01 seconds, or just 0.01 s.

0.01 s might not sound very long, but a sprinter can travel 10 centimetres in that time. 10 centimetres, and 0.01 s, means the difference between winning and losing.

One of the longest athletics events is the 10 000 m. Usually we'd call that 10 km, but the tradition in athletics is to use metres as the unit of distance. It's a long way to run, and top athletes take about half an hour, but still the timing is done to a precision of 0.01 s. The women's record in the year 2004 was set by Paula Radcliffe at 30 minutes and 17.15 s.

The total time for the race is what everybody is interested in. From this, it's possible to work out an athlete's **average speed** for the race. Average speed is found from total distance divided by total time, as usual.

$$\text{Average speed} = \frac{\text{total distance}}{\text{total time}}$$

Total distance is 10 000 m and total time is 30 minutes, 17.15 seconds (or 1817.15 seconds).

$$\text{average speed} = \frac{10\,000}{1817.15}$$

$$\text{average speed} = 5.50 \text{ metres per second}$$

But the athlete doesn't run at exactly 5.50 metres per second for the whole race. Her speed changes. As the starting gun goes off, she's not moving at all. Then it takes her a second or two to accelerate to running speed. As all the athletes jostle for position, lap by lap, sometimes she is running more quickly and sometimes more slowly. In the last part of the last lap she finds herself taking part in a sprint for the finish line. So all through the race her speed can change from one instant to the next. The speed she has at one particular instant is called her **instantaneous speed**.

a) Starting off – speed increases instant by instant.

b) Speed during the race fluctuates from one instant to another as athletes jostle for position.

c) Speed increases during the final sprint.

Figure 2 An athlete has only one average speed for a whole race, but has lots of different instantaneous speeds.

Questions

1 Write these times in decimal form:

  a) one hundredth of a second

  b) two hundredths of a second

  c) a tenth of a second.

2 For the sprinter running 10 cm in 0.01 s, what is their speed in:

  a) centimetres per second?

  b) metres per second?

3 What is the athlete's speed at the instant that the gun goes off?

4 Two seconds before she finishes, is the athlete's instantaneous speed likely to be bigger or smaller than her average speed for the whole race?

Remember

Complete the sentences using the words below.

**average speed   metres per second
instantaneous speeds   total distance
precision   total time**

Athletics events are timed to high _____**1**_____, usually to the nearest 0.01 s.

For a complete race, an athlete has an average speed which can be worked out by dividing _____**2**_____ by _____**3**_____.

At different instants of time, the athlete might have different _____**4**_____. Sometimes this is bigger than the _____**5**_____ and sometimes it is smaller.

All speeds, average speed and instantaneous speed, can be measured in _____**6**_____.

High Street travellers

We can use graphs to show the stories of different journeys.

Milford High Street is a 500 m strip of shops, banks and cafés. It has a couple of busy junctions with traffic lights and pedestrian crossings. It's a lot like any other shopping street.

Matt, Vicky, Ellie and Ali don't know each other, but they all travel along Milford High Street at about the same time on a busy Saturday afternoon. Matt is walking, Vicky is on a bike, Ellie is riding on a bus and Ali is in a car. They take different times to travel the length of the street, so they have different average speeds for their journeys. They also stop and start in different ways. Their instantaneous speeds have different patterns.

Matt stops to cross roads and to look in shop windows. Ellie stops at the bus stops. Ali's car stops to let his brother get out to go into a shop.

We can tell the stories of these four High Street travellers in pictures. The pictures show how far they've travelled at different times. The pictures are called **distance–time graphs**.

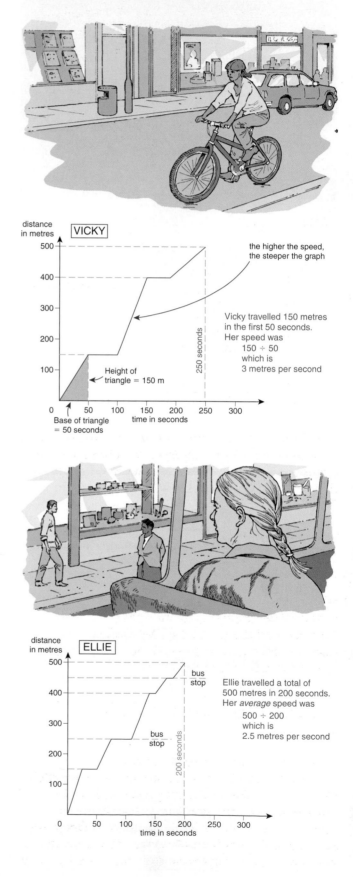

the higher the speed, the steeper the graph

Vicky travelled 150 metres in the first 50 seconds. Her speed was
150 ÷ 50
which is
3 metres per second

Height of triangle = 150 m

Base of triangle = 50 seconds

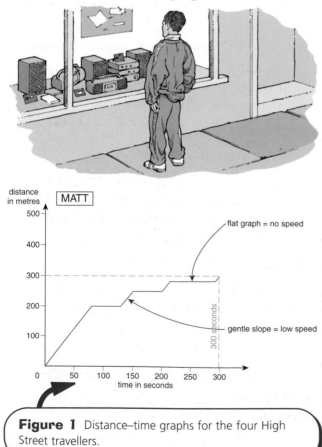

MATT

flat graph = no speed

gentle slope = low speed

ELLIE

bus stop

bus stop

Ellie travelled a total of 500 metres in 200 seconds. Her *average* speed was
500 ÷ 200
which is
2.5 metres per second

Figure 1 Distance–time graphs for the four High Street travellers.

the line of the graph as part of a triangle. From the graph we can measure the height of the triangle to find out distance and we can measure the base of the triangle to find out the matching time. We divide the height (distance) by base (time) to work out the speed.

The distance–time graphs show where the travellers have stopped. When they stop, the distances don't change and the graphs become level lines. When they set off again, the lines become slopes. The faster they go, the steeper the slopes.

Average speed for the whole journey

We can use the graphs to work out average speeds. The graphs tell us the total distance travelled and the total time. We divide total distance by total time to work out the average speed for each of our travellers.

Speed for part of the journey

We can also work out speed at any section of a journey. We can look at the steepness or **gradient** of the graph. Where the graph is flat there isn't any steepness – the gradient is zero and this matches the speed. Where the graph is steep, the speed and the gradient are large. We can work out just how large the speed and gradient are by using

Air speed I

Any kind of object will move at a steady speed when the forces on it are balanced. Speed can only change when forces are unbalanced.

Figure 1 This bird is using the force of gravity to dive down to catch fish. The force of gravity that pulls the bird downwards is also called its **weight**. There is not enough upwards force acting on the bird to balance its weight. The bird's motion changes – it gains speed. The bird **accelerates**.

Figure 2 A bird in steady flight has forces under control. The force of gravity, or weight, acts to pull the bird towards the Earth's surface. But the bird uses the flow of air across its wings to create forces of **lift**. Lift is a force that acts upwards. Weight and lift can be forces of the same size. Then the up–down, or **vertical**, forces are in balance.

The bird in Figure 2 experiences up–down (vertical) forces. There are also backwards–forwards, or **horizontal**, forces. One of these is air resistance – a force of **drag**. You can feel the same kind of force when you ride a bike. Air resistance or drag acts in the opposite direction to the motion. On its own it always causes slowing down or **deceleration**. Deceleration is like a negative acceleration. It's not what you want when you're in a hurry.

To keep going forwards at a steady speed the bird needs to use its wings to create a forward force. The forward force is called **thrust**. Only when thrust and drag are in balance can the bird keep a steady horizontal speed.

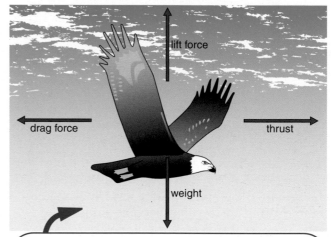

Figure 3 The vertical forces are balanced. The horizontal forces are balanced. The bird flies at a steady speed, without acceleration or deceleration.

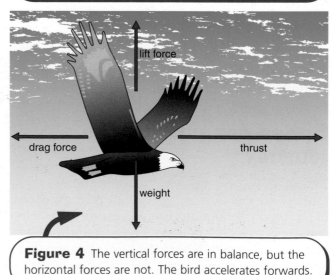

Figure 4 The vertical forces are in balance, but the horizontal forces are not. The bird accelerates forwards.

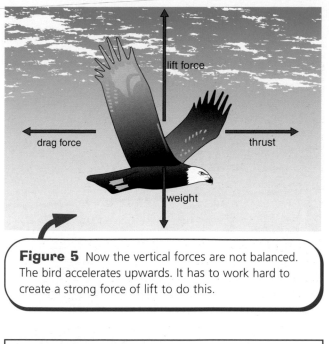

lift force

drag force

thrust

weight

Figure 5 Now the vertical forces are not balanced. The bird accelerates upwards. It has to work hard to create a strong force of lift to do this.

Acceleration: Any object that's changing either its speed or its direction, or both, is accelerating.

Bird speed

Bird	Maximum speed in metres per second
Swift	45
Pigeon	28
Sparrow	8

Table 1 Bird speed

You've worked out speeds before. Here is some more practice. To work out the average speed of an object, we divide the distance it travels by the time it takes. For example, if a bird travels 100 metres in 5 seconds, then,

$$\text{average speed} = \frac{\text{distance}}{\text{time}}$$

$$\text{average speed} = \frac{100 \text{ metres}}{5 \text{ seconds}}$$

That's 100 metres divided by 5 seconds. 100 divided by 5 is 20. So,

$$\text{average speed} = 20 \text{ metres per second}$$

1 Sort these words into correct matching pairs:

up	thrust
down	drag
backwards	lift
forwards	weight

2 What happens to a bird when:

a) drag is bigger than thrust?

b) thrust is bigger than drag?

3 Sketch a diagram to show the forces acting on a bird that is accelerating forwards.

4 Make a table to show the distances travelled by a swift, a pigeon and a sparrow, flying at maximum speed, in: 1 second, 2 seconds, 3 seconds, 4 seconds, 5 seconds.

5 Work out the average speed of a bird that flies 55 metres in 5 seconds.

Remember

Unscramble the anagrams to complete the word list.

L_ _ _

B_ _ _ _ _ _

H_ _ _ _ _ _ _ _

D_ _ _

A

F_ _ _ _

M_ _ _ _ _

D_ _ _ _ _ _ _

A flying bird experiences vertical forces of weight and <u>FLIT</u>. When it flies without accelerating up or down, these forces are in <u>CLEAN BA</u>.

It experiences <u>A THIN ZOO RL</u> forces of thrust and <u>GRAD</u>. When it flies without experiencing backwards or forwards <u>O CLEANER CAT</u>, then these forces are in balance.

Balanced <u>REFCO</u> always results in no acceleration.

Speed is measured in <u>STREEM</u> per second. You can work out average speed by dividing <u>SAND ICE T</u> by time.

Air speed II

Cars and aircraft are designed for high speed. They must push against strong forces of air resistance.

The faster you travel through the air, the faster you have to push air out of the way. You can feel this happening when you ride a bike. Your hair isn't very good at pushing air out of the way and it blows out behind you. You can feel the wind in your face. You are feeling a force of air resistance or drag.

Figure 2 A good car design makes the air flow across the surface in smooth streamlines. This car has tapes fixed to it to show which way the air is moving at different places.

Figure 1 You have to pedal to provide a force of thrust to balance the drag force.

Air resistance isn't a serious problem when you're on a bike. But cars go faster and they're much bigger. The more air resistance there is, the more work the car and its engine have to do to overcome it. That means that the car uses more fuel, which costs more and produces more pollution. So car makers try to design cars so that the force of air resistance, or drag, is as low as possible.

The car companies put their car designs into wind tunnels and blast air at the cars. Sometimes they put smoke into the air so that they can see the flow of air and smoke across the surface of the car. The lines of smoke show the air's **streamlines**. If the streamlines are smooth, then drag forces are not too big. Then we might say that the car is well **streamlined**. But if the streamlines break up into chaotic swirls, the drag forces become a lot bigger. This breaking up of streamlines is called **turbulence**. Cars are designed to stop turbulence happening too much.

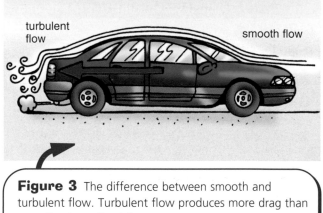

Figure 3 The difference between smooth and turbulent flow. Turbulent flow produces more drag than smooth, streamlined flow.

Air resistance and particles

An airliner flies across the Atlantic Ocean from New York to London, a distance of 5580 km, in 6 hours 40 minutes. It goes very fast so it has to push air out of the way *very* quickly. It collides with the particles of the air. These particles might not be very big, but there are a lot of them and the plane hits them hard. The result of all these particle crashes is that particles in the plane's metal are made to vibrate more rapidly. The particles have high energies of vibration. That means that the metal gets hotter.

Figure 4 A plane needs special design features to solve problems caused by air resistance.

drag force

thrust

Figure 5 Drag and thrust on a plane. At high speed the drag force is high, so the plane's engines must provide a strong thrust force to balance the drag and keep going at steady speed.

Questions

1 Why does a plane experience *much* more drag force than a person riding a bike?

2 What is the cause of drag?

3 A body can only go at a steady speed if the forces on it are balanced. What force acts to balance drag force

   a) for a person riding a bike?

   b) for a plane?

4 If a car is 'streamlined', what does that mean?

5 What is turbulence? Why is it often a problem?

6 **a)** What is the airliner's average speed for its journey from New York to London?

   b) Use distance = average speed × time to work out how far the plane would travel in 10 hours if it kept the same average speed.

7 Is the plane's average speed always the same as its instantaneous speed? Explain your answer.

Remember

Complete the sentences using the words below.

**drag   thrust   collisions   streamlines
turbulence   balanced**

A cyclist, a car and a plane can only go at steady speed if the forces acting on them are

_____**1**_____. That means that they must exert a

forwards _____**2**_____. This is a force that

balances the backwards force of _____**3**_____.

Drag is caused by air resistance.

Air resists the motion of cyclists, cars and

planes because air must be pushed out of the

way. This involves _____**4**_____ between air

particles and particles in the moving body.

_____**5**_____ show flow of air. Car makers use

smoke to help them to study streamlines. If the

streamlines are smooth, then drag is quite low.

If the streamlines show _____**6**_____, then drag

increases.

Closer

Powers of prediction

The distance from Cardiff to Newcastle upon Tyne is about 480 kilometres. By car the journey will take about 6 hours. That's an average speed of 80 kilometres per hour.

$$\text{Average speed} = \frac{\text{distance}}{\text{time}}$$
$$= \frac{480}{6}$$
$$= 80 \text{ kilometres per hour}$$

Calculations allow us to make predictions about journeys.

(Map of the United Kingdom showing Newcastle and Cardiff connected by a line)

Activity

1 We can use the same sort of calculation to predict times for the same journey using different forms of transport. Copy the table below. Make your predictions to complete the table.

Remember that all you have to do is to follow the same pattern each time. This is the pattern to use:

$$\text{Journey time} = \frac{\text{distance}}{\text{average speed}}$$
$$= \frac{(number)}{(number)}$$
$$= (number) \text{ hours}$$

Write the whole pattern down every time you work out a prediction.

Method of travel from Cardiff to Newcastle	Average speed in kilometres per hour	Predicted journey time in hours
Walking	4	
Riding a bike	12	
By car	80	6
By train	100	

2 Use the Internet to research the bullet train, Maglev transport or electric cars.

Find a good picture. Download it or use it to make your own artwork. Then write some words to go with it. Your words could be a couple of paragraphs or a bullet-point list. Explain what the picture shows, where in the world it is, and what makes it special.

3 Think about how much transport has changed in the last 100 years. 100 years ago there were steam trains, but there were very few cars and they were very slow. How do you think transport will change in the next 20 years and the next 100 years? Why will it change? Make a poster of 'Transport Futures'.

4 These are key terms from Chapter 9, in jumbled order:

> **weight   streamline   average speed
> drag   gradient   force
> distance–time graph
> metres per second   unit   thrust
> instantaneous speed   balanced
> acceleration   lift   turbulence
> unbalanced**

a) Match the terms to make eight pairs.

b) Explain why you put each two terms together.

Forces in action

Opener Activity
Shoe technology

Every Akibide shoe has a gas-filled heel – the bubble that you squash at every step. Particles of gas get closer together when your weight comes down on the bubble. And since there's plenty of space between the particles in the gas, there's plenty of room for them to get closer together. You get a nice soft landing, even on the hardest of surfaces.

Akibide

Every time your foot comes down, the ground pushes upwards. If it pushes in the wrong place, the upward force combines with your weight to twist your foot. But with Akibide shoes, there's no turning effect and you keep your balance.

Questions

1 The panel above shows an advert for running shoes. Advertisers often use 'scientific' information to help them to sell their products. Think of some more examples. What 'science' do the advertisers use?
(*Hint*: there are plenty of different types of products to choose from, such as cleaning materials, cars or cosmetics.)

2 Particles in a liquid are very close together. How does this explain why the shoe designers don't use bubbles of liquid in the heels of their shoes?

3 Write down another example of the use of bubbles of gas (big or small) to provide cushioning.

4 A foot and shoe experience a downwards force and an upwards force when a person puts their foot down.

a) What is the cause of the downwards force?

b) What is the cause of the upwards force?

Elephant pressure

The effect of a force on a surface depends on the area of contact with the surface.

If you're an elephant, you need the right kind of feet. Little pointy things wouldn't do at all. With all that weight pushing down on them, they'd always be sinking into the ground. There'd be too much **pressure**. To be a self-respecting elephant you need big, big, flat feet. Four is a good number, and the more of them you keep on the ground, the better. The size of the surface in contact with the ground matters. The size of a surface is called its **area**. For an elephant's feet in a muddy place, big area is good and small area is bad.

There is an **inverse relationship** between pressure and area – the bigger the area, the smaller the pressure. When one gets bigger, the other gets smaller. So when you want to exert a small pressure, be like an elephant and make sure the area is as big as possible.

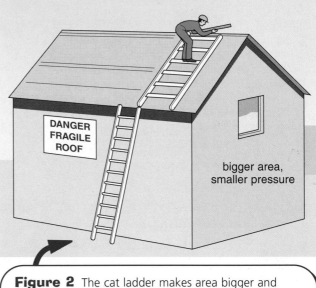

DANGER FRAGILE ROOF

bigger area, smaller pressure

Figure 2 The cat ladder makes area bigger and pressure smaller. It does what an elephant's feet do.

If you WANT to dig into the ground then high pressure is a good thing. If you want to get at tasty roots then your pointed tusks are very convenient. Small area produces big pressure for the same force, so sharp tusks have a larger effect than blunt ones. For digging, small area is good, big area is bad.

Figure 1 The pressure that an elephant exerts on the ground depends on the force, which is the big weight of the elephant. But it also depends on the area of foot that is touching the ground. The large feet of an elephant spread its weight over a large area so that the big weight doesn't have too much effect on the ground below. The pressure is not too big.

smaller area, bigger pressure

Figure 3 If you want to exert a large pressure, think about the tusk and get sharp. A knife uses the small area of its sharp edge to create a big pressure.

Your personal pressure

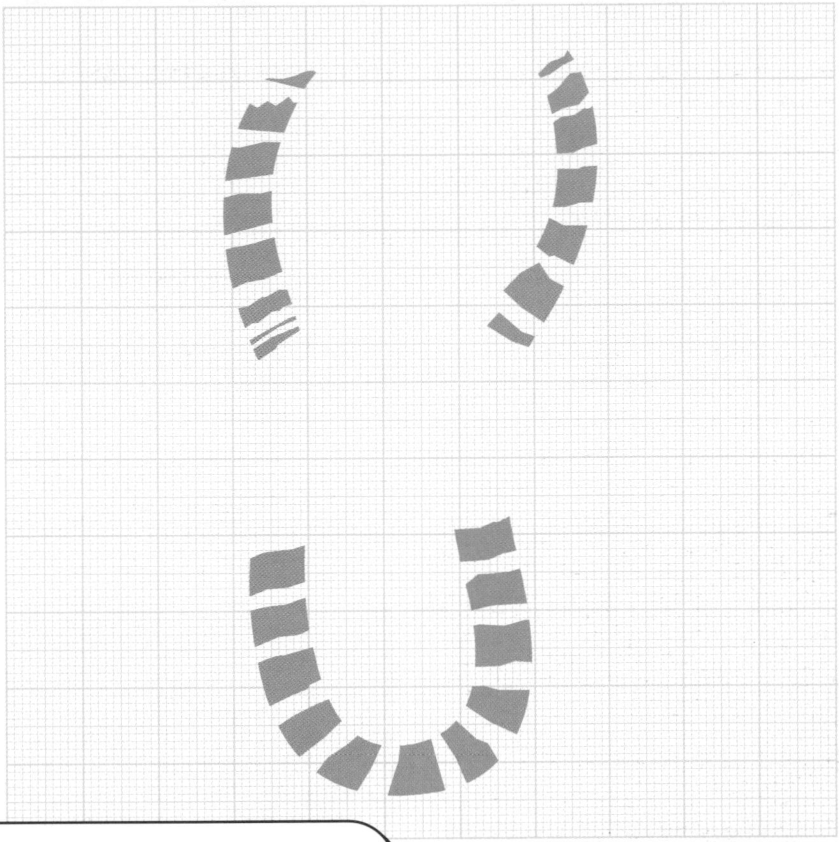

Figure 4 You can use squared paper and coloured chalk to measure the area of contact between your feet and the floor. You can use a forcemeter to measure your weight.

The force you exert on the floor is your weight. Your weight stays the same from one minute to the next. But the pressure you exert on the floor can easily change.

The pressure depends on force and area. It depends on the area of your shoe or foot that is in contact with the ground.

You can change the area of contact by standing on your toes or by standing on the edges of your shoes. Pointed high heels have a small area and so people who wear them can exert a lot of pressure. The pressure can be enough to damage surfaces like wooden floors. An ice-skaters' blades also have a small area. The high pressure helps them to make the ice more slippery.

In all cases we can work out the pressure from the size of the force and the area of contact.

$$\text{Pressure} = \frac{\text{force}}{\text{area}}$$

That is, pressure = force divided by area.

Questions

1. When you are standing up, you usually have your feet flat on the floor. What can you do to increase the pressure that you exert on the floor? Use the words **weight** and **area** to explain how this works.

2. a) What is an inverse relationship?
   b) Name two variables that have an inverse relationship.

3. Use the words **area** and **pressure** to explain how a knife can cut through cheese.

Remember

Unscramble the anagrams to complete the sentences below.

EAR A is the size of a surface. SUPER RES is a measure of the possible effect of a force on a FUSE CAR. If the force acting on a surface doesn't change, then when area gets bigger, pressure gets REL SLAM. There is an SERVE IN relationship between pressure and area.

Working under pressure

Pressure is related to force and area. Safety often depends on controlling the pressure that's acting.

Atmospheric pressure

We all live at the bottom of a sea of air – the Earth's **atmosphere**. The air presses on our bodies. It exerts an **atmospheric pressure**.

The surface area of a human body is, very approximately, 1 square metre or 1 m². The total force exerted by the air on that surface is very large – about 100 000 newtons. That's a force of 100 000 newtons on every square metre.

100 000 newtons per square metre is also called 100 000 **pascal**. The pascal, or Pa for short, is the international unit of pressure. The pressure of the air at or close to sea-level is about 100 000 Pa.

Water pressure

Air exerts pressure on all of the skin of our bodies. So does water when we go below the water's surface. The deeper we go under water, the higher the pressure. About 11 metres under water the pressure is double that at the surface. At 22 metres it's trebled.

Divers can't go very far under water before the pressure starts to present a hazard. Bubbles of nitrogen can start to form in their blood if they come back to the surface too quickly. These bubbles are like the ones that form when you reduce the pressure acting on a fizzy drink by opening the bottle. Divers call it 'the bends' – it's painful and it can kill.

Figure 2 The deeper a diver goes, the greater will be the pressure on them.

Figure 1 We are used to the 100 000 Pa of atmospheric pressure acting on our skin on Earth. Our bodies on the insides of our skin push out to balance the pressure. For an astronaut in space there is no atmosphere so there is no air pressure. The astronaut's body would explode were it not for special pressurised space suits.

Working out pressure

$$\text{Pressure} = \frac{\text{force}}{\text{area}}$$

There is an **inverse relationship** between pressure and area. That means that the bigger the area over which you spread a force, such as your weight, the smaller the pressure.

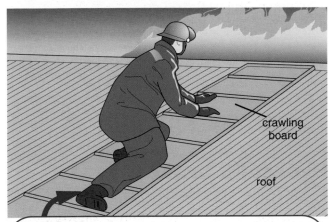

Figure 3 The crawling board reduces the pressure of the firefighter on the roof below by spreading out his area.

We can calculate the pressure exerted by the firefighter in Figure 3 as follows:

Weight of firefighter
= 800 N

Area of feet in contact with roof when standing
= 0.01 m²

Area when on crawling board
= 1 m²

Pressure on roof when standing
= force/area = 800/0.01 = 80 000 Pa

Pressure on roof when on crawling board
= force/area = 800/1 = 800 Pa

Figure 4 Smaller area results in bigger pressure. The edge on a firefighter's axe has a small area, so the force has a big effect on the surface it hits.

Questions

1 What is the unit of each of these quantities:
   a) force, **b)** area, **c)** pressure?

2 What does it mean that there is an 'inverse' relationship between pressure and area?

3 What does it mean that there is a 'direct' relationship between pressure and force?

4 Calculate the pressure exerted by a 600 N person standing on a floor. The area of the bottom of their shoes, touching the floor, is 0.01 m².

5 Diving is hazardous. Illness or death caused by the bends are particular risks. How does a diver reduce these risks?

6 Explain, in terms of pressure, why a sharp point on a drawing pin is better than a blunt one.

Remember

Match the words below to the spaces in the sentences.

    a   *b*   *c*   *d*
inverse pascal atmosphere depth
pressure increases square force
            f   *g*   *h*
newtons

___1___ *e* = force/area. There is a direct relationship between pressure and force.

Increasing the force ___2___ *f* the pressure, provided that area stays the same. There is an ___3___ *a* relationship between force and area. Increasing the area decreases the pressure, provided that ___4___ *h* stays the same. If force is measured in ___5___ *i*, N, and area is measured in ___6___ *g* metres, m², then the unit of pressure is the ___7___ *b*.

The atmosphere exerts a pressure. Outside the Earth's ___8___ *c*, there is no air and no atmospheric pressure. Water also exerts pressure. Water exerts more pressure at greater ___9___ *d*.

Robot force

Pressure applied to gases reduces their volume. Pressure applied to liquids does not reduce their volume. The liquid pushes out on its container.

Hydraulics

Figure 1 Many robots use **hydraulics** or liquid pressure. There are two cylinders – a master cylinder and a slave cylinder – connected by a sturdy pipe. The slave does everything that its master tells it to do, but it does it with more force than the master could manage.

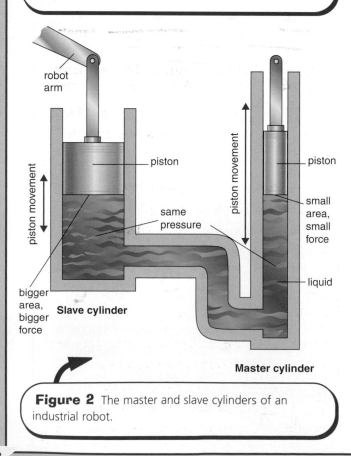

Figure 2 The master and slave cylinders of an industrial robot.

A hydraulic master cylinder has a piston with a small area. The piston is pushed and so pressure acts on the liquid. The liquid volume can't change. The piston can't compress the liquid into a smaller volume. So the liquid presses on the piston in the slave cylinder. The liquid 'transmits' the pressure from one piston to the other.

The pressure on the piston is the same as the pressure provided by the master cylinder. But the same pressure acting over a bigger area provides a bigger force. The force that the slave piston can exert is bigger than the force acting on the master piston. Using hydraulics in this way a small force is magnified.

Hydraulic brakes

A car's brakes also work by using a hydraulic system. The driver's foot goes down on the brake pedal and that pushes a piston inside a master cylinder. The pressure acts on the liquid in the pipes. It exerts force on four pistons in slave cylinders – one for each wheel. The four pistons push the brake blocks to stop the wheels turning.

It is dangerous to get air into the brake pipes. Air is *not* like a liquid and its volume *does* change when pressure is applied to it. So if a driver presses on the brakes when the pipes have air bubbles in them, mostly what happens is that the air bubbles get squashed. All of the pressure is not transmitted to the wheels.

Figure 3 Hydraulics are involved in the workings of a car's brakes.

Using gas pressure

Gases like air can change their shape and their volume under pressure. They are **compressible**. Liquids, like hydraulic fluid or water, can change their shape but not their volume. Liquids are **incompressible**. This is why liquids are good for hydraulic systems but gases are not. There are, however, times when the compressibility of gas is a good thing. Using gas pressure is called **pneumatics**.

Figure 4 The compressibility (or sponginess) of gas in the tyres gives a less bumpy ride on a bike.

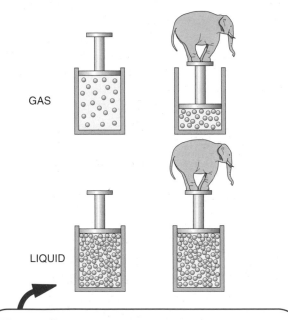

GAS

LIQUID

Figure 5 In a gas, the particles are a long way apart compared with their size, and it's not too hard to push them closer together. In a liquid, it's very hard to push particles much closer together. So the particle idea can explain the different behaviour of gases and liquids under pressure.

Questions

1   In a hydraulic system, what design feature makes the force exerted by the slave piston bigger than the force exerted on the master piston?

2   Give an example of situations in which the compressibility of air is

  a) a good thing,

  b) a bad thing.

3   a) If you put your finger over the end of a bicycle pump and push the handle, you can feel the sponginess or compressibility of the air inside. What would happen if you filled the pump with water and tried to do the same thing?

  b) Some water pistols use an air pumping system so that the water comes out 'under pressure'. Explain the behaviour of the air and the water in one of these water pistols.

4   Explain, using the idea of particles, why it's dangerous to have air inside a car's braking system.

Remember

Match the words below to the spaces in the sentences.

compressible incompressible particles liquid hydraulic force area pressure

A ____1____ system can convert a small force into a bigger force. The system is filled with liquid, which is ____2____.

The force acting on the piston in the master cylinder acts over a small ____3____. The ____4____ is transmitted through the liquid, so the same pressure acts on the piston in the slave cylinder, but it acts over a bigger area. The same pressure acting over a bigger area produces a bigger ____5____.

A gas is of no use in a hydraulic system because it is ____6____. Pressure acting on a gas pushes the ____7____ closer together. In a ____8____ the particles are already close together and it's very hard to make them closer.

Safe forces at play

In playgrounds, children play with the force of gravity. On see-saws, forces can have turning effects. The principle of moments can be used to predict when a beam will be in balance.

Most of the time, your weight is not the only force acting on you. For example, there is usually a floor pushing up on you to balance your weight. Sometimes forces combine together to put you into a spin, like the gymnast in Figure 1. Forces can have **turning effects**.

upwards force exerted by bar

weight of gymnast

Figure 1 The arrows show the size and direction of the forces. Although they are the same size, they do not act at the same point on the gymnast's body and so they make her turn.

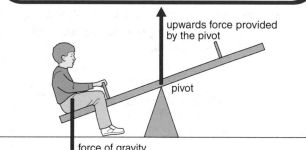

upwards force provided by the pivot

pivot

force of gravity (weight)

Figure 2 On a see-saw, the force of gravity can produce a turning effect.

Figure 3 The force of gravity acting on a second person can also produce a turning effect.

The variables that affect the size of a turning effect are:

- the **size** of the force – more weight means more turning force.

- the **distance** of the force from the pivot – bigger distance means more turning effect.

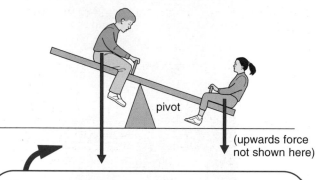

pivot

(upwards force not shown here)

Figure 4 A smaller person can have a bigger turning effect than a big one by sitting far enough from the see-saw **pivot**.

We can measure the turning effect of a see-saw force by combining the size of the force with its distance from the pivot. We say that the size of the turning effect on a see-saw is the force multiplied by the distance from the pivot.

For a see-saw:

turning = force × distance of force
effect   from pivot

Another name for the turning effect of a force is the **moment** of the force. Forces are measured in newtons and distances are measured in metres. So turning effects or moments are measured in **newton metres**.

Designing for fun and safety

Jeff is a designer who's been given the job of creating some new see-saws for a woodland play area. He wants to use big logs to make the see-saws, as logs will fit in with the forest environment. He knows that the see-saws must be fun but most of all they must be safe.

Jeff needs to think about **clockwise** and **anti-clockwise** moments. A force that has a clockwise turning effect has a clockwise moment. He knows that a see-saw will be balanced when the total of the clockwise moments is the same as the total of the anti-clockwise moments. That is, for balance,

> **total clockwise moments =
> total anti-clockwise moments**

This is called the **principle of moments**. With this information, Jeff can start to sketch some initial ideas.

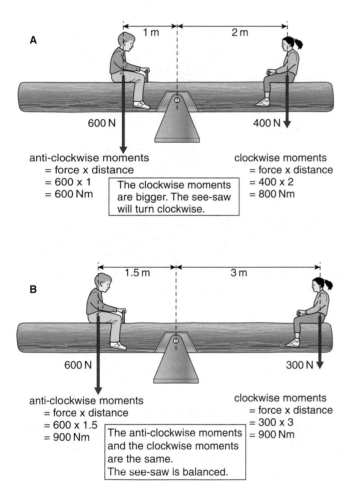

A

1 m   2 m

600 N   400 N

anti-clockwise moments
= force × distance
= 600 × 1
= 600 Nm

> The clockwise moments are bigger. The see-saw will turn clockwise.

clockwise moments
= force × distance
= 400 × 2
= 800 Nm

B

1.5 m   3 m

600 N   300 N

anti-clockwise moments
= force × distance
= 600 × 1.5
= 900 Nm

> The anti-clockwise moments and the clockwise moments are the same.
> The see-saw is balanced.

clockwise moments
= force × distance
= 300 × 3
= 900 Nm

A beam that swings up and down is a hazard. Now Jeff needs to consider how to reduce the risks of harm as much as possible. He writes a list of the hazards and risks:

> falling off, with special risk to head
>
> being hit by beam moving up and down, again with special risk to head
>
> sudden movement, with special risk of neck damage if very sudden

Jeff incorporates design features to minimise risk:

- extra weight at the bottom of the beam to prevent sudden movement
- pits under the seats filled with log shavings.

Questions

1 a) Make a table to show the moment of a force of 100 N when it acts 1 m, 2 m, 3 m, 4 m and 5 m from a pivot.

b) Add another line or column to your table to show the distances that a 50 N force must be from the pivot to produce balance for each position of the 100 N force.

2 a) What will be the moment caused by a person who has a weight of 500 N sitting 2 m from the pivot of a see-saw?

b) If they sit on the right-hand side, will this be a clockwise or anti-clockwise moment?

3 a) Calculate the total moment in each of these situations:

    i) a 250 N force 3 m from the pivot

    ii) a 140 N force 2.5 m from the pivot

    iii) a 38 N force 1.2 m from the pivot.

b) Calculate the distance that a 100 N force must be from the pivot to balance each of these moments.

Remember

Match the half sentences together.

a) We measure force in units . . .
b) We draw arrows to compare the . . .
c) The size of the turning effect of a force depends on . . .
d) The turning effect of a force about a pivot . . .
e) A moment is equal to the size of a force . . .
f) The unit of moment is the newton metre, and it can be clockwise . . .

i) . . . or anti-clockwise.
ii) . . . called newtons.
iii) . . . is called its moment.
iv) . . . the size of the force and on the distance of the force from the pivot.
v) . . . sizes and the directions of forces.
vi) . . . multiplied by its distance from the pivot.

Body balance

We can use the principle of moments to think about turning effects and a wide range of situations, including hazardous situations.

Figure 1 The unbalanced force of gravity is giving the gymnast an anti-clockwise moment. Her hands on the bar act as the pivot. The principle of moments is not being satisfied:

total clockwise moments are not equal to total anti-clockwise moments.

The result of this is that the gymnast experiences a turning (rotational) acceleration.

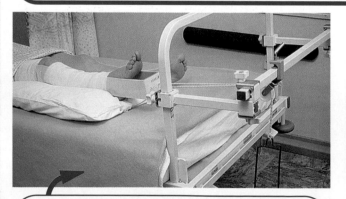

Figure 2 The idea of suspending the leg is to keep it pulled straight so that it can heal properly. Turning motion is certainly not what's wanted. The moments acting on the leg must satisfy the principle of moments. The joint at the person's hip acts as a pivot.

total clockwise moments = total anti-clockwise moments

Figure 3 This tightrope walker is using a pole to make smooth and well-controlled adjustments to the moments acting – avoiding too much violent arm-waving.

total clockwise moments = total anti-clockwise moments

Levers

Some people are stronger than others, but nobody is so strong that they don't need to use levers. We can use them to magnify the size of forces. Something as simple as a screwdriver used to take the lid off a tin is one sort of lever. The longer the screwdriver the more 'leverage' there is.

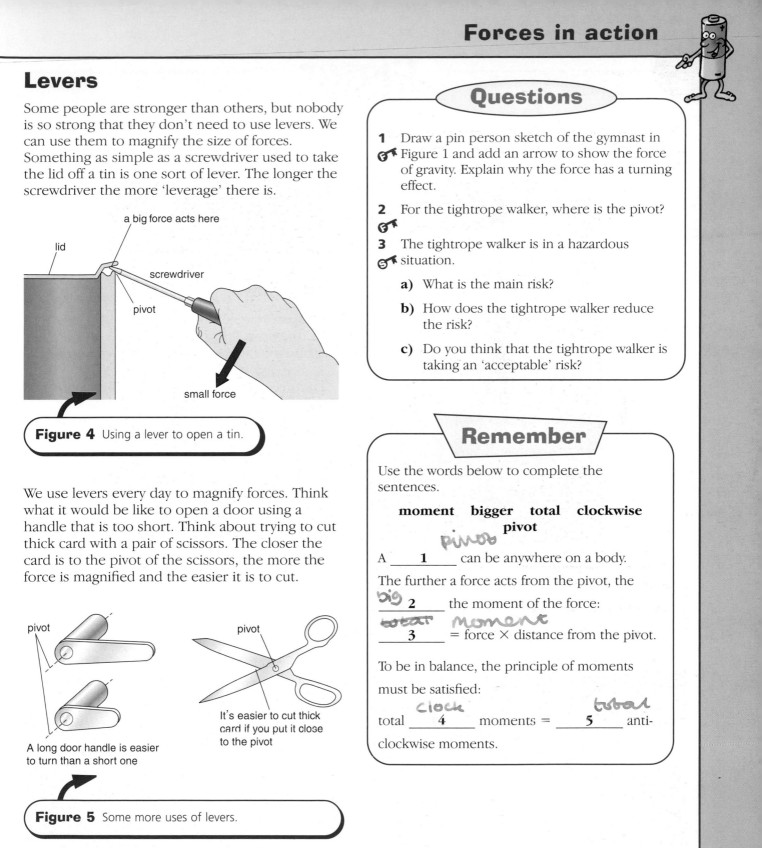

Figure 4 Using a lever to open a tin.

We use levers every day to magnify forces. Think what it would be like to open a door using a handle that is too short. Think about trying to cut thick card with a pair of scissors. The closer the card is to the pivot of the scissors, the more the force is magnified and the easier it is to cut.

A long door handle is easier to turn than a short one

It's easier to cut thick card if you put it close to the pivot

Figure 5 Some more uses of levers.

Closer

Activity

Moving house

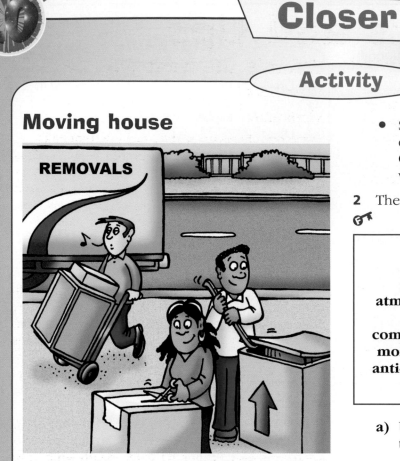

1 Imagine that you have to move house. There are heavy things to move such as a washing machine, and a lot of boxes all taped shut.

- What mechanical devices, such as levers, wheels, or hydraulic systems, will you use to help you to move?

- In your new home you have lots of boxes to open. What mechanical devices will you use?

- As you put things away in your new home you will sometimes want to 'spread the weight'. Give some examples of when low pressure at home is good.

- Sometimes you want to 'focus the weight' onto a small area, and use high pressure. Give some examples of when you might want to do this.

2 These are key terms from Chapter 10:

> area   pressure   surface
> inverse relationship   weight
> newton   pascal   atmosphere
> atmospheric pressure   square metre
> hydraulics   pneumatics
> compressible   pivot   incompressible
> moment   newton metre   clockwise
> anti-clockwise   principle of moments
> lever   force multiplication

a) Use a table or lists to sort the terms into these categories:

- quantities (things we can measure)
- units
- describing words
- objects or parts of objects
- other.

b) Choose one term from each category. Write a sentence that includes this term. Compare your sentences with the ones that other people have written.

Revision hints and tips

This page will help you to find the revision method that suits you.

- Simply reading about a subject is not revising. Revision is about learning facts but it is also about understanding the work that you have done.

- Having a TV on will distract your attention, but there is evidence that music can help you concentrate. The type of music that works best is soothing music. If you have music on with words that could distract you.

- The best revision is done over the period of time leading up to the exam. Leaving it until the last minute is not helpful. There will be too much to learn in one evening.

- A good exercise book will help a lot. But think carefully, will your exercise book contain everything that you need?

- Bedtime is for sleeping. You are unlikely to revise well if you are sleepy.

How should I plan my revision?

- Draw up a timetable for revision. Your timetable should revisit topics regularly.

- Plan your timetable so that you have regular breaks and don't exclude all the fun things you enjoy. Plan to revise topics for no more than half an hour and have a 10-minute break between each half-hour session. If you don't like a topic, revise it between two that you do like.

- Rather than resenting having to revise while your favourite TV programme is on, arrange it so that you do work before the programme, take a break, watch the programme, then go back to work.

Where's the best place to revise?

Organise a space for your revision. Make sure you have everything before you start, like your textbook, revision guides, some paper or file cards and pens (at least two different colours or perhaps a highlighter). Make sure the room is comfortable but not too warm.

What's the best way to revise?

Method 1

Some people revise best by making thinklinks charts. First read through your notes on a topic and any other information. Write the name of the topic in the middle of a clean page. Write as many words down on the paper around the topic that are linked to that idea. Now join the words up, making connections between them.

Method 2

Read through a whole topic. Break the topic up into sections and re-read the section. Make short notes about each section or use a highlighter. Now re-read the topic again and then on a fresh piece of paper, write down what you know without looking at your notes. Keep the notes to revise from in the future.

Method 3

Use file cards to organise your revision. At the top of the file card write the name of the topic and an important word or phrase. Underneath write down the meaning of the word or phrase and how it links with other words or phrases in the topic. Soon you will have lots of file cards. You can build up different boxes of file cards for all subjects.

Different people learn in different ways:

- Some people like to record notes on a cassette and listen to them on the way to school or when they have a free moment.

- Some people like to see how things work or like to learn using diagrams. If this is you, use Method 1 and learn by drawing little pictures and diagrams.

- Other people learn by doing things. Remember activities you did in class? When you revise, try and picture what happened in the class on that day.

Whichever method you use, **good luck** in all of your exams and tests!

Experimental skills – a checklist for experiments

Use these points to help you when you write up an account of your experiments.

◆ Have a clear question in your mind that you want an answer to.

◆ Make a list of the apparatus you want to use.

◆ Write an outline of the way to find the answer.

◆ Identify the key variables that affect your experiment.

◆ Make a prediction about how these variables affect your question.

◆ Give an explanation of the science in your question using proper scientific language.

◆ Do trial runs of your experiments to see if you get some data.

◆ Find information from textbooks and other sources about your question.

◆ Say how you will work safely.

◆ Carry out experiments that are fair tests and explain why they are fair.

◆ Decide how many readings, observations or measurements you need to take for accurate results.

◆ Explain how your experiment can be made more accurate.

◆ Make tables of results and observations.

◆ Decide whether there are enough results to build an accurate answer, and repeat your readings.

◆ Decide on the accuracy of the equipment you were using.

◆ Make charts or graphs to illustrate your results.

◆ Draw lines of best fit on graphs.

◆ Explain how the pattern on the graphs relates to the answer you have found to the question.

◆ Present all your calculations.

◆ Explain how the answer given fits with the data collected.

◆ Reject doubtful results, i.e. results which don't seem to fit your pattern. Don't include them in averages; do more repeats.

◆ Suggest ways in which you could improve on the method or equipment used.

◆ Decide whether the range of your results was enough to be certain of a pattern.

◆ Decide how similar your repeats of results were.

Physics Post-test chapter

Seeing

Figure 1 Sometimes we simply look and record what we see. Sometimes our eyes can see more with some help. Telescopes provide one kind of help. The astrophysicist Dominique Bockelee-Morvan studies comets using the radio telescope shown behind her.

Figure 2 The stars as you've never seen them. Photographs provide our eyes with extra help. You can't see the colour of stars, but a photograph shows that the colour is there. One way to study stars is to compare the colours of their light. We can classify stars according to their size and their colour. One type of star is a **red giant**. Another is a **white dwarf**.

Questions

1 Telescopes and photographs help our eyes to see things that they can't see without help. What can we do to help our ears to hear?

2 Can you think of any other ways of using photographs to help us to see things that our eyes can't see on their own?

We see the light that objects reflect. We can shine a torch into the darkness to find out what's there. Or we can make sound and then detect its reflections, or **echoes**. Submarines and fishing boats do that too. So does a radiographer in hospital, to examine an unborn baby inside its mother.

A geological surveyor also sends sound and detects the reflections, looking for layers of rock under the ground. The geologist makes the sound using explosives. You can't do that to examine unborn babies! You use an ultrasound probe instead.

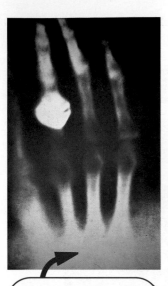

Figure 3 X-rays are one way to probe hidden places. X-rays travel through most parts of your body much better than through your bone. So X-rays make shadow pictures of your bones. Anything else that absorbs the X-rays also makes a shadow, like the ring on the photo above. We make the shadow visible by using photographic film.

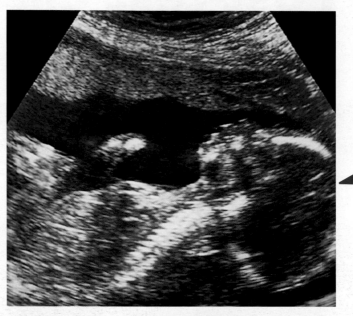

Figure 4 A radiographer uses high frequency sound, or ultrasound, so that the reflections provide the data for making an image of an unborn baby.

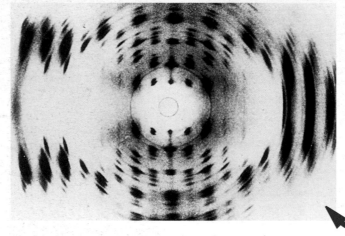

Figure 5 Atoms are much too small to see, but we can probe arrangements of atoms with X-ray beams. We can shine a beam of X-rays into a crystal. We find the X-rays that come out of the crystal have been arranged into patterns. The patterns tell us about the arrangements of atoms inside the crystal.

Questions

3 From these descriptions

a) describe how ultrasound and X-rays are similar

b) describe how ultrasound and X-rays are different.

Measuring

As far as we know, cows and sheep don't count. Birds don't count. Counting is a human thing. And very useful it is too.

But we don't just count, we **measure**. Measuring is a way of comparing. With the right measurements of materials we can predict how some things, like cakes that we bake and bridges that we build, will turn out.

When we make measurements we usually use **units**. Metres, seconds, kilograms and °C are all units. We have to use units sensibly.

2 metres + 2 metres = 4 metres

but

2 metres + 2 seconds doesn't equal anything at all.

Figure 6 We can make measurements to test predictions and to find out about relationships between variables.

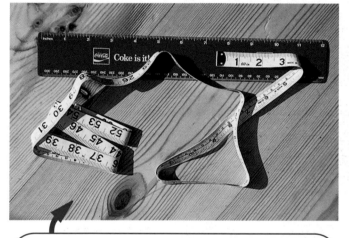

Figure 7 We measure length using numbered scales. The markings on the scales are evenly spaced. All rulers have the same spacing system so we can all agree on our measurements, whichever ruler we use.

Figure 8 To measure volumes of liquids we use measuring cylinders, which also have scales.

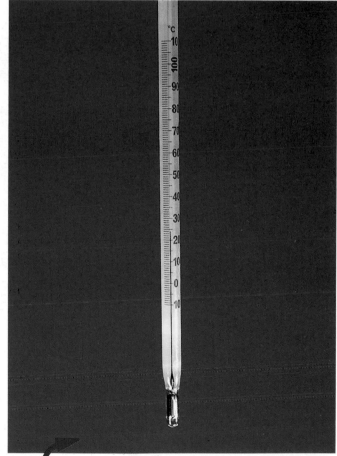

Figure 9 Measuring other quantities, such as temperature, is not quite so straightforward. To measure temperature we use the expansion of a liquid in a tube.

The length of a thread of liquid in a tube is not temperature, but it is related to temperature. We use the length of the thread as an analogue of temperature. The liquid-in-glass thermometer is an **analogue** measuring instrument.

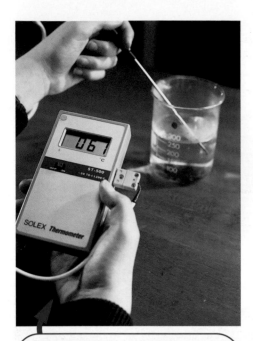

Figure 10 Some thermometers are not analogue but **digital** measuring instruments.

Figure 11 Electrical measuring instruments, like ammeters, can also be either analogue or digital. An analogue ammeter tells us a measurement from how far a needle moves around a scale. A digital ammeter is usually easier to use.

Questions

4 We know that 2 + 3 = 5. But can
a) 2 dogs + 3 cats = 5 camels?
b) 2 cm + 3 mm = 5 mm?

5 What DOES 2 cm + 5 mm equal
a) in cm?
b) in mm?

6 What are the readings on these instruments?

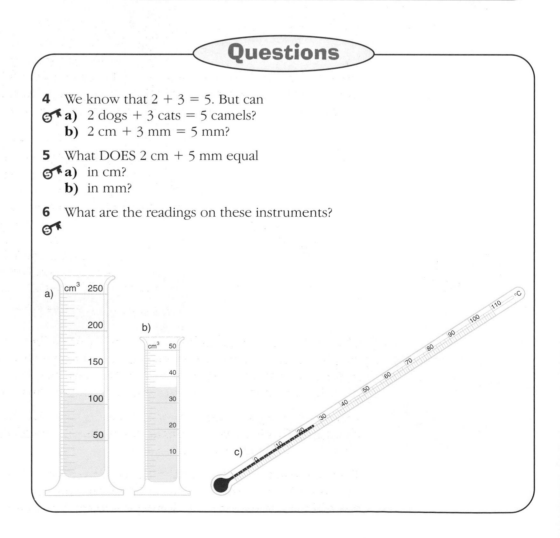

Questions

7 These are some measuring instruments with different **ranges**.
Which instrument is most appropriate for measuring
   a) 20 cm³ of water?
   b) 120 cm³ of water?
   c) A temperature of 35°C?
   d) An increase in temperature from 35°C to 120°C?

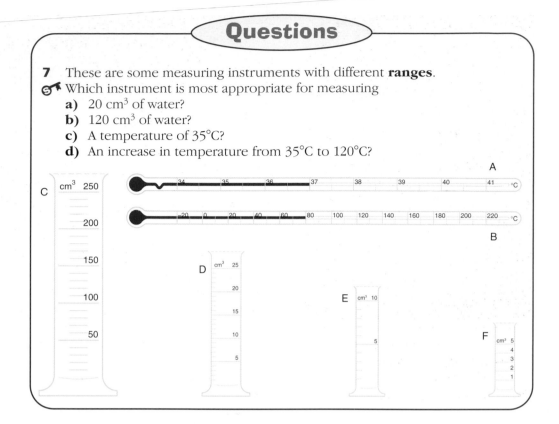

Investigating variables

Your height has varied since you were born. But if it hasn't stopped changing already, then it will stop some time in the next few years. Then it won't vary any more. It won't be a **variable** but will be **constant**. Variables are quantities that we can measure, and they are quantities that can change.

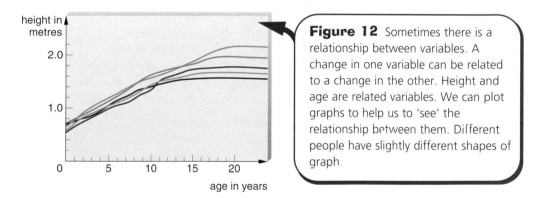

Figure 12 Sometimes there is a relationship between variables. A change in one variable can be related to a change in the other. Height and age are related variables. We can plot graphs to help us to 'see' the relationship between them. Different people have slightly different shapes of graph.

The world is complicated but science helps us to find simple patterns. To find simple patterns we have to investigate variables just two at a time. If we try to make an investigation with more than two variables that change, its impossible to make any conclusion. An experiment with only two variables is a **fair test**.

Usually, in an experiment we control one variable. We decide exactly how to change it. This is called the **input variable**. You could also call it the *controlled* variable or independent variable.

Then we watch what happens to the other variable. We have no direct control over this. We just wait to see what happens. This variable is the **output variable** of the experiment. Some people call it the dependent variable.

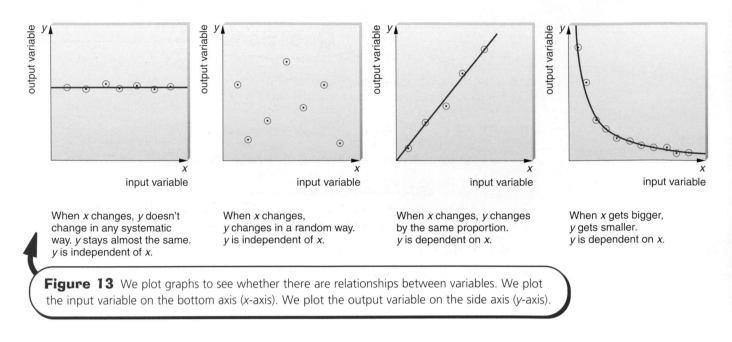

When *x* changes, *y* doesn't change in any systematic way. *y* stays almost the same. *y* is independent of *x*.

When *x* changes, *y* changes in a random way. *y* is independent of *x*.

When *x* changes, *y* changes by the same proportion. *y* is dependent on *x*.

When *x* gets bigger, *y* gets smaller. *y* is dependent on *x*.

Figure 13 We plot graphs to see whether there are relationships between variables. We plot the input variable on the bottom axis (*x*-axis). We plot the output variable on the side axis (*y*-axis).

When the graphs show that both variables change in a clear way, that means that the input variable makes a difference to the output variable. The output variable is **dependent** on the input variable.

If the output variable doesn't change when we change the input variable, then the graph suggests that the variables are **independent** of each other.
If the output changes in a random way when we change the input variable, that also suggests that the variables are independent.

Questions

8 **a)** For each of the graphs below
   i) name the input variable
   ii) name the output variable.
  b) Which of the variables do you control when you do an experiment?
  c) For each graph, say whether the output variable is *dependent on* or *independent of* the input variable.

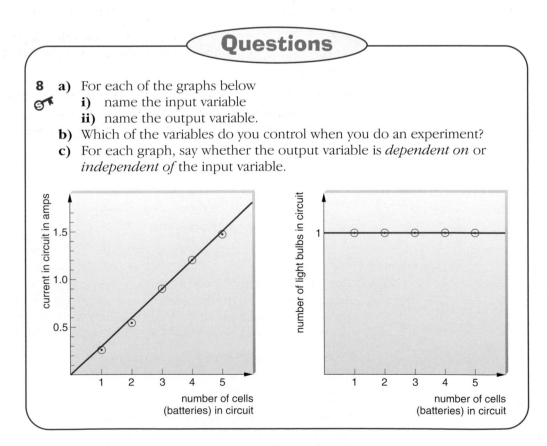

Asking scientific questions

A scientific question is one that we can investigate by doing an experiment.

These are some scientific questions:

- Does a wet surface cool down more quickly than a dry one?
- How can we make water evaporate more quickly?
- What is the relationship between saltiness of water and how high ships float?
- How do fish control upthrust?

These are some questions that are not scientific. They are still important questions, but we cannot find out the answers from experiments:

- Who is the world's best singer?
- Are elephants beautiful?
- Who should win the next election?

The purpose of an experiment is to answer a question. An experiment works in stages something like this:

Step 1: I have an idea that's based on what I know so far. I'm not sure if it's a good idea. I can write my idea as a question.

Step 2: Depending on the answer to my question, if I do _____**X**_____ . . .

Step 3 . . . then I'd expect _____**Y**_____ to happen. This is a testable prediction.

Step 4: If **Y** does happen then my idea is probably a good one.
(This is usually good because it says that you may well be on the right lines with your idea.)

Step 5: If **Y** doesn't happen then my idea must be wrong. I need a new idea.
(This is almost always good, because it makes you have to think about new ideas. Being wrong can be the start of new ideas. It can be very useful to be wrong!)

Here is an example:

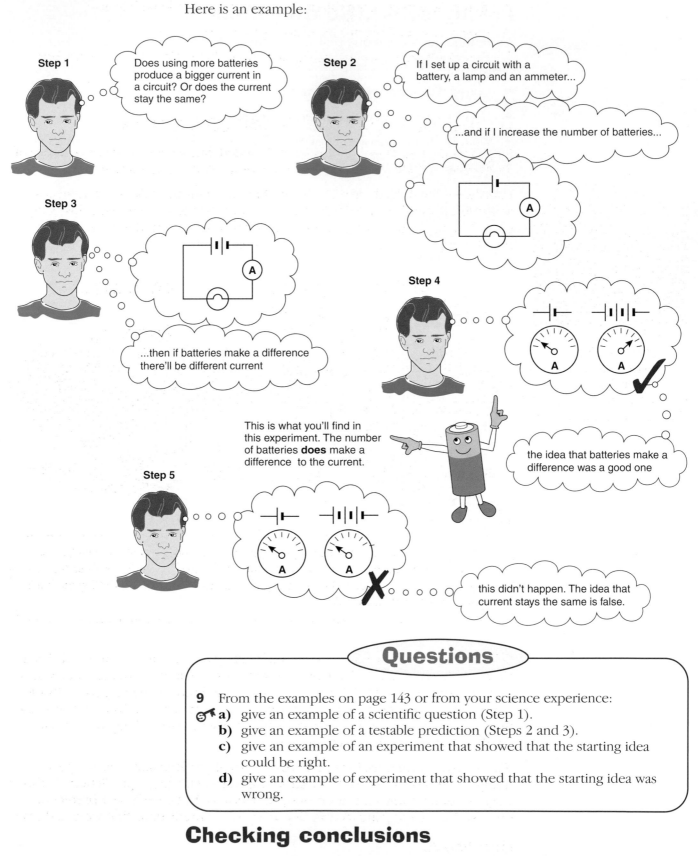

Step 1

Does using more batteries produce a bigger current in a circuit? Or does the current stay the same?

Step 2

If I set up a circuit with a battery, a lamp and an ammeter...

...and if I increase the number of batteries...

Step 3

...then if batteries make a difference there'll be different current

Step 4

the idea that batteries make a difference was a good one

This is what you'll find in this experiment. The number of batteries **does** make a difference to the current.

Step 5

this didn't happen. The idea that current stays the same is false.

Questions

9 From the examples on page 143 or from your science experience:
   a) give an example of a scientific question (Step 1).
   b) give an example of a testable prediction (Steps 2 and 3).
   c) give an example of an experiment that showed that the starting idea could be right.
   d) give an example of experiment that showed that the starting idea was wrong.

Checking conclusions

One problem is that if you do an experiment and write about it, people might not believe you. Scientists don't believe each other until many scientists have repeated the experiment to see if they get the same result. This is called **replicating** the results.

If different scientists reach different conclusions it could be because:

- their measurements are unreliable, or because
- they don't have enough measurements so that their conclusions are not valid.

Figure 14 This elephant is squirting water over itself to try to cool it down.

Some BIG questions for elephants

Elephants are big. They are also warm-blooded, like we are. The temperature of an elephant's body has to stay the same, or it will die. The same goes for you.

Usually, elephants' bodies are warmer than the air around them. That means that energy transfers *outwards*. The elephants then have to replace this energy or their temperatures will decrease. Their food reacts with the oxygen they breathe to provide the source of energy they need.

Figure 15 Energy transfers are happening in elephants' bodies all of the time, just like ours. On a cooler day, that's fine. Energy will transfer out into the surroundings so that the elephants don't get too hot. But on hotter days, there can be a problem. Getting too hot is as dangerous as getting too cold.

Different animals have different ways of making energy transfer outwards faster. Dogs do this by panting. They breathe hard over their wet tongues. It may seem that they're working hard, but this is their natural way of keeping cool. People cool down by sweating. Salty water comes out from our skin. Elephants can use their trunks to squirt water over themselves. These ways of keeping cool all involve evaporation from wet surfaces.

We can investigate questions that are important to elephants (and people) trying to keep cool. For each question, we start by making a prediction. At this stage we don't know how good our prediction is. But if we have a prediction, then we have something to test. These are some predictions that we could test:

Question A:

How do we know when evaporation is taking place?

Testable prediction A: If evaporation is taking place, then mass of liquid should decrease.

Question B:

How do we know that evaporation causes cooling?

Testable prediction B: If evaporation causes cooling, then we should be able to measure a bigger fall in temperature from a wet object than from an identical dry object.

Question C:

Does evaporation cause cooling only of hot objects?

Testable prediction C: If evaporation only causes cooling of hot objects, then fall in temperature will be the same in cooler objects whether they are wet or dry.

Question D:

Does surface area make a difference? If so, how much?

Testable prediction D: If surface area makes a difference, then the bigger the surface that is wet, the more fall in temperature we should see.
We could control the size of the wet surface (the input variable) and then measure what happens to the size of the temperature fall (the output variable). This will need to be done as a **fair test**. That means that other variables must *not* be allowed to change.

Question E:

Does a flow of air make evaporation happen more quickly?

Testable prediction E: We can measure how quickly evaporation takes place by measuring a change in mass of water. Then we can make measurements using identical conditions but with and without a flow of air.

Question F:

Does faster evaporation have more cooling effect?

Testable prediction F: If evaporation has a cooling effect, and we make it happen more quickly, then there will be a bigger fall in temperature.

Questions

10 For each of Questions A, B and C, write down what variables need to be measured.

11 Choose one question, and write down a plan for an experiment. In your plan you should include:
  a) what variables you will measure
  b) which is the input variable and which is the output variable
  c) the approximate range (i.e. the difference between the biggest and smallest) of values each variable will have (you may not know this very precisely)
  d) what measuring instruments you will use
  e) how you will record your results
  f) what you will do with the results to look for a pattern
  g) what pattern you think you are likely to find. (It doesn't matter if your experiment shows that you are wrong on this.)

Some questions for sailors and salmon

A liquid provides a force of **upthrust**. It is this force that balances weight so that objects can float.

Fish like salmon can vary the size of the upthrust to help them move up and down in water. One problem that salmon have is that they spend part of their lives in the sea and part in rivers. The sea is salty water, but rivers have fresh water.

Some ships also move between rivers and the sea. They have to be able to float in sea water and in salty water.

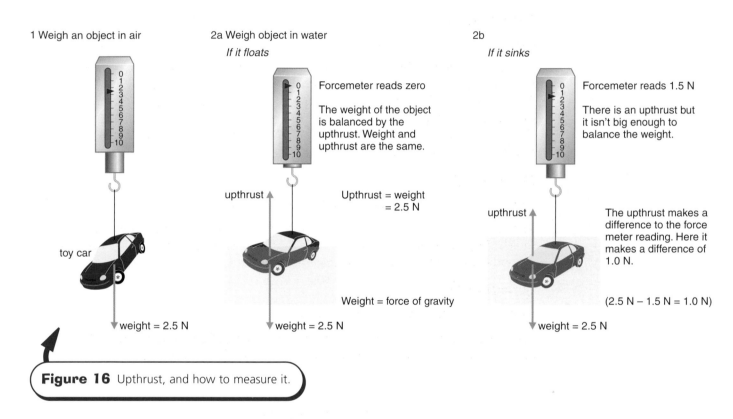

Figure 16 Upthrust, and how to measure it.

Variables that *might* affect upthrust include:

* the saltiness of the water
* the weight of the object
* the volume of the object.

Questions

These are some important questions for these ships, and for salmon.

A   Does salty water provide more or less upthrust on a body than fresh water?

B   What happens to the upthrust as we vary the saltiness of water?

12   For each question suggest some testable predictions. You could then go on, with guidance from your teacher, to make practical investigations of your predictions, and write a report on this.

Chemistry Post-test chapter

Science and experimenting

Science is about explaining how things happen.

Part of science is about gathering information. This information is often called data. The information has to be gathered carefully, so that it is accurate and reliable. People working scientifically need to know how it is collected, so they keep accurate records of everything they do.

Often the data has to be turned into another form. Calculations can be carried out from the data, and it can then be used to make graphs and charts. Our brains work better with pictures than with numbers.

This information is used to find patterns in the way natural things work. If they can find a pattern, people working scientifically can use that pattern to make predictions about the way things will happen in the future.

Not all scientists look like the person in Figure 1.

A nurse is a scientist. Nurses have to monitor data to try to make patients better.

A gardener is a scientist. Gardeners monitor data about how much fertiliser to add to soil to produce the best crop.

A chef is a scientist. Chefs must choose the right mixture of ingredients to make the perfect meal.

A builder is a scientist. Builders have to make the correct concrete mix to ensure safe buildings.

Figure 1 Is this a scientist?

Stuff is made of particles because ...

Science is about using models.

Models are one way of thinking about how things work. In science, the small particles, like atoms and molecules, are far too small for us to see. Particle models can be used to help us explain the behaviour of most materials.

Chemistry is about understanding how substances behave. To do that we have to see patterns in how substances change, and explain them, using the 'because' word.

Figure 2 People do chemistry to make better materials. Materials for better clothes, for cosmetics, for people's health, for improving crops, for counteracting pollution – the list is endless.

Questions

Complete the explanation for each of these observations. If possible, try to use a particle model explanation.

1 Solid substances often form crystals with regular shapes because…

2 Candle wax melts at 58°C because…

3 A block of steel stays the same shape even when hit hard because…

4 A bike tyre feels hard even though it is full of air because…

5 A peeled orange smell spreads across a room because…

6 Water is a compound because…

7 Copper conducts heat and electricity because…

8 Sulphur does not conduct heat well because…

9 In Africa, evaporation is used to extract salt from sea water because…

10 Petrol can be separated from crude oil because…

11 Black ink can be separated into many colours because…

12 Nail varnish is cleaned off by nail varnish remover but not by water because…

13 When water evaporates from your skin, you feel colder because…

14 Rocks get broken up by water freezing because…

15 Igneous rock gets turned into sedimentary rock because…

16 Lava rock has tiny crystals because…

17 Metal can be produced from metal ores because…

18 Iron rusts and cream goes sour because…

19 Burning oil releases light and heat because…

20 Burning fossil fuels causes several different types of pollution because…

21 When heated, magnesium flares up and becomes a white powder because…

22 Sodium will displace titanium from titanium compounds because…

23 Gold is said to be unreactive because…

24 Litmus paper turns blue in soapy water because…

25 Pure water has a pH of 7 because…

26 Magnesium reacts with acids because…

27 Tartaric acid and sodium hydrogencarbonate (baking powder) makes scones spongy because…

28 Vinegar will cure wasp stings because…

29 Powdered lime is put into lakes affected by acid rain because…

30 All acids react in the same way because…

A family of non-metals

Science is about finding patterns.

The halogens are a family of reactive non-metals. They all occur in the same column or period of the Periodic Table, just before the noble gases. This means that the halogens have an outer shell of electrons with only one empty space in it. Because they all have this structure, they have very similar chemical reactions. This is one of many 'patterns' that can be found in the Periodic Table.

Eating into glass

Glass, like diamond, is a very hard material. Unlike diamond, which will burn in air if heated, glass is almost totally chemically unreactive. That's why we use it so much as containers for food and chemicals. Glass is much less reactive than metals or plastics. Both of these can give nasty tastes to food, but glass does not. To attack glass, you need a really reactive chemical. That chemical is hydrofluoric acid.

The halogens

The halogens are a group. They are **Group 7** of the **Periodic Table**. They are typical **non-metals**: low melting points, do not conduct electricity or heat, and react strongly with **metals**.

As explained earlier, they have similar chemical reactions, but they do vary in reactivity. Because of their different reactivities, they react differently with living things. They range from very dangerous to a strong antiseptic. There is a **reactivity series** for halogens, as they will displace each other from solution.

Fluorine

This is the most reactive and, therefore, the most dangerous. It will make wood and rubber burst into flame. Fluorine molecules are so small that they diffuse through flesh and attack your bones directly! This is one chemical you never want to see in the laboratory. It is used to make the Teflon coating on non-stick frying pans.

Figure 3 When car windows are marked with their registration number, a mask is used to protect the surrounding glass. The chemical is put on as a jelly so it stays in one place. It eats into the glass, dissolving the surface and leaving a rough patch that is a contrast to the smooth surface.

Figure 4 The halogens: chlorine, bromine and iodine.

Chlorine

Chlorine gas is dangerous. If you get it into your lungs it attacks the flesh, causing septic pneumonia. Asthmatics beware! When it is diluted, it is used as a disinfectant because it kills bacteria easily. When it has reacted, it forms all the different chlorides you have met in science lessons. You will know the smell of chlorine from visits to the swimming pool. Domestic bleach also contains chlorine.

Bromine

Bromine is a liquid element at room temperature. It gives off a choking red gas as it vaporises. This gas is harmful. Bromine dissolves in water to form a dilute solution called 'bromine water' that we often use in science labs.

Iodine

Iodine is the pretty one in the family. At room temperature it is shiny grey crystals. But when you heat it, it turns into a beautiful purple-coloured vapour. It goes directly from solid to vapour with no liquid phase. This is called **subliming**. Iodine is one of the elements needed by our bodies. Small traces of iodine are used to make your thyroid gland work properly. For many years a solution of iodine was used to clean cuts and wounds. It's antiseptic, but it really stings!

Some other uses for the halogens are shown in Figure 5.

Figure 5 Some uses of halogens.

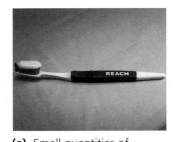

(a) Small quantities of fluoride make your teeth much stronger and resist attack by tooth decay.

(b) Silver bromide is used in photographic film and paper. Silver bromide decomposes when light falls on it.

(c) People need some iodine ions in their diet. It is one of the minerals we need for health. Iodine is needed for the thyroid gland to work properly.

Questions

31 What are the typical properties of a non-metallic element?

32 Why is the glass etching chemical in the form of a jelly?

33 The people who do the security marking wear rubber gloves and eye protection. Explain why.

34 Read about the different halogens and put them in order with the most reactive first.

35 What does subliming mean?

36 All the halogens can be used to kill germs. Find and write out evidence for this from the text.

37 Why can silver be extracted from discarded photographs?

38 What halogen is needed to make the thyroid gland work properly?

39 'Teeth are made of a mineral called apatite. Chlorapatite flakes easily, but fluorapatite is strong and hard.' Use this chemical idea to explain why compounds containing fluorine are added to drinking water.

40 What plastic material contains chlorine atoms?

How fast?

Science is about applying theories.

Chemical reactions are all about losing, gaining or sharing electrons. For this to happen, particles have to hit against each other with enough energy to shake some of their electrons free.

The more collisions there are, the faster the reaction will be. The harder the collision, the more likely it is that a reaction will happen. This is called the **collision theory** of chemical reactions.

Cooking spuds

Ever since Sir Francis Drake brought the potato plant to Europe, potatoes have been part of our diet. They provide high carbohydrate bulk and are very easy to grow. They are also easy to harvest, need no special machinery and can be cooked in many ways.

Cooking potatoes is a chemical change that sometimes takes ages and sometimes a minute or two. The cooking process breaks down the potato cells, making them easier to digest. It also releases the pleasant tastes from inside the cells. Cooking potatoes follows the same rules as speeding up any chemical reaction. If you make the potatoes hotter, they cook faster.

Chips that are deep-fried in oil cook in 2–3 minutes, but it takes about 20 minutes to boil potatoes. That's because deep-fat fryers work at a much higher temperature than boiling water.

If you cut the potatoes up smaller, they cook faster. Crisps only take 20–30 seconds to deep fry. The thin slices cook through much faster. Crinkle-cut chips cook faster than straight chips. The crinkle cut exposes much more of the surface to the cooking oil so the chips cook quicker.

This all fits with the collision theory for reactions.

Figure 6 Spuds with everything.

- **Higher temperature** means the particles are moving faster. This causes more collisions AND collisions with more energy.

- Smaller pieces or crinkle-cut pieces mean **more surface area** exposed. This means there are more potato cells exposed, so the cooking reaction happens faster.

Get your concentration right

Chlorine is a greenish-yellow gas. In low concentrations, a chlorine solution is used to clean surfaces in restaurants, to purify tap water, and of course to kill germs in swimming pools. But chlorine is also a respiratory irritant. The gas attacks the mucous membranes in the lungs. It is so dangerous that it was used as a war gas in 1915. More concentrated chlorine mixtures react much faster and can be very dangerous. When there are more particles in the area, there are more collisions, so the reaction is faster.

Use of chlorine	Concentration in parts per million (ppm)
To clean drinking water	0.001 ppm
In swimming pools	1 ppm minimum level
Minimum level to detect smell	3.5 ppm
As a restaurant surface cleaner	50–200 ppm
As a poison gas	Over 1000 ppm. Fatal after a few deep breaths.

Table 1 Some uses of chlorine.

Figure 7 Chlorine is used in solution to kill germs in swimming pools.

Below is an extract from *Dulce et Decorum Est* by Wilfred Owen. He wrote poetry about his experiences in the Great War (1914–18). This extract describes the effect of a chlorine gas attack on the troops in the trenches.

'GAS! Gas! Quick, boys! – an ecstasy of fumbling,
Fitting the clumsy helmets just in time;
But someone still was yelling out and stumbling
And flound'ring like a man in fire or lime.
Dim, through the misty panes and thick green light,
As under a green sea, I saw him drowning.

In all my dreams, before my helpless sight,
He plunges at me, guttering, choking, drowning.

If in some smothering dreams, you too could pace
Behind the wagon that we flung him in,
And watch the white eyes writhing in his face,
His hanging face, like a devil's sick of sin;
If you could hear, at every jolt, the blood
Come gargling from the froth-corrupted lungs,
Obscene as cancer, bitter as the cud
Of vile, incurable sores on innocent tongues,

My friend, you would not tell with such high zest
To children ardent for some desperate glory,
The old Lie: Dulce et decorum est
Pro patria mori.'

Questions

Explain the different observations in Questions 41–48 using ideas about the collision theory.

41 Food goes off slowly in the fridge.

42 Wood shavings catch fire easily.

43 Exhaust pipes on cars rust quickly.

44 Motor fumes cause bronchitis. There is more bronchitis in city centres.

45 Powdered limestone, rather than lumps, is used to treat lakes affected by acid rain.

46 You rub pure soap on the dirty collars of shirts.

47 If you get acid on your hands, you should pour lots of water over them.

48 You should use a hot wash for very dirty clothes.

49 What is the surface area of a 5 cm cube of potato (a cube in which each side is 5 cm long)? If this was cut into 1 cm cubes, what would be the total surface area now?

50 Draw a diagram to show the increased surface area of a crinkle-cut chip.

51 Read the extract from the Wilfred Owen poem on page 153. Draw a picture of what the scene would be like.

Summary of the collision theory

- Particles can only react if they collide with each other.

- Some of the particles have to be either a liquid or a gas, as their particles move about.

- Not all collisions result in a reaction. There has to be enough energy transferred as the particles smack together to make the reaction happen.

- To make reactions happen faster you can do three things:
  - increase the number of collisions OR
  - make the collisions have more energy OR
  - reduce the energy needed to react.

Biology Post-test chapter

What is biology?

Biology is a science that looks at how living things work: plants, animals (including humans), bacteria, viruses, single-celled organisms and fungi. Biology uses knowledge from other sciences: for example, chemistry to explain how chemical reactions take place in living things and physics to explain how living things move. Knowledge and understanding of biology is also used to explain how living and fossilised organisms are related to one another.

Science is about asking questions and finding the answers if at all possible. It is also about solving problems. In biology there are a lot of questions that scientists can ask about how living things work and how and where they live. Scientists test their ideas by experimentation. An experiment is a controlled test to check out the scientist's theory or explanation of what they think is happening.

Monera (bacteria)

Protista (single celled organisms)

Animals

Fungi

Plants

Insects

Figure 1 Representatives from some of the kingdoms of living organisms.

Look at the questions below. Which ones do you think are scientific questions that we could find the answers to by experiment and which ones are questions that cannot be answered by doing experiments?

For the questions that you decided could be investigated by experiments, choose one and design an experiment or series of experiments that could give you an answer. Remember to use the checklist for experiments.

Where do living things come from?

For thousands of years, people believed that many living things just 'appeared'. This sounds silly to us today, but in times when scientists didn't know about cells or how living things reproduced, it wasn't silly. They called their theory **spontaneous generation**. The word 'spontaneous' means that something just happens. In the 17th Century, there was a recipe for the spontaneous production of mice. The recipe needed some sweaty underwear and the husks of wheat. These were placed in an open jar and, after about three weeks, the theory was that the sweat from the underwear would soak into the husks of wheat and they would change into living mice!

It wasn't until the scientist **Louis Pasteur** scientifically investigated questions such as "why does food go off if it is left in the open air?" that he came up with a theory that microbes were responsible. He also found that microbes were responsible for some diseases like cholera and rabies. The following account tells how scientists investigated spontaneous generation before Pasteur. It goes on to show how Pasteur used experiments to prove his theory that microbes caused food to go off and made people and animals ill from diseases such as cholera and rabies.

Figure 2 The recipe for mice?

Experiments before Pasteur

In 1668, an Italian scientist called **Francesco Redi** set out to prove that maggots didn't 'just appear' in rotting meat. He had a theory that flies laid eggs on the meat and that the maggots came from the eggs. He put meat into a number of flasks – some open to the air, some sealed from the air and others covered with gauze to prevent the flies landing.

Think about the following questions and write down your answers. Remember to give reasons for your answers.

Questions

1 Do you think maggots appeared on the meat in the open flasks?

2 Do you think maggots appeared on the meat in the sealed flasks?

3 Do you think maggots appeared on the meat in the flasks covered with gauze?

4 Why did Redi use sealed flasks as well as open ones and ones covered in gauze?

Figure 3 Francesco Redi was a physician and poet.

But Redi's experiments didn't settle the argument over spontaneous generation. Nearly 80 years later an English clergyman claimed that he could prove the theory of spontaneous generation with an experiment that showed that life did 'just appear'. **John Needham** wanted to test whether or not micro-organisms would appear after they had been heated. By this time many people knew that in order to kill micro-organisms, they needed to boil things. He boiled some chicken broth, put it into a flask and then sealed the flask. He waited and just as he had predicted, micro-organisms grew.

Questions

5 Heating micro-organisms to a high enough temperature does kill them. Try to give two explanations why they grew in Needham's broth.

6 Needham only did one experiment. How would you improve on his experiment?

An Italian priest, **Lazzaro Spallanzani**, was not convinced by Needham's experiment. He suggested that the micro-organisms might have got into the broth after it had cooled but before it was sealed in the flask. He tried a different experiment. Spallanzani put the broth into a flask, sucked out the air, then sealed the flask and boiled the broth. No micro-organisms grew in the broth.

Questions

7 Why did Spallanzani suck the air out of the flask?

8 What might have happened if he had not sucked out the air?

9 People were not convinced by Spallanzani's experiment. They said that it only proved that micro-organisms could not grow without a vital substance. What do you think that 'vital substance' was?

Pasteur's experiment

The theory of spontaneous generation was finally disproved by Louis Pasteur in 1859. He had decided to design a series of experiments for a contest run by the French Academy of Sciences to either prove or disprove the theory of spontaneous generation. His experiments were a combination of those carried out by Redi, Needham and Spallanzani.

Figure 4 Pasteur made special swan necked flasks for his experiment.

Pasteur placed some meat broth into a glass flask and heated the broth to make it sterile. He then heated the neck of the flask until the glass began to melt and curved the neck into the shape of an 'S' or a swan's neck. Pasteur then sealed the flask by heating the end until the glass melted and fused. No micro-organisms grew in the sealed flasks.

He then nipped the end of one of the flasks. This would allow air into the flask, but the curved swan-like neck would trap any micro-organisms floating in the air. They would settle in the neck of the flask because of gravity. No micro-organisms grew in the sterile broth, but when Pasteur tilted the flask and let the broth come into contact with the neck area where the micro-organisms had settled, the broth very quickly went cloudy. Pasteur had proved that spontaneous generation had *not* taken place in the broth, and he had also proved that micro-organisms are everywhere, even in the air that we breathe.

Questions

10 What variables (factors) was Pasteur trying to control in his experiments?

11 Why did he start off with sealed flasks?

12 Why was it important for Pasteur to let air get into one of the flasks?

13 In what ways was Pasteur's experiment similar to and different from the experiments of Redi, Needham and Spallanzani? (You could make a table of similarities and differences.)

14 Why did all three use meat or broth and not just water?

15 Why was Pasteur's experiment more of a fair test than the experiments of the others?

Pasteur's work led to many things. He concluded that fermentation is carried out by micro-organisms, and found that different types of fermentation take place according to the type of micro-organism present. For example, yeast (the micro-organism) produces alcohol as a waste product which is useful in brewing, but other micro-organisms – bacteria – produce chemicals that can make wine taste like vinegar. Pasteur also linked microbes to disease and developed vaccinations against chicken cholera, anthrax and, most importantly, against rabies.

In all of his work, Pasteur used experiments to test his ideas (what he thinks will happen and why – his hypothesis) and used the results of his experiments to provide explanations for what was happening (his theories).

Questions

16 What other micro-organisms do you know of that can cause illness or disease?

17 What does the word hypothesis mean?

18 What is a theory?

19 What is the difference between an hypothesis and a theory?

Maggots and murder

Believe it or not, the police often use maggots to help solve serious crimes like murder. When a murder takes place and the murderer tries to hide the body by dumping it or burying it, insects are the first things to settle on the body. Trained scientists, called **forensic scientists**, examine the scene of the crime looking for evidence to tell them how the person was murdered, where and most importantly when. Flies are always looking for somewhere to lay their eggs and a dead body is ideal. Forensic scientists will look for evidence such as fly eggs, maggots, dead flies or other insects. By studying them carefully they can work out what species they are and how old they are. The scientists can work backwards and pinpoint when the first flies laid their eggs and so determine the time of death. The number of different insects can indicate if a person was killed in the spring or summer, autumn or winter. More than one murderer has been caught by a maggot on a dead body!

Figure 5 Maggots have helped the police to solve many murders.

Humans as organisms

Nutrition

Fifty years ago, science fiction films and stories would often have humans eating pills instead of real food. Looking into the future, writers would sometimes see us wearing silver suits, flying around in 'hover cars' and getting all of our nutrients from a single pill, washed down with a glass of water. Would you like to live in a world like this?

In order to travel in space, astronauts need to have a balanced diet. They cannot take lots of fresh food into space. Inside the space shuttle there is only a limited amount of space to prepare and cook the food. Much of the food astronauts eat is dehydrated (all of the water is removed). It is pre-packed and in order to 'eat' the food, they simply rehydrate it by adding either hot or cold water in pre-measured amounts through a special nozzle that makes sure the water doesn't escape into the cabin.

Figure 6 Food is kept in packs like the one the astronaut is holding and water is added to re-hydrate the food.

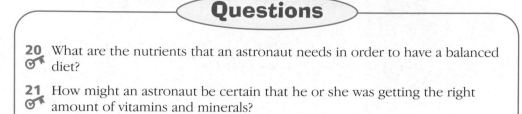

Questions

20 What are the nutrients that an astronaut needs in order to have a balanced diet?

21 How might an astronaut be certain that he or she was getting the right amount of vitamins and minerals?

22 What problems might astronauts have eating and drinking in a weightless environment?

Movement

Many of our muscles work in pairs. Our arms are a good example. The muscles are attached to our skeleton by tendons. The diagram below shows how these muscles work. Biologists call pairs of muscles that work in this way **antagonistic pairs**.

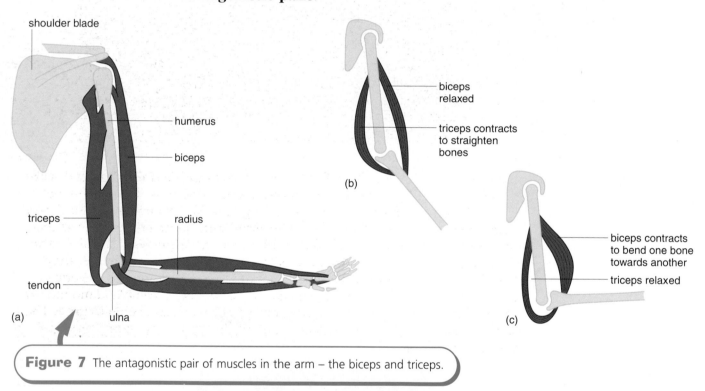

Figure 7 The antagonistic pair of muscles in the arm – the biceps and triceps.

We rely on our skeleton and muscles working together to produce movement. If we damage a muscle or break a bone, it can make even simple movements very difficult.

Questions

23 When the biceps contracts, what happens to the triceps?

24 Think of another pair of muscles that could work in the same way as the arm muscles. Write down where you would find them (you don't need to know the actual names of the muscles).

25 What sort of movements would be difficult if you broke a bone in your wrist? What help would you need to do everyday things?

Reproduction

Sadly some couples are not able to have children. Often they will approach their doctor to try fertility treatment. The newspapers used to refer to children born this way as 'test-tube babies'. This is misleading. Fertility treatment is not about creating babies in test tubes. Many cases of infertility can be treated with drugs. Sometimes men can be infertile and unable to produce sperm. Sometimes it is the woman who cannot produce eggs. Hormones can be given to encourage the body to produce either sperm in men or eggs in women.

Figure 8 Sperm is added to the eggs and left for 40 hours.

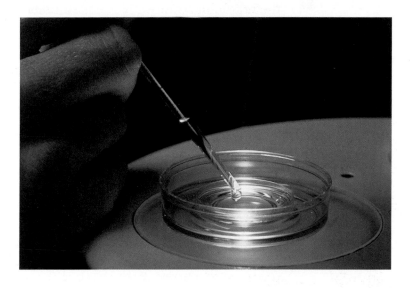

Another method of treating infertility is known as *in vitro* **fertilisation** (**IVF**). This involves taking some eggs from the woman on day 14 of her menstrual cycle. The woman is given a hormonal drug to make her ovaries produce more than one egg at a time. The eggs are fertilised with sperm taken from the man or from a sperm donor in a glass Petri dish (the words '*in vitro*' actually mean 'in glass'). After about two days, the eggs are examined to see whether they have been fertilised by the sperm and started to grow as embryos. Several of these embryos are then placed back inside the woman's womb and monitored to see if any attach themselves to the wall of the womb and begin to grow. The success rate of IVF is quite small and multiple births are common. It is also a very expensive procedure.

Questions

26 If a woman who had received IVF treatment had a multiple birth, are the children more or less likely to be identical twins? Explain your answer.

27 Why do you think several embryos are implanted back into the woman's womb instead of just one?

Breathing

Our lungs are continually exposed to tiny particles in the air that we breathe in – bacteria, viruses, spores, dust and lots of different pollutants and particles that we may be allergic to such as pollen, the commonest cause of hay fever. The lungs work hard to provide us with oxygen and to get rid of the waste gas

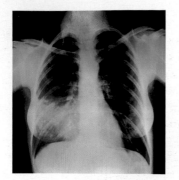

carbon dioxide. Any lung disease or disorder can be serious. Infections such as tracheitis (inflammation of the trachea), bronchitis (inflammation of the bronchi) and bronchiolitis (inflammation of the bronchioles) are common after colds and 'flu. Pneumonia (inflammation of the lungs) is usually caused by bacteria or viruses and is more serious (*itis* means inflammation).

A common lung problem is **asthma**, where the muscles of the bronchi contract and restrict the flow of air into and out of the lungs. The cause of asthma can be pollen, house mites, fungal spores and animal dander (tiny scales shed from the skin, hair or feathers of animals). The dander from humans makes up most of the household dust we have in our homes.

Figure 9 An X-ray of the lungs can be used to check out respiratory tract diseases, such as bronchiolitis.

Questions

28 What do we normally call the condition where people are allergic to pollen?

29 Explain why some asthma sufferers cannot have household pets such as cats and dogs.

Respiration

Respiration provides the body with all of the energy we need. For quick access to energy, we need to take in **glucose** – many energy drinks contain glucose. To release energy more slowly, we can take in starch that is broken down by digestion to glucose. Both starch and glucose are called **carbohydrates**, because they contain the elements carbon, hydrogen and oxygen. The energy is produced in our cells, where glucose is combined with oxygen. This produces water, the waste gas carbon dioxide, and releases energy. It can be summed up in the following equation:

$$\text{glucose} + \text{oxygen} \rightarrow \text{carbon dioxide} + \text{water} + \text{ENERGY}$$

$$C_6H_{12}O_6 + 6O_2 \rightarrow 6CO_2 + 6H_2O + \text{ENERGY}$$

The energy is needed for a number of things – to maintain our breathing, heartbeat, body temperature and other functions. These all contribute to what we call our **metabolism**. People often talk about having a high or low **metabolic rate**. What they are referring to is how quickly we use up the fuel that provides us with energy. When we exert ourselves during exercise or if we are under stress, our metabolic rate increases. When we are resting or sleeping, our metabolic rate slows down.

Questions

30 What common name do we give chemicals such as glucose, sucrose and fructose?

31 What are the three basic elements needed to produce chemicals called carbohydrates?

Health

We have come a long way from the days when doctors prescribed leeches for almost every disease. The leeches were placed on the sick person and allowed to suck the 'bad blood' out. They dropped off the patient's body once they had had their fill of blood. It often had little to no effect, but modern medicine is now learning a thing or two from the past. Medical leeches are still used today, though only to drain collections of partially-clotted blood (a haematoma) from a wound. The leech has a painless bite and its saliva has a chemical that stops blood from clotting. This can cause a leech wound to bleed for several hours after it has filled with blood and dropped off. Leeches do not carry any infections and are not thought to transmit any diseases.

Doctors also use maggots to clean infected wounds. Maggots only feed on dead and rotting flesh. When someone has a bad wound that is infected, special sterile maggots are placed in the wound and they will literally eat the infected flesh, leaving behind the healthy flesh. This helps the wound to heal a lot faster and is more effective than treating the wound with antibiotics or other drugs.

Figure 10 This medical leech will suck blood from the patient and drop off when it is full.

Questions

32 What sort of medicine is used to treat someone who has a bacterial infection – an antibiotic or an antihistamine?

33 What are the different ways in which diseases can be spread among humans?

Plant biology

Versatile cellulose

Cells are the building blocks of life. Groups of cells make tissues and tissues make up organs. Biologists use their knowledge and understanding of science to work out the functions or jobs that different cells have, but they can also use some of the properties of cells to make useful products that we use everyday. There are many similarities between plant and animal cells, but one major difference is that plant cells have a cell wall that is made up of a type of sugar called **cellulose**. Cellulose is a very useful chemical and scientists have managed to adapt it to make many useful things.

Questions

34 What are the things that plant and animal cells have in common?

35 Which part of the cell controls what it does (its function)?

Cellulose acetate

This is a man-made chemical. It is used as the raw material for photographic films as it makes a film that is like plastic. This see-through film is also used on laminated car windscreens to stop the glass from breaking into sharp pieces and flying about. The glass is covered by layers of cellulose acetate, called **laminations**. Cellulose acetate can also be made into fibres that can be used in the manufacture of textiles and made into clothing.

Figure 11 One of the uses of cellulose acetate.

Questions

36 What other plant fibre is commonly used to make clothing?

Cellulose lacquers and paints

Cellulose lacquer is also a man-made chemical that can be used to put a clear plastic-like coating on top of paints. The cellulose paints are often the ones used to paint cars. The paint is more durable than ordinary house paint and gives a better finish.

Questions

37 What is meant by the term 'durable'?

Figure 12 Playing cards and staples used to be coated with cellulose nitrate.

Cellulose nitrate

You might have heard of the term 'celluloid'. It is often used in connection with Hollywood films. The film used in these professional cameras is cellulose nitrate. This man-made chemical was also used in the past to coat playing cards and staples. The coating allowed the cards to slide over one another easily and made sure they didn't stick to one another. The coating also helped the staples work smoothly in the staple gun. Today newer plastics have replaced much of the cellulose nitrate.

Cellulose xanthate

You are probably wearing some of this man-made chemical today. We know it as **viscose**. It is used in hundreds of garments and is often combined with cotton – another fibre obtained from plants.

Photosynthesis

Plants make their own food by combining water and the gas carbon dioxide to make sugar using the energy from sunlight. The green chemical **chlorophyll** is also needed as a place for this to happen. The process is known as **photosynthesis** and because plants make their own food they are called **autotrophs** (*auto* means self and *troph* means feeding, so they are self-feeding).

The formula for photosynthesis is:

$$\text{carbon dioxide} + \text{water} \xrightarrow[\text{chlorophyll}]{\text{sunlight}} \text{glucose} + \text{oxygen}$$

$$6CO_2 + 6H_2O \xrightarrow[\text{chlorophyll}]{\text{sunlight}} C_6H_{12}O_6 + 6O_2$$

Many people think plants are quite boring as they never move. But this is not actually completely true. Plants do move. They don't pick up their roots and walk, but they do move to face the light. If you leave a potted plant on a windowsill facing in one direction, the plant will bend towards the light. If you then turn the plant around, it will bend back towards the light. Try this out at home.

Did you know that some German and Japanese scientists now think that plants can tell the difference between being eaten and being trodden on? They also claim that they have evidence that lima beans that are attacked by spider mites release chemicals that not only attract the insects' natural predators but also warn nearby plants that they might also be in danger.

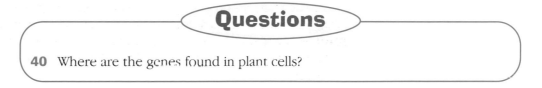

Questions

38 Apart from those things listed in the formula, what else do plants need in order to photosynthesise well?

39 What do farmers and gardeners often add to the soil to help plants grow and what are the three elements they contain?

Genetically-modified plants

Plants are also being **genetically modified** to produce varieties that make a type of human growth hormone. The plants can be grown quickly and cheaply and the hormone can be extracted for use in drugs that help children with growth problems.

Some plants, in particular potatoes, have had inserted into them genes that are naturally found in rice. These genes make the plants produce extra vitamin A and this helps to reduce the number of people suffering from a deficiency of this vitamin.

Finally, plants are being used to make plastics. Plastic is normally made from crude oil, but some bacteria naturally produce a type of plastic. Genes from these bacteria have been inserted into rape seed plants that would normally produce rape seed oil but instead start to make plastics that can be extracted from them. Whatever plants are, they most certainly are not boring!

Questions

40 Where are the genes found in plant cells?

Ecology

Ecology is the study of plants and animals, the environment in which they live and how they interact with each other. Ecology is a very important branch of biology. Until scientists began to understand how living things affected each other and how changing the environment in which things lived affected them, we caused many problems and our action probably made many thousands of plants and animals extinct.

We now have laws both in this country and abroad, designed to protect and save plants and animals from extinction. The problem is that many of us are willing to save what we think of as cute or cuddly animals, such as the panda, from extinction, but we don't feel as strongly about an ugly reptile or a boring plant.

Zoos are places that today spend a lot of time and money protecting thousands of different species from extinction. At Kew Gardens, a Millennium Seed Bank has been created to carefully store the seeds from thousands of different species and varieties of plants just in case they one day become extinct.

Activity

Write a short (roughly 300 word) article on why we must save plants and animals from becoming extinct. You can choose a particular plant or animal if you wish and illustrate it with pictures, clipart etc.

Figure 13 The Millennium Seed Bank at Kew.

Periodic Table of the elements

Group	1	2				Transition elements								3	4	5	6	7	Group 'O'

Period 1

1 ★																			2 ★
H Hydrogen 1																			He Helium 4

Period 2

| 3 Li Lithium 7 | 4 Be Beryllium 9 | | | | | | | | | | | | | 5 B Boron 11 | 6 C Carbon 12 | 7 ★ N Nitrogen 14 | 8 ★ O Oxygen 16 | 9 ★ F Fluorine 19 | 10 ★ Ne Neon 20 |

Period 3

| 11 Na Sodium 23 | 12 Mg Magnesium 24 | | | | | | | | | | | | | 13 Al Aluminium 27 | 14 Si Silicon 28 | 15 P Phosphorus 31 | 16 S Sulphur 32 | 17 ★ Cl Chlorine 35.5 | 18 ★ Ar Argon 40 |

Period 4

| 19 K Potassium 39 | 20 Ca Calcium 40 | 21 Sc Scandium 45 | 22 Ti Titanium 48 | 23 V Vanadium 51 | 24 Cr Chromium 52 | 25 Mn Manganese 55 | 26 Fe Iron 56 | 27 Co Cobalt 59 | 28 Ni Nickel 59 | 29 Cu Copper 63.5 | 30 Zn Zinc 65.4 | 31 Ga Gallium 70 | 32 Ge Germanium 73 | 33 As Arsenic 75 | 34 Se Selenium 79 | 35 Br Bromine 80 | 36 ★ Kr Krypton 84 |

Period 5

| 37 Rb Rubidium 85 | 38 Sr Strontium 88 | 39 Y Yttrium 89 | 40 Zr Zirconium 91 | 41 Nb Niobium 93 | 42 Mo Molybdenum 96 | 43 Tc Technetium | 44 Ru Ruthenium 101 | 45 Rh Rhodium 103 | 46 Pd Palladium 106 | 47 Ag Silver 108 | 48 Cd Cadmium 112 | 49 In Indium 115 | 50 Sn Tin 119 | 51 Sb Antimony 122 | 52 Te Tellurium 128 | 53 I Iodine 127 | 54 ★ Xe Xenon 131 |

Period 6

| 55 Cs Caesium 133 | 56 Ba Barium 137 | 57 ► La Lanthanum 139 | 72 Hf Hafnium 178 | 73 Ta Tantalum 181 | 74 W Tungsten 184 | 75 Re Rhenium 186 | 76 Os Osmium 190 | 77 Ir Iridium 192 | 78 Pt Platinum 195 | 79 Au Gold 197 | 80 Hg Mercury 201 | 81 Tl Thallium 204 | 82 Pb Lead 207 | 83 Bi Bismuth | 84 Po Polonium | 85 At Astatine | 86 Rn Radon |

Period 7

| 87 Fr Francium 223 | 88 Ra Radium 226 | 89 ►► Ac Actinium 227 | 104 Rf Rutherfordium | 105 Db Dubnium | 106 Sg Seaborgium | 107 Bh Bohrium | 108 Hs Hassium | 109 Mt Meitnerium | 110 Uun Unnnilium | 111 Uuu Unununium | 112 Uub Ununbium |

Lanthanoid elements ►

| 58 Ce Cerium 140 | 59 Pr Praseo-dymium 141 | 60 Nd Neo-dymium 144 | 61 Pm Promethium | 62 Sm Samarium 150 | 63 Eu Europium 152 | 64 Gd Gadolinium 157 | 65 Tb Terbium 159 | 66 Dy Dysprosium 163 | 67 Ho Holmium 165 | 68 Er Erbium 167 | 69 Tm Thulium 169 | 70 Yb Ytterbium 173 | 71 Lu Lutetium 175 |

Actinoid elements ►►

| 90 Th Thorium 232 | 91 PA Protactinium 231 | 92 U Uranium 238 | 93 Np Neptunium 237 | 94 Pu Plutonium | 95 Am Americium | 96 Cm Curium | 97 Bk Berkelium | 98 Cf Californium | 99 Es Einstein-ium | 100 Fm Fermium | 101 Md Mendel-evium | 102 No Nobelium | 103 Lr Lawrencium |

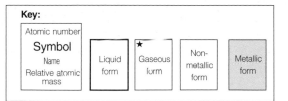

Key:

Atomic number
Symbol
Name
Relative atomic mass

Liquid form

★ Gaseous form

Non-metallic form

Metallic form

Confused words

Don't be caught out when these words are used. They have a special meaning in science.

Word	Common English meaning	Science meaning
Absorb	He used a cloth to absorb the water he'd spilt.	Most substances absorb light.
Acid	She has a very acid tongue.	Acids are corrosive substances that taste sour.
Atmosphere	They didn't stay at the restaurant because it had no atmosphere.	Atmosphere is the layer of gas around a planet.
Boiling	It's boiling hot!	The boiling point of water is 100°C – the weather is almost never that hot.
Cell	He was locked away in a cell for five years.	A cell is an electrical energy store. A group of cells make a battery. OR The basic unit of which plants and animals are made up.
Concentration	Homework needs concentration.	Concentrated solutions have a lot of solute dissolved in them.
Condensing	I am condensing my argument into one sentence.	When a vapour turns into a liquid it is condensing.
Conductor	The conductor was in charge of the orchestra.	An electrical conductor lets electric current flow through it and a thermal conductor lets energy flow through it.
Current	The current situation is difficult.	Current is an electrical flow.
Dense/density	He's really dense.	Density is heaviness for its size.
Drag	She had to drag the truth out of him.	Drag is a force that resists motion.
Efficiency	He works with efficiency.	The vacuum cleaner has an efficiency of 40%.
Elastic	You use elastic in clothes.	Elastic means a substance stretches but goes back to its original shape.
Element	I think the element in the kettle has burned out.	A substance that contains only one type of atom.
Energy	That boy has got too much energy!	Heating and cooling involve transfer of energy. When a force acts and something moves, that also involves transfer of energy.
Evaporate	She could feel her enthusiasm evaporate.	Particles of a liquid escape into the surroundings when it evaporates.
Force	The police force.	A force is a push or a pull.

Word	Common English meaning	Science meaning
Freezing	It's freezing cold.	The freezing point of water is 0°C – it can be that cold when it's frosty.
Gas	Light the gas (for a cooker).	A gas can be many substances e.g. oxygen.
Habitat	Shall we go to Habitat and buy some furniture?	A habitat is the home for a group of organisms.
Hip	That's quite a hip outfit you're wearing!	A part of the skeleton that supports the legs.
Host	Will you be the host of the party on Saturday night?	The animal that a parasite lives inside.
Humerus	That comedian thinks she's humerous. (Note the different spelling.)	The bone that connects the shoulder and elbow.
Impulse	I feel a little impulsive today. I might have an impulse buy in the shops!	The electric charge that travels along a nerve fibre.
Indicator	Indicators are orange winking lights on cars.	An indicator is a material that changes colour in solutions of different acidity.
Ions	Iron is a metal that can go rusty.	Ion sounds similar to iron, but it is a particle in a chemical change.
Irritant	That boy is an irritant!	An irritant is a chemical that affects the skin – it is a hazard.
Kingdom	As your sovereign I rule this kingdom!	All living things are divided into five kingdoms.
Lift	They took the lift to the fourth floor.	Lift is an upwards force on the wings of a bird or a plane.
Lime water	Lime is a green fruit like a lemon, and a white chalky powder.	Lime water is made with chalky powder not with fruit.
Liquid	I need a drink of liquid.	Liquids can be many different substances – not just water based.
Mass	She goes to Mass every Sunday.	Mass is a measure of the amount of material an object has.
Material	What colour material do you want for your new dress?	All the stuff things are made from.
Matter	What's the matter?	Matter is the stuff we are made from.
Moment	Wait just a moment!	A moment is a turning effect of a force.
Negative	He felt very negative about going to school this morning.	A battery has a negative terminal.
Net	The net had holes so the fish escaped.	With an upwards force of 10 newtons acting on a ball and a downwards force of 3 newtons, there is a net upwards force of 7 newtons.

Confused words

Word	Common English meaning	Science meaning
Neutralise	A large police force will neutralise the threat of disorder.	Acids will neutralise alkalis in a chemical change.
Normal	Everything is normal here.	A normal is a line which is at 90° to a surface.
Organ	On Sundays I play the organ in church.	A group of tissues working together.
Parallel	The wallpaper has nice parallel stripes.	You can connect lamps in parallel.
Peat	Hi Pete, where are you going? (Note the spelling.)	Rotted vegetable matter formed thousands of years ago.
Pest	You are a pest during the summer holidays!	An animal, often an insect, that is a nuisance.
Plastic	A plastic washing up bowl.	Plastic means a substance stretches and stays in the new shape, like putty.
Positive	The results of the test were positive.	A battery has a positive terminal.
Power	We have the power to arrest you.	Power is a measure of how quickly energy is transferred, such as by a kettle or a lamp.
Pressure	I feel under pressure to pass exams.	Pressure is the force per unit of area.
Pure	Not harmful.	Contains only one substance.
Range	The eggs are free range.	A range of values is the difference between the highest and the lowest.
Ray	You are my little ray of sunshine.	A ray is a very thin line that we draw to show a pathway of light.
Reflect	Reflect on your behaviour.	Surfaces can reflect light.
Renewable	His membership of the sports club is renewable every year.	A renewable energy resource is one that will not run out.
Salt	Salt and vinegar on chips.	Table salt is one kind of salt made in neutralisation reactions.
Saturated	I got caught in the rain and I'm saturated!	A saturated solution will not dissolve any more solute.
Scale	Fish have scales on their skin.	Measuring instruments have scales with marks and numbers.
School	Off you go to school today, no arguments please!	A group of animals that live in water, e.g. a school of dolphins.
Series	That was a great TV series.	You can connect lamps in series.
Solution	Have you found the solution to the puzzle?	A solution is made by dissolving a solute in a solvent.
Thrust	She thrust her face into other people's business.	Thrust is a driving force.
Transfer	Blogtown United have put their goalkeeper on the transfer list.	Energy can transfer from place to place and from system to system.

Word	Common English meaning	Science meaning
Unbalanced	If I have to put up with much more of this my mind will become unbalanced.	Unbalanced force produces acceleration.
Unit	They've chosen some nice new kitchen units.	Degrees Celsius, newtons, metres and seconds are all examples of units of measurement.
Vacuum	He decided to vacuum the floor.	A vacuum is a space with no air or other material.
Variable	The weather was variable when I went on holiday.	A variable is a quantity that can change.
Weight	The scales said that she had a weight of 140 pounds. She could lose weight by going on a diet.	Her weight was really 650 newtons, and she could lose weight by going far from the Earth.
Work	I did eight hours hard work today.	Work is a kind of energy transfer that happens when force changes the motion of an object.

Glossary

Hydraulic	Transferring force by liquid pressure	128, 129
Hydroelectric	Type of power which uses the potential energy of water	38
Hypochondriac	Somebody who always thinks they are ill.	13
Hypothesis	What you think will happen in a experiment.	158
Identical twins	Twins produced from one sperm and one egg	3
Incompressible	Not able to be squeezed	129
Insulation	Slowing down the transfer of energy	43
Ion	Particle with an electrical charge.	18, 107
IVF	*In vitro* fertilisation – fertilising an ovum with sperm outside the womb.	161
Kilowatt-hour	Unit of electrical energy.	41
Kinetic	About movement	36, 40
Laminations	Layered	163
Leech	Animal that sucks blood from bodies	163
Lift	Upwards force due to action of a bird's or aeroplane's wing.	118
Ligaments	String-like tissue that joins bones to bones	47
Maggot	Larval stage of house fly.	159
Malleability (malleable)	Able to be hammered into flat sheets	17
Mass	How much of an object there is	72
Melanin	Dark coloured pigment in the skin.	64
Micro-organisms (microbes)	Tiny organisms not visible with the naked eye – bacteria, viruses and fungi	156, 157, 158
Minerals	Chemicals needed by plants in small amounts	87
Model	Way of visualising something in science.	148
Moment	Turning effect of a force	130
Monomer	Single unit of a polymer.	104
Natural selection	The main idea in the theory of evolution produced by Charles Darwin and Alfred Russel Wallace.	12
Neoprene	Synthetic rubber material	108
Neutralisation	Reaction between an acid and an alkali to produce a salt and water	18
Newton metre	Unit of turning effects or moments	130
Newton	Unit of force	72
Nicotine	The addictive drug in cigarettes	50, 54
Nitroglycerine	Dangerously explosive liquid.	108
Osmosis	Movement of water	106
Ovules	Female plant sex cells.	8
Oxidation	Reaction where oxygen combines with other material to make new substances called oxides	102
Ozone	Oxygen molecule with formula O_3; poisonous to humans but absorbs harmful ultraviolet radiation high in the atmosphere.	64–65
Parachute	Device with lots of air resistance that slows the motion of an object falling through air.	70–71
Pascal	Unit of pressure – 1 newton per square metre	126
Passive smoking	Breathing in the tobacco smoke of someone else, although you are not a smoker.	51
pH	A measure of how acid or alkaline a solution is	59, 60
Photosynthesis	Process by which a plant makes its own food	82, 83, 164